Esports

by Phill "DrPhill" Alexander

for
dummies®
A Wiley Brand

Esports For Dummies®

Published by: **John Wiley & Sons, Inc.**, 111 River Street, Hoboken, NJ 07030-5774, www.wiley.com

Copyright © 2020 by John Wiley & Sons, Inc., Hoboken, New Jersey

Media and software compilation copyright © 2020 by John Wiley & Sons, Inc. All rights reserved.

Published simultaneously in Canada

For general information on our other products and services, please contact our Customer Care Department within the U.S. at 877-762-2974, outside the U.S. at 317-572-3993, or fax 317-572-4002. For technical support, please visit https://hub.wiley.com/community/support/dummies.

Wiley publishes in a variety of print and electronic formats and by print-on-demand. Some material included with standard print versions of this book may not be included in e-books or in print-on-demand. If this book refers to media such as a CD or DVD that is not included in the version you purchased, you may download this material at http://booksupport.wiley.com. For more information about Wiley products, visit www.wiley.com.

Library of Congress Control Number: 2020934234

ISBN 978-1-119-65059-1; ISBN 978-1-119-65056-0 (ebk); ISBN 978-1-119-65061-4 (ebk)

Manufactured in the United States of America

V10018184_032220

Contents at a Glance

Table of Contents

Introduction

The last decade has belonged to esports. Whereas many industries face downturns, esports has been in a steady, almost exponential growth pattern since 2010. This past year, the *League of Legends* World Championship had more viewers than every sporting event but the Super Bowl. Franchises for the professional *Overwatch* League sold for $50 million. Esports is a exploding.

Yet, as a professional in the field, I am still asked almost daily, "What is esports?" People sometimes guess, "Is it like *Madden?*" The answer is yes, kind of, but also no. Esports involves competitive gaming, but the term represents so much more. The fact that you picked up this book means you're curious. Within these pages, you can learn all about the esports world.

About This Book

Esports is a multifaceted ecosystem of players, developers, organizations, and fans. Entering into an esports conversation can be intimidating without knowing the lay of the land. *Esports For Dummies* means to give you exactly that: a basic overview of how the esports world works.

This book doesn't have the space to make you an expert on esports, but it gives you the road map to navigate the terrain, and more than enough information to speak intelligently about it. It also offers guidance for developing a career as an esports professional, for players and others in the industry. *Esports For Dummies* can help you lock in on your own goals and know how to start developing expertise. The rest is up to you.

A word of caution: If your goal is to be a professional within the esports space, you don't need to know every type of game or title, or how every organization runs. Most professionals focus on a specific game or specific genre of games and develop their skills based on that smaller subsection. Don't feel like you need to know every single thing there is to know about esports games. Knowing too much about too many games but not having mastery over one game can make you less effective.

Because esports is growing at such a staggering rate, bear in mind that some parts of this book could become outdated within months of publication. If you find that information you read about here has changed, don't feel misled. The esports world and details of various games and organizations change quickly. I was actually teaching a class on key esports titles when *Fortnite* was released, and I had a week to develop an entire new section of the class. Change is the nature of the beast. With this book, you discover the key information you need to know, and Google is your best friend for keeping abreast of the latest developments.

Foolish Assumptions

Because I get questions about esports almost every day, I try not to make too many assumptions. Here are the assumptions I do make about you:

>> You have high-speed Internet access and a computer (though I suggest computers you might buy).

>> You know how to connect all your devices to power and displays so that they can operate.

>> You know how to browse the Internet and visit web pages.

>> You know how to download and install games and software.

>> You have an email account.

>> You have access to all your passwords (email, computer, network).

Icons Used in This Book

Occasionally you encounter icons in the margins of this book's text, and here's what those icons mean:

TIP

The Tip icon marks tips (duh!) and shortcuts that you can use to make your esports activities easier.

REMEMBER

This icon marks information that's especially important to know. To siphon off the most important information in each chapter, just skim through these icons.

TECHNICAL STUFF

The Technical Stuff icon indicates information of a more technical nature that you can normally skip over unless you find yourself confused about what's going on or want to know more.

WARNING

The Warning icon tells you to watch out! It marks important information that may save you headaches.

Beyond the Book

In addition to the book itself, this product also comes with an online Cheat Sheet that includes a list of terms you encounter in the esports world, some professional esports teams to know about, and tips to get started playing a game called *Clash Royale* right from your smartphone or tablet. To get this Cheat Sheet, go to www.dummies.com and enter **Esports For Dummies Cheat Sheet** in the Search box. Then scroll down the page that appears.

Where to Go from Here

Esports For Dummies is designed for you to read in any order you want; you don't have to read it in linear fashion. If you're not familiar with esports, however, I recommend that you read Chapter 1 first to find out what esports is all about. If you know that you're interested in a particular game or type of game, you might want to start with the chapters in Part 2. To learn about streaming, Chapter 14 is the place to start. If you need equipment to play and want recommendations, Chapter 2 will come in handy.

Remember that esports is a big business, but it's a business based on having fun! Dive in wherever you want and see where your interests take you. Remember that you can't win if you don't play, so play on!

1

Getting Started with Esports

IN THIS PART . . .

Understand what esports are.

Prepare and gather all the gear you need to play esports.

Chapter **1**

What Are Esports?

The first event that could claim to be an esports competition was organized by Stewart Brand at Stanford University on October 19, 1972 (https://www.rollingstone.com/culture/culture-news/stewart-brand-recalls-first-spacewar-video-game-tournament-187669/). The game being played was a science fiction spaceship combat game called *Spacewar*. The Stanford AI Lab was one of only a few places in the world that could have held such a competition at the time. None of the gamers played with their own machines or peripherals; such things would have been unheard of then. The *Spacewar* game consisted of little more than white pixels on a black screen.

That *Spacewar* event would barely fit any of the criteria that the industry or fans apply to esports now. It bears a passing resemblance to a fighting-game LAN (local area network) tournament in which consoles or computers are set up on a private network within a venue so that competitors can play matches, but at today's esports events, the competitors still bring their own peripherals at the very least, and the games are played on commercially available machines, whether those are Xbox or PlayStation consoles or PCs. But at the core of it all, that moment at Stanford was, in the most technical of senses, an esports competition.

In this chapter, you find out what the term *esports* refers to and explore what it takes for a game to be considered an esport. Along the way, you encounter some of the language surrounding esports and get a general sense of the history of what many call the biggest sport some people have never heard of.

Defining Esports

Esports is the competitive play of video games. Quick read, right? End of chapter! Now you know!

If only the answer could be so simple. It's not so simple, however. The one aspect that has remained true since the origin of what people call esports is that it involves, and always will involve, players competing against each other in a video game. This aspect was true of *Spacewar*; it was true of the era of competitions to reach the highest possible score with games like *Pac-Man* or *Donkey Kong*; and it remains true today for *Overwatch* League and the *League of Legends* World Championship, more commonly referred to as "Worlds" by players and fans.

Defining esports as competitive video gameplay no longer works, however. Nearly every video game that exists — including games like *Minecraft* that were not initially designed to be competitive — has players who elevate a more casual game to an ultra-competitive level. Also, not every game is an esport. Following are the five key criteria that determine whether a game truly qualifies as an esport. An esport has

» Regular publisher support and updates

» A massive fan base with the desire to watch competition

» A clear ranking or ladder system so that players know where they stand relative to other players

THE IMPORTANCE OF HIGH SCORES IN VIDEO GAME HISTORY: *THE KING OF KONG*

To the current generation of gamers, it might seem crazy that people once dedicated their lives to having the highest possible score on a one-player arcade video game. That culture, however, is the one that spawned the esports world we know today. If you'd like to learn more about those crazy days of record keeping and the use of officials and pre-game hardware inspection, check out the 2007 documentary *The King of Kong: A Fistful of Quarters*. Written and directed by Seth Gordon, the movie is the real-life story of the competition between Steve Weibe and Billy Mitchell to secure the world record high score in *Donkey Kong*. In addition to providing an interesting overview of esports before the Internet, the movie is highly entertaining in the same spirit as reality television competition shows are. The feud between Weibe and Mitchell is reminiscent of professional wrestling, complete with hype interviews and accusations of cheating and foul play.

>> Frequent competitions from reputable tournament organizers

>> Longevity as a reliable, quality game

Before I elaborate on these criteria in the upcoming sections, note that all these rules have exceptions. The most obvious one is the fighting game *Super Smash Bros. Melee*. Released for the GameCube in November 2001, *Melee* has been out of print for a decade and the GameCube console hasn't been manufactured since 2007. Nintendo has since released its popular *Super Smash Bros. Ultimate* game for the Nintendo Switch, but even without support from Nintendo, *Smash Melee* still sees regular competition. It is, however, a true rarity in that sense, and it is the only major esports game in the current landscape to go through such a long period without updates or development changes.

Regular publisher support

Prior to the mid-2000s, the marketing model for video games was relatively simple. A company would release a game and, depending on the level of interest from fans, it might patch errors. Less often, the company offered expansion package content either by download or through the purchase of another game disc. Most often, though, the company chose to create a sequel or follow-up or to let a game run its course. You see the more traditional spirit of creating a follow-up in sports-based games like the EA Madden NFL franchise or 2K's NBA or WWE games. Each year, a new version of those games is released with updated rosters and some new features, but for the most part, the games themselves haven't changed dramatically from the previous year.

Popular esports titles break this mold. For some examples, look at the five esports games based on prize pools in the first half of 2019, according to *Esports Observer*: *Fortnite, CS:GO, Dota 2, League of Legends*, and *Overwatch* (https://esportsobserver.com/top10-prize-pools-h1-2019/). Take a look at the dates of release and the most recent update for each of those games as of February 2020 (as you read this, I offer a personal guarantee that each game will have been updated again).

Although *League of Legends* is ten years old, as of the writing of this chapter, it had been updated with fresh content just weeks before. This frequent updating is one of the most important parts of esports because the constant updates allow the games to evolve but also allow for tweaking and balancing so that if a competitor finds an unexpected loophole or exploit, the company can quickly identify and correct it. Games without this level of support also decay quickly because the meta — or the current best practices — for the game grows stale and competition becomes highly predictable.

Also, all the titles listed in Table 1-1 have major tournaments that are administered by their publishers. *Overwatch* even has its own professional league with franchised teams, as you can read more about in Chapter 4. These events, known as first-party tournaments, are critical to the success of each game.

TABLE 1-1

Original Release Date and Date of Last Update for Major Esports Titles

Game	Release Date	Most Recent Update as of February 20, 2020
Fortnite	July 21, 2017	February 20, 2020
CS:GO	August 21, 2012	February 11, 2020
Dota 2	July 7, 2013	February 11, 2020
League of Legends	October 27, 2009	February 19, 2020
Overwatch	May 24, 2016	February 12, 2020

A large fan base

Two major metrics determine how popular a game is: how many people play it and how many people watch other people play it. With the current status of Twitch.tv as far and away the largest live-streaming service in the world, you can easily see a snapshot of how games are doing with regard to those metrics. Table 1-2 presents the same five games listed in Table 1-1 in the previous section to show who is playing and watching as of October 2019.

TABLE 1-2

Twitch Streamers and Viewers for the Five Most Popular Esports*

Game	Average Number Streaming the Game	Average Number of Viewers
Fortnite	6,429	196,905
CS:GO	1,310	52,862
Dota 2	612	32,784
League of Legends	2902	217,359
Overwatch	974	16,924

*https://twitchtracker.com/statistics/games

To give the numbers in the table some context and perspective, at any given time during the week of October 13–19, 2019, just a bit more than 200,000 people were watching someone play *League of Legends,* and just a bit fewer than 200,000 people were watching someone play *Fortnite.* Those are strong audience numbers. Those might not seem like strong Nielsen ratings for television, but TV programs are measured by the half-hour or hour, and the Twitch.tv numbers are based on the entire day. In the month of October 2019, *Fortnite* had a maximum peak viewership of 1,611,930 (https://twitchtracker.com/statistics/games). The 2018 *League of Legends* World Championship had 60 million viewers at one point, which exceeded the number of viewers of the 2018 BCS College Football Championship Game, the Winter Olympics, and the 2018 NBA Finals combined.

Added to those impressive statistics are the numbers for the player bases themselves. Table 1-3 again presents figures for the five top games.

TABLE 1-3   **Registered Average Monthly Players and Prize Money for the Five Most Popular Esports in 2019***

Game	Number of Registered Players	Total Prize Money
Fortnite	78,000,000	$64,198,550.25
CS:GO	411,000	$14,108,415.95
Dota 2	422,000	$43,807,673.09
League of Legends	80,000,000	$6,531,481.20
Overwatch	20,000,000	$9,078,716.77

*https://yourmoneygeek.com/esport-games-

For perspective, when Blizzard's *World of Warcraft* cracked 10,000,000 users in 2014, that number of players was considered to be unheard of in the video game industry (https://investor.activision.com/news-releases/news-release-details/world-warcraftr-surpasses-10-million-subscribers-warlords). The growth shown by top-tier esports games in the last five years is staggering, and that growth speaks to what makes those games top esports titles.

The installed base makes a game viable as an esport. Newer games may find breaking into the space difficult. This difficulty is particularly true for the newest of the esports genres, the battle royale. Numerous games have attempted to sway a portion of that 250 million player base away from *Fortnite* (https://www.engadget.com/2019/03/20/fortnite-250-million-epic-games-sweeney-interview-gdc/). You can read more about *Fortnite* in Chapter 7.

A clear ranking system

Before 1978, games didn't record scores. With the release of *Space Invaders*, games started to retain a tally of who had managed to score what, displaying those scores on a screen when the game wasn't in play, and cementing the early legacy of PMA in arcades across my region of central Indiana and southern Ohio, for example.

High scores mattered because they were the way to know who was skilled at a specific game. After a time, though, mere scores didn't really do the job. After the Internet became widely accessible and could aggregate all the scores, the tradition of walking into an arcade and looking at a screen to see who was the highest scorer on that machine paled in comparison to being able to see where your score stood against, well, everyone.

Almost every competitive esports game today has some manner of publicly accessible, criteria-based ranking system that can be used to determine how good a player is relative to competition. These ladders, or Elo scores, have become so pervasive that they're a vocabulary of their own.

To convey how a ladder system words, here's a look at the system that *Overwatch* uses. The process itself is relatively easy to understand. To play in competitive mode, a player must reach level 25. The player can do so simply by playing. Skill can help to speed the process, but anyone who is persistent will get to level 25 without major problems. After a "season" starts (seasons begin every three months and come close to mirroring the actual seasons of the year), a level-25 player must play a set of ten competitive "placement" matches. Based on those placement matches, the player receives an initial score between 1 and 5,000. Those scores map to the ladder rankings shown in Table 1-4.

TABLE 1-4   *Overwatch* **Ladder Rankings***

Rank	Score Range	Percentage of Players at Rank
Bronze	1–1,500	8
Silver	1,500–1,999	21
Gold	2,000–2,499	32
Platinum	2,500–2,999	25
Diamond	3,000–3,499	10
Masters	3,500–3,999	3
Grandmaster	4,000–5,000	1

https://www.pcgamesn.com/overwatch/ranks-explained-how-to-get-ranked

After players have placed, their matches throughout the season allow them to climb the ladder or fall depending on their talent, the way matches play out, and other factors. A player's rank, and more specifically, in most cases, the number that goes with the ranking, reveals how talented a player is compared to the rest of the player base.

Again, figuring out how talented a player is becomes a matter of understanding how all the numbers go together. Having a rating of Grandmaster in *Overwatch* is quite impressive. Only 1 percent of players rank that high. But if you look back at the number of active players and do the math, that number means that there could be up to 400,000 players in the world who have obtained the Grandmaster rank and are ranked 4,000 or higher. Based on the numbers, if you're at the Platinum rank, you could also very easily be the best player in a rather large group because more than half the competitive population is at Gold or below.

The *Overwatch* system represents just one of the many ladders in the esports world, but knowing how to determine what the scores mean and where you stand is a critical part of finding competition. The difference between a team of six with an average of 3,500 and a team of six with an average of 4,000 is the difference between a competitive college-level team and potentially professional team.

Frequent competitions

At the collegiate level, the teams that I help to coach play in at least one, if not two or three, leagues weekly. The college has had difficulty with our efforts to build a *Fortnite* team because at the collegiate level, the competitions, as of 2020, just aren't frequent enough. Frequency of competition is key for three reasons:

» Building a fan base and a routine for competition requires regularity. When teams don't play for weeks on end, they must rely on practice to keep their skills sharp, and they have to work double time to keep their fans engaged.

» Establishing that a team is a "thing" requires regular competition and scheduled events. With traditional sports, scheduled events are a given, but imagine if your favorite basketball or football team didn't have a clear schedule that you could consult to find out when the next game was.

» Regular competitions almost always result in playoffs or elimination rounds, and winning titles and prizes is how a team or individual player gets established. Any win is a good win, but trophies and titles build reputations and legacies.

Use caution if you're looking to start a long-term career playing a particular game but have difficulty in finding regular competitions for that game. It isn't the kiss of death, but you'll need some luck finding competitions, or you'll need to travel frequently or even relocate to a different region to overcome the fact that games like *League of Legends* and *Overwatch* offer weekly competitions at multiple levels.

Longevity

Esports is still a relatively new thing, but at the same time, competitions have happening since the 1970s, and most of the big-name games currently being played in major competition have been around for at least five years. As Table 1-1, earlier in this chapter, shows, three of the five most popular esports titles in the world have been around and offering regular competitions for fans since 2013. In the case of *League of Legends*, Riot is entering the second decade of League competition. Also, even though it has fallen from the top ranks of esports, Blizzard's *World of Warcraft* has been offering events for its Arena player-versus-player game mode since 2005 and has offered the Mythic Dungeon International, a competition in which two teams of five players each run the same five-player dungeon side by side with the quickest time winning, since 2016.

Each of the major games in the esports space has faced the launch of numerous similar games. The established titles usually win the "war" for competitive space, even when heavy competition seems to arise. For example, over the summer and fall of 2018, a number of battle royale games popped up to challenge *Fortnite* for its spot. One predated *Fortnite* — the more tactical shooter styled *PlayerUnknown's Battlegrounds*. Another was *Realm Royale*, a more fantasy-based battle royale from Hi-Rez Studios. The presumed juggernaut of that period was the battle royale Blackout mode in *Call of Duty: Black Ops 4*. None of those games managed to dethrone *Fortnite*, nor did EA's more recent release, *Apex Legends*. The staying power of each of these games is explored in more depth in Chapter 7.

Similarly, *League of Legends* and *Dota 2* have maintained their status as top esports in spite of a large number of other MOBA games entering the space. *League of Legends* even managed to fend off Blizzard's *Heroes of the Storm*. I talk more about MOBA games in Chapter 3.

The tried-and-true rule in the esports space is that games that have been around for a while tend to stick around, and older games fade only when their platform becomes completely antiquated. Starting competition in a newly released game is always a risk, but staying on current consoles and not picking an older game in a hotly contested market can guide you toward the best new titles to try. For example, if you track *Overwatch* based on who made it and where the maker distributed it, you find that it was viewed as competition for *CS:GO*, *CoD*, and *Team Fortress 2*, a game that has fallen away from the mainstream. *Overwatch* was a slam dunk in the other four categories, however. It launched with a clear ladder and ranking system; Blizzard already had an established history in esports and knew how to offer the correct support as well as organized competitions; and within days of its release, *Overwatch* had a large and enthusiastic installed audience.

By way of comparison, Nintendo's shooter *Splatoon 2,* which was hyped as an esports title as part of the Switch console release, had the wind of organized events and the promotional powers of Nintendo behind it coming out of the launch gate, but it didn't take off with fans and as a result has failed to become an upper-level title.

Being a Gamer versus an Esport Player

Early in the chapter, I start with the most bare-bones definition of esports: the competitive play of video games. By this point in the chapter, the definition has taken a more layered form. Esports, as the industry and competitors understand it, is competitive play of a title with a large fan base, a clear way to understand player skill, and the backing of a publisher that frequently updates the game and is a supportive part of the tournament and competition scene. In terms of what the vast majority of people mean when they use the term esports, this is definition to take to heart. You can even think of it as a sort of simple math equation: Competitive Game with Ladder + Large Fan base/Player base + Frequent Competition + Publisher Support = Esports.

But wedged between the general "competitive video games" definition and the one I just spelled out is a massive debate in the esports realm that also needs to be acknowledged: What is the difference between a gamer and an esports player?

The word *gamer* comes with a tremendous amount of baggage, owing in no small part to the 2014 (and ongoing) Gamergate debate (see the "Gamergate" sidebar). That baggage sometimes makes discussions of gamers and gamer culture difficult and troubling as the stereotype emerges of the gamer as Eric Cartman from South Park, a young, white, affluent male in his parents' basement covered in cheese powder and guzzling caffeinated soda. That same stereotypical gamer is presumed to be misogynistic, homophobic, and racist, generally rude, and in almost every other way immature.

The gamer stereotype isn't at all accurate, but the baggage that comes from it can be troubling in the esports world. More important, though, is the fundamental difference between a gamer (not the stereotype but any of the many diverse people who would claim to be gamers) and an esports competitor. That difference can be summed up in a short sentence, but it has a profound impact on how each of those groups understands itself and the others: Gamers love to play games, but esports players train and practice to win above all else.

GAMERGATE

If you spend any amount of time reading about games and esports, you'll quickly come across Gamergate. Although whole books have been written about the topic, here are the key points about Gamergate that anyone entering the esports world should know:

- Gamergate was a reaction to the advancement of feminism in online games spaces. Most specifically, it was a reaction to a game called *Depression Quest*, which was made and distributed by Zoe Quinn.

- *Depression Quest* won awards, and some people in the community claimed that Quinn received those awards and the positive reviews of the game because Quinn was female. (She was even accused of exploiting male reviewers.)

- A second person, a scholar named Anita Sarkeesian, came to Quinn's defense. Later, a game developer named Brianna Wu would be pulled into the debate, as would well-known games influencer Felicia Day.

In the ongoing debate about the merits of female creators and the rights of female creators to be part of the gaming world, two major threads emerged:

- Harassment — including illegal and reprehensible behavior like death threats, stalking, public disgrace, and over-the-top sexual harassment — proliferated in online gaming discourse spaces.

- A debate began over whether the "gamer" as a stereotype is dead.

The debate continues to this day in some corners of the Internet. Just know that when the subject of Gamergate comes up, it represents two polarizing issues to some degree: problems of diversity and inclusion, and the desire of some members of the gaming world to retain the label of "gamer" as a badge that essentially represents membership in a boy's club. If you are interested in learning more about Gamergate, take a look at *Gamergate: First Battle in the Culture War,* by Kevin McDonald (*independently published,* 2019) or *Crash Override: How Gamergate (Nearly) Destroyed My Life,* by Zoe Quinn (*PublicAffairs,* 2017). Before wading into additional reading, however, bear in mind that most written accounts of Gamergate show a bias.

The ecosystem around games is so large and diverse that attempts to make such clear and absolute definitions can in itself be a problem, though. If a group of people staged a *Pokémon* event with competition and prizes, it wouldn't be considered "esports" by the same community that grinds the ladder in a game like *League of Legends* and participates in sponsored events with huge prize pools. No one can deny that *League of Legends* is an esport. The slippage occurs when, for example, an organization puts on a *Pokémon Go* competition and calls it an "esports event." By many definitions, it would be fair to call the *Pokémon Go* event an esports event, but many hardcore esports advocates would claim that a game that is that "casual" without the rigor of a game like *League of Legends* isn't actually an esports title. The tension between the big-tent view of esports and a more defensive view of what can and cannot be considered esports is something you are likely to encounter when entering the esports space.

When looking at esports as a larger concept, that level of diversity in what can be considered an esport is a great thing. One of the many hats that I wear at my day job at a university is advising the campus Esports Club. The club openly accepts any students who want to come and play a game they love competitively. That acceptance is part of what is amazing about the esports world. It's one of the most collaborative and kind groups of people you could ever encounter. But that wonderful fuzziness makes nailing down a definition of esports difficult.

In this book, I include games that some people who are deeply involved with professional esports would say are not esports. However, the people who are involved in them refer to them as esports.

Most often, though, when people talk about esports, they mean players who practice their game the way athletes practice their sport, on teams or as solo players with large fan bases and regular competitions. To be an esports player requires time and dedication.

I was once in a lecture by a famous author who visited our campus. He asked at the start, "How many of you write for eight hours a day?" No one raised a hand. He followed with, "Then you'll never be as good as I am. I write. That's what I do." Likewise, I was once told by NBA Hall of Famer Earvin "Magic" Johnson that the secret to being a great free-throw shooter is shooting free throws for hours every single day. Esports excellence requires the same kind of effort. If you're not practicing your game 3–4 hours a day, you'll never be as good as the people who do. But we can't all be professional players, which is why there are fans. It's also why being a gamer is not a bad thing. In other words, you don't have to want to win every game to play and enjoy, but if you want to be an esports champion, you shouldn't feel good about losing.

Chapter **2**

Gearing Up to Play

When you decide to dive into the world of esports, you may find that the computer and video game systems you have on hand don't measure up to the level of performance you want. To dominate the competition, you need quality hardware.

That isn't to say that you need an extremely expensive computer. Although PCs exist that retail for more than $8,000, you don't need to spend nearly that much to be competitive. The secret is in looking for the right components. You have many items to think about beyond the PC, too, such as all the peripherals (keyboard, mouse, and headset, among others).

In this chapter, you find out about all the gear you need to have great gaming experiences, whether you're playing competitively or just on your home turf. The chapter also delves into the best types of televisions for esports, along with gaming consoles and controllers.

REMEMBER

As you read this chapter, you see that I mention the specific gear I use. Don't take any of what I'm saying as a blanket endorsement of the gear I take into virtual battle. I'm not trying to push any particular product. At the same time, I did pick the gear I carry for a reason, and I hope that talking through those reasons can help you to make your own selections.

Discovering PC Must-Haves for Esports

For the majority of esports players, the most important preparation you can make for playing is picking the right computer. Although a great many different options are available, for esports, you want to focus on a few specific key elements: a powerful processor, a high-quality graphics card, a versatile networking card, and a gaming-quality monitor.

Computer processor

As a general rule, you want to get the fastest computer processor you can afford for your esports gaming rig. That said, you shouldn't target the newest, fastest processor on the market unless you have money to burn. The newest processors always have premium pricing. If you shop for the processor just one step below the fastest, you can save yourself significant money. For example, at the time of this writing, *PC Magazine* lists the Intel Core i9-9980XE Extreme Edition for $1,999, but the slightly lower-powered Intel i9-9900K for $499 (see https://www.pcmag.com/roundup/366303/the-best-cpus). Although the 9980XE is faster, the speed difference isn't nearly significant enough to pay four times the price.

REMEMBER

Computer processor information can quickly become confusing. Reading the name and specifications for a processor isn't difficult as long as you know what you're looking at. All this information, however, varies by manufacturer and line. Your best bet while shopping is to look at benchmarks and reviews to see how machines perform. You can use sites like CPU Boss (http://cpuboss.com/) to compare processors.

You want to know five aspects of any PC processor you look at:

>> **Who is the manufacturer?** If the processor isn't made by AMD or Intel, steer clear. Intel processors are considered more favorable, but most AMD products perform just as well. If it's from some other company, avoid it for gaming.

>> **What is the clock speed?** This is the single biggest indicator of how fast the computer processes data, but it is also dependent on the processor's generation and manufacturer. For example, a 3.5GHz Intel Core i9 might not be slower than an AMD 4 GHz Ryzen. To get exact numbers, you have to dig deeper. But a 4 GHz AMD Ryzen is much faster than a 3.5 GHz AMD Ryzen.

>> **How many cores does the processor have?** Possessing more processor cores means that the computer has the capability to run more processes. How much this issue matters across lines can be debated because speed and

general processor power usually mean more for gaming than the number of cores, but when looking at processors within a line (for example, if you are shopping for an Intel Core i9), the more cores, the better.

» **Can the processor multithread?** A processor that can multithread can run more than one process on a core at any given time. Multithreading can double your computer's processing capability.

» **Is the processor locked or can it be overclocked?** In some cases, you can set a computer to attempt to run faster than its listed clock speed. Some games and software can make this happen.

Graphics card

The next most important consideration for an esports computer is the graphics processor card. Being able to compete at the highest level is all about resolution and refresh rate. You want high resolution and high frame rate. The standard for esports as of early 2020 is the NVIDIA GeForce GTX 1080. For top esports titles like *Fortnite, League of Legends,* and *Overwatch,* this card is more than powerful enough, but the GeForce RTX 2080 has hit the market and is a popular card. Alternative video cards are on the market as well, but almost all esports professionals favor the NVIDIA GeForce. You're well advised to go with a version of the 2080.

TIP

You have various options from which to choose for the GeForce 2080 card, but you should always favor more memory and more cooling options.

Networking card

Also critical to an esports machine is the networking card. For most computer users, whatever networking card comes with the system will likely suffice. In esports, however, the difference of a tenth of a millisecond of speed can be the difference between victory and defeat. You should not plan to play highly competitive games over a Wi-Fi network. You should play from a wired connection, with a network card like the Killer Ethernet E3000 card, an adapter that allows for 10/100/1000 Mbps so that the card can prioritize your network access and keep your ping (time from your machine to the game) and latency (delay from your input to the information leaving your machine and entering the network) as low as possible.

CONSIDERING PRICE AND LONGEVITY

You will have important decisions to make about the concept of trying to buy a machine that is "future proof." One option is to seek a top-end system that is expected to last for several (5–10) years. Although this longevity is certainly possible, your decision also involves a gamble because you obviously can't see the future and know what might be developed next. Computer companies, likewise, cannot know for certain what will advance, so even systems with price tags above $8,000 are not a sure bet to last more than 2–3 years.

The other option is to buy a machine that is ready for current competition but might be obsolete sooner. To give you a sense of where most professionals and collegiate players position themselves, people generally expect a PC to last two to three years in competitive esports before technology advances enough to need a replacement (or an upgrade of many of the key components). Sticking with that pattern can allow you to buy a computer in the $1,500–$2,000 range. Purchasing at the other end of the current retail spectrum may result in needing to replace your computer less often, but consider that an $8,000 computer would need to last you four times as long as a $2,000 machine to be worth it.

Deciding Whether to Build or to Buy

It is beyond the scope of this book to show you how to build a PC. If you are interested in learning to build a PC, or if you already know how, you will find yourself at a crossroads as you consider your esports PC: Should you make your own or buy a prebuilt one?

Considering the pros and cons of the DIY esports computer

You can experience two major benefits from building your own esports rig. The first is that you can save money. In many cases, you can save quite a bit of money, in fact, because you can choose your parts from various suppliers online. You can also choose what to spend big on and what to minimize. The other major advantage is that you can choose when and what to upgrade. That flexibility can mean that your machine may last longer than it typically would.

If you built the computer you are currently using, you can even replace a few key components and be ready for esports competition. Some games in particular, like *League of Legends* or *Hearthstone*, can be played with much less powerful overall computer systems.

Building your own machine comes with potential pitfalls, though. The first is that it's up to you to ensure that all the parts you buy will work together. Sadly, that's not always the case. It also falls on your shoulders to make sure that you put things together correctly, and if you make a mistake, it's your responsibility to figure out what is incorrect and to fix it or replace the defective piece. You also find yourself without a warranty to cover the machine.

Buying a prebuilt computer

Another alternative to building your own machine is to buy a prebuilt one. The only real detriments to buying a prebuilt machine are that you will spend more money than you would on the parts alone (if you built your own), and you won't get the satisfaction of assembling it yourself. Assuming that you're not itching for a DIY project and you're not so budget strapped that you need to get the absolute lowest price, buying a preassembled esports computer is much safer than building your own. You don't take a chance on incompatibility of the individual components; the machines undergo a rigorous presale testing process that you couldn't replicate on your own without risking damage; and, most important, not having to assemble it yourself removes the chance of user error, which can be particularly hazardous when working with computer components.

If you decide to buy a prebuilt computer, you still have a wide range of hardware options to choose from. Many companies offer gaming and esports computers, from brands that exist to cater to gamers, such as Alienware, Razer, and Omen, which build high-end PCs, to companies like iBUYPOWER or CyberPowerPC, which build machines targeted to gamers but allow them to choose among a variety of components.

TIP

People often say that in buying a computer from Alienware or Razer, you're paying for the logo and branding. Although you can certainly find cheaper alternatives, if you're not a person who tinkers with computers, you're best off going with a company with a reputation and a product that you like. Having a multiple-year warranty in particular is beneficial if you are considering a two- to three-year replacement schedule. Never being out of warranty means having no unexpected expenses pop up.

Also, just between you and me, there's something to be said for the cool factor of high-end gaming PCs. Part of enjoying the esports world is enjoying the look and feel of your technology. Make sure to think through whether you see yourself as a DIY gamer; or as a budget-conscious gamer who seeks to avoid corporate logo-laden machines from big name companies like Dell (which owns Alienware) or HP (which owns Omen); or as someone who wants a machine with all the lights and logos and bells and whistles. Only you can determine the right answer as to what you want in a computer, but remember that your PC will be your home in the esports world. You should think of it the way athletes think of their equipment.

Considering Three Levels of PC Power and Expense

The previous sections in this chapter consider whether to build your new esports rig from scratch, buy from a company that assembles machines and lets you pick your components, or buy a high-end build from one of the major companies. After you make your decision, you need to figure out how much you want to spend and how much computer you want. Bear in mind that I'm just talking about the computer itself — the tower, as some call it. I talk about monitors and peripherals later in the chapter.

Also note that many companies now offer laptops that serve as desktop computer replacements. (See the "Do you want a gaming laptop" sidebar, later in this chapter, for more about laptops.) Gaming laptops are typically a wise investment only for people who need the mobility. That said, I spent more than a year playing nearly professional-level *World of Warcraft* on a laptop, so it is entirely possible. Note that the computer specs suggested in the following sections are current as of the writing of this book. Look for updates to be posted every six months or so on this book's page at www.dummies.com.

Keeping it affordable: The bargain esports rig

If your goal is to play *League of Legends, Fortnite, Overwatch, Hearthstone, CS:GO, Apex Legends,* or *Rainbow Six: Siege,* your computer will need to perform at the minimum level to be competitive. The specifications listed in this section are for what is quite literally a minimal machine. With the following specs, you shouldn't face massive lag or processing bottlenecks, but you sacrifice high-end graphics settings and will need to make sure that you don't overheat during long sessions.

The minimal rig requires the following:

>> Windows 10 operating system.

>> Intel Core 5 or AMD Ryzen 7 processor. Scale the GHz based on your budget because either of these families of processors should suffice at entry level.

>> At least 8GB of RAM. The higher the speed, the better.

>> A NVIDIA GTX 1070 graphics card with 8GB of onboard memory.

>> A 500GB hard drive at minimum.

>> A Killer NIC gaming network card with 10/100/1000 Mbps or the equivalent.

>> A 24-inch, 144Hz monitor.

Note that not every component to build a computer appears in this list. If you're building the computer yourself, you need a motherboard that will allow all your components to interface. You also need a power supply, an optical drive, a sound card if you want better than the motherboard's onboard offering, and so on.

Also missing from the list of components in this section are peripherals like a keyboard, mouse, or headset. I cover peripherals in later sections of this chapter, but because peripherals are so personal to the player, these tend to remain static across systems. Price points vary for each of the key gaming items you might buy, but those don't map directly to the quality of your PC. Some players use a $200 keyboard and $200 mouse with an $800 computer, whereas others will play on a $6,000 PC with a $20 keyboard. That's all about player preference.

An example of an entry-level PC that's ready to go out of the box is the following configuration from Alienware (https://www.dell.com/en-us/shop/gaming-and-games/alienware-aurora-gaming-desktop/spd/alienware-aurora-r8-desktop/wdshatcrr811s?view=configurations). Similar systems are available from other retailers, such as Omen, CyberPowerPC, iBUYPOWER, or Origin.

A system like Alienware Aurora allows you to play any of the currently popular esports titles. The vendor's page even lets you see the system's performance by game by using a drop-down menu in the top-left area of the screen. Paired with a monitor like the BenQ Zowie 24 inch XL2411P (https://www.benqdirect.com/monitors/gaming/xl2411p-esports-monitor.html), this system would cost roughly $1,000 plus peripherals. For that entry price point, you can play all the top titles comfortably with some room for growth. The system also allows for upgrading, meaning that you can add RAM, swap video cards, and so on to keep up with the times. Realistically speaking, however, you would be looking at a three-year life span before this computer begins to struggle to keep up with future esports titles.

Moving up to the next level

As with computers purchased for productivity, most serious esports gamers want to have more power than they need in a computer system. Although more power holds an intrinsic appeal, some practical reasons make people want a machine that can handle more of a load than the current big-name games require. Most esports players also watch and create streaming content, play other games that require more processing power than the typical esports titles, and even run or play more than one game at any given time.

You might also take comfort in having a higher-end machine so that you might not need an upgrade as soon as a new "killer app" game is released that increases demands on a system. One of the major demands to think about is virtual reality (VR), which is currently in esports infancy. Having a computer that could run a VR headset is a wise choice for anyone looking to buy a machine that will last more than three years.

A PC that is ready to play esports, create media, run VR, and won't wilt under the pressure of higher-end games has the following specs:

>> Windows 10 operating system.

>> An Intel Core 7 or AMD Ryzen 9. Scale the GHz based on your budget, but you want to look close to the highest-end processor available. The newest processor will have a premium price, but the release just before it will be the best value for the dollar.

>> At least 16GB of RAM. The higher speed, the better.

>> An NVIDIA GTX 1650 graphics card with 8GB onboard memory.

>> At least a 500GB solid-state hard drive.

>> A Killer NIC gaming network card with 10/100/1000 Mbps or the equivalent.

>> A 24-inch, 144Hz monitor.

The biggest differences between this system and the budget-conscious configuration are the following: You want to consider buying a much newer processor, as close to the most recent release as possible; also, you want more RAM and a solid-state hard drive. The speed you gain from these items is one of the most critical upgrades. In addition, you need to upgrade to a higher-end graphics card. At the time of this writing, an NVIDIA 1650 can easily handle any game you might throw at it, but six months before that was how gamers and developers viewed the GTX 1080, which was considered overkill in comparison with the GTX 1070. With the GTX 2060 recently released, keeping a close eye on NVIDIA's cards is a wise idea as you shop.

A system like the HP Omen (https://store.hp.com/us/en/pdp/omen-by-hp-desktop-pc-880-175x?jumpid=ma_weekly-deals_product-tile_desktops_14_3uq94aa_omen-by-hp-desktop-p) is a fantastic example of a system in this category, though similar systems can be found from the other vendors named previously.

Again, the BenQ Zowie XL2411P would pair well with this system, though potential upgrades would include a monitor like the Razer Raptor (https://www.razer.com/gaming-monitors/razer-raptor-27?utm_source=affiliates&utm_mediu=CJ&CJEVENT=4f577a2f34ae11ea82cb034a0a240612). Depending on their competitive game of choice, some gamers don't want to upgrade their monitor size. In fact, I had complaints from my *CS:GO* players when we purchased 27-inch gaming monitors for their practice arena because the difference in size can change redraw and reaction time. Your best option here is to pick a monitor that suits you and stick with it, but if you're looking to compete widely, you should check this book's chapter that covers your preferred game to see what the competition standard monitor is for your game. If you plan to play more casually, and are interested in media production as well, consider a widescreen monitor. And finally, if cost isn't an issue, your absolute best option is to have multiple monitors.

Spending it if you've got it: The computer your friends will envy

A wonderful aspect of computer technology is how often it brings out a hot new component or processor. Having the best computer with all the top-end components is a costly process, however, involving curating your technology and following websites and trends to see when new items release. And even though you can't future-proof a computer because you can't know what the next big thing might be, some computers are so loaded with advanced components that their obsolescence before wearing out from use is unlikely. This is the sort of computer you'll still be playing with when the actual zombie apocalypse hits.

iBUYPOWER's Titan RTX Ultimate Gaming PC (https://www.ibuypower.com/Store/Titan-RTX-Ultimate-Gaming) is an example of a high-end gaming rig. The issue with the highest-end gaming computers is that a new one comes out almost every month. Although the Titan RTX is an absolute beast of a machine at the time that I'm writing this, long before this book is considered old, a PC that makes the Titan RTX look weak by comparison will appear. By the same token, if I bought a Titan RTX today, the odds would be good that I'd still be playing competitive esports games on it in 2030.

Buying this machine means that you're done buying computers for a while. You're ready for the next wave of VR. Barring a quantum leap in technology, you're ready for the next five years of games at the least. You're even ready to stream a movie on Netflix while playing *Overwatch* in one window and *Hearthstone* in another, all the while streaming yourself live on Twitch and Mixer while compressing a video to upload to YouTube. This machine can get it.

DO YOU WANT A GAMING LAPTOP?

Using a laptop for gaming has limitations, and one of the major trade-offs with a laptop relates to price. If you want the level of computing power that a top-of-the-line laptop offers you, the price point will be roughly double that of a desktop with the same specifications.

A recent development in gaming laptops is worth considering. In an effort to compete with Apple's line of MacBook computers, companies like Razer have developed sleek, thin, lightweight gaming laptops. These systems lack some of the power of a desktop, but they can be viable if you're looking for ultra-portable esports computing.

Although Apple makes a great laptop for content creation, you should never buy any Macintosh computer for esports. A very small number of *Hearthstone* pros play on MacBooks, but seeing an esports gamer on a Macintosh is almost unheard of.

Part of my day-to-day work involves working on audio, video, and visual content creation. Alongside my gaming PCs, I own and regularly work with a top-end MacBook Pro. It's fantastic for streaming and for doing all my video work, and it will run a number of games, but the only esport I can play at a competitive level on it is *Hearthstone.* I can also play *Hearthstone* competitively on my phone and on the bargain Asus tablet I purchased for $80 on vacation last year. Macs and gaming are just not a good match.

The most promising thin gaming laptop is the Razer Blade Pro 17 (`https://www.razer.com/store/gaming-laptops`), which comes in multiple configurations from $2,500–$3,700. The highest-end model includes a touchscreen, something that hasn't been an option on any of the other machines discussed in this chapter so far. Although a touchscreen isn't of tremendous value for most current esports titles, as mobile games advance, touchscreens could become an important element because PCs will need to mimic phone and tablet screen interactivity.

The Razer laptop's greatest strength is having its components made by Razer, a company that is focused on gaming peripherals. The screens, although smaller than gaming monitors, are gaming resolution and refresh focused. The keyboard, often a weakness in a laptop, is configured like a high-end gaming keyboard. The Razar laptop also does lots of cool lighting effects (the Alienware does as well). The Razer machine does all this at six pounds of total weight. That's roughly half the weight of most desktop replacements. The price tag is still twice that of a desktop with comparable specs, but if you want a light, mobile gaming machine — for example, if you're about to go off to college and want a machine that you can also take to class — systems like this Razer Blade are worth your consideration.

Setting Up for Today's Console Gaming

Console gaming holds an interesting and sometimes confusing spot in the esports world. If you're interested in more discussion of this dichotomy, see Chapter 1 definitions of how games become classified as esports. In short, though, you should think of it like this: Any game that has competitive play can be defined by certain groups as an esport, including games like *Mario Kart* or *MLB: The Show*. But in the most specific sense, only a few console titles exist among the highly competitive and widely considered high-level esports games. Also worth noting again is that games like *Overwatch* and *CS:GO*, which exist across multiple platforms, have thriving console player bases but are almost never played on consoles at major tournaments. The reason is the massive difference between console and PC-based play. For more on those differences, see Chapter 4 on first-person shooters.

In spite of the usual bias toward PC gaming, enough console games are major esports titles for serious gamers to need access to the current generation of video game consoles. Each console has at least one key title, as described in the following sections.

Playing on Sony's PlayStation 4 Pro

Sony's console remains popular, particularly among *Call of Duty* (*CoD*) players and those who play fighting games. The only PlayStation exclusive game you might think of as an esports title is *MLB: The Show*, one of the only highly developed baseball games with the support of Major League Baseball.

Players interested in fighting games and shooters like *CoD*, as well as players who might want to play *Fortnite* with the popular Sony DualShock 4 controller, should invest in the PlayStation 4 Pro console. Although the Pro model is slightly more expensive than the original PS4 and the PS4 Slim, the added benefits are well worth the cost to gamers. The PS4 Pro outputs in 4K video, whereas the other models output only in 1080p High Definition. The PS4 Pro ships with a larger internal hard drive.

TECHNICAL STUFF

One of the key factors to consider with console gaming is the output quality to the television. PC games allow for resolutions to be set by the software and governed by the computer hardware, but console hardware is locked. In this current generation, the major difference between the available PlayStation 4 and Xbox One consoles is that the higher-end, newer versions of each console output 4K video whereas the older versions output only in 1080p HD. If your television supports 4K, the difference in resolution between 4K and 1080p is significant. (One has double the pixels of the other, allowing for nearly twice the definition.) Even if your TV cannot display 4K, a small upgrade in graphic quality occurs with the 4K-compatible machines because they downsample, meaning that while displaying at 1080p, the source is 4K and contains more detail.

Buying a PlayStation 4 Pro isn't a must for esports, but that doesn't mean that you won't find numerous PS4 esports players and fans. For a player with an esports PC and an Xbox One, the PS4 might be a piece to skip. For a serious console gamer, or for someone who wants to play esports but doesn't want to invest in a PC, the PS4 is a solid purchase.

Gaming on Microsoft's Xbox One

The Microsoft Xbox One X, the newest version of the Xbox console, is the primary fighting game and console shooter competition for Sony's PS4. Although hardcore esports gamers and fans debate about which console has the best controller, with many leaning toward the Sony side of the console "war," the esports reality is that Xbox One has key exclusive titles that make it an esport must for those interested in certain shooters, namely *Halo* and *Gears of War*, though Microsoft has moved to releasing these games on Windows PC as well in recent years.

As with the PS4, multiple versions of the Xbox One are on the market. The best choice for esports gamers is the Xbox One X. Like the PS4 Pro, it ships with a larger hard drive and allows for 4K resolution. It also has a slightly faster processor and graphics core than the initial-launch Xbox consoles. If you know which games you might want to compete in, be aware that Microsoft tends to create bundles, and often even unique consoles with impressive visual appearance differences like colors of custom case art, for major releases, such as this now highly collectible *Gears 5* edition.

REMEMBER

A word of caution regarding the Sony versus Microsoft debate. One of the longest-running contemporary online gaming debates exists between supporters of each console company. Looking at the consoles objectively, they are roughly equal, with some games looking better on one console or the other mostly because games are developed for one console and "ported" to the other and hence use one system more efficiently. In the esports argument, Microsoft gets the nod because of *Gears of War* and *Halo*, but without those exclusive titles, the two consoles would be on equal footing. For people interested in overall gaming, Sony has the advantage because of high-caliber exclusive games like *Spider-Man*, *Horizon: Zero Dawn*, and *God of War*. Because those games aren't esports titles, however, they don't weigh into the commentary here.

Gamers who want to play fighting games on console and who are interested in console *Fortnite* will find the Xbox One X to be a solid choice. If you want to play *Gears 5* or *Halo Infinite*, the Xbox One X is a must.

Enjoying Nintendo's unique esports offerings

Nintendo has a spotty history with esports, as I describe in more detail in Chapter 5. One of Nintendo's older titles, *Super Smash Bros. Melee*, still has something of a powerful esports scene but is played on the Nintendo GameCube, a console that is several generations old and hasn't been sold retail since 2009. Because the console is no longer on the market and *Smash Melee* is 18 years old, Nintendo doesn't support *Melee* competition.

Nintendo has redoubled its efforts to be a part of the esports landscape with the release of its newest console, the Nintendo Switch. Unlike the other consoles listed here, the Switch is both a television-tethered console and a mobile device, allowing for playing on the go. Although numerous games on the console could be considered esports, such as *Fortnite, SMITE,* and the only nonmobile version of the Tencent Games MOBA *Arena of Valor,* the Switch is a must-have for two games: *Super Smash Bros. Ultimate* and *Splatoon 2.*

Smash Ultimate is Nintendo's most recent entry in the *Super Smash Bros.* series and regularly appears at major fighting game tournaments like EVO. For more on *Smash Ultimate,* flip to Chapter 5. In contrast, *Splatoon 2* is a game that Nintendo has pushed as an esport but which hasn't, to this point, taken root in the community as a major title.

Gamers who want to play *Super Smash Bros. Ultimate* and who like the idea of a portable console will find the Switch to be a must-have. Nintendo has recently introduced a cheaper version of the Switch called the Switch Lite, but serious esports gamers want the original version, because the Switch Lite cannot dock and be played on a television and has a less powerful overall processor. You should also invest in a large-capacity SD card to add to the system's internal storage, along with some manner of controller so that you aren't trying to play competitive *Smash Ultimate* on the functional but small Joy-Cons that come connected to the console. The most recommended controller for competition is the Nintendo Switch Pro Controller (https://www.nintendo.com/switch/buy-now/?cid=A1000-01:ch=pdpd).

WHAT YOU NEED TO PLAY *SMASH MELEE*

Playing *Super Smash Bros. Melee* is an exercise in retro gaming. To be able to play competitively, you need to obtain the following items, which are somewhat rare but not particularly expensive in some cases:

- **A functioning Nintendo GameCube console:** The best places to look for these are eBay.com or a local retro game shop. You should be able to find one for less than $100.

- **A copy of *Super Smash Bros. Melee*:** It still fetches nearly its original retail price but can be bought for $35–$45.

- **At least one quality GameCube controller:** Nintendo replicas (not produced by Nintendo) and newer versions of these controllers made for systems like the Switch can be found for $25–$50, but highly competitive players favor original controllers or refurbished and modified controllers like the ones for sale at sites like Multishine (https://multishine.tech/). A quality, tournament-ready GC controller can cost as much as $200.

- **A Cathode-Ray Tube (CRT) television:** Once the most common type of TV set, these are the heavy TV sets you might have watched your parents or neighbors toss away when they upgraded to their current model. If you're older, you probably had one of these as a kid. The size of CRT you want depends on whether you prefer to be able to easily take your TV to a tournament. Unlike current TVs and monitors, most CRTs have the same display ratio, so the size matters only in terms of the actual size of the display. Finding a CRT can be tricky, but sites like Craigslist can be your friend on your search. You might be lucky enough to find a friend or family member who has an old one they just want out of their way. Although not usually expensive, this item is often the most difficult one to find for a *Melee* gamer.

Smash Melee can also be emulated on PC, though the legality of playing that way is questionable. Because CRTs are difficult to find, many retro arcades and local game shops offer *Smash Melee* events where the TVs are provided.

Playing Big: Nothing Says Esports Like a Large TV

Esports computer monitors tend to stick to a specific size, hovering at around 24 to 27 inches, but televisions run to a much wider range of sizes, both in competition and for home use. Here are four factors to consider as you seek the perfect television to pair with your esports consoles:

>> **Is the TV 4K?** Although the current Nintendo Switch does not output in 4K, the PS4 Pro and Xbox One X do, and that change in resolution makes a dramatic difference. A year ago, 4K might have seemed like a luxury, but for competitive gaming, 4K is a must.

>> **Does the TV have high dynamic range (HDR)?** HDR allows for brighter colors and darker blacks. Although this feature might seem like a luxury, it's a key element for gaming because of the importance of color and contrast to many titles. In shooter games like *Gears 5,* for example, the capability to reproduce low-light environments with a wider gray and black scaling range means that players can see parts of the environment and other key indicators that would be difficult if not impossible to properly discern on a television with washed-out color.

>> **Does the TV have a solid refresh rate and response time?** These are key measurements for computer monitors, but historically these measurements have been less critical to television because of the relatively low importance of response time in watching (as opposed to playing). TVs on the market today still lag behind television monitors, but you should try to find a TV that runs at 60Hz.

>> **Do you need a large TV or are you better off gaming on a computer monitor?** Your answer depends on the size of the space in which you intend to play and what else you plan to use the TV for. If you're just going to play games and you plan to play close to your PC gaming area, you could get by with using your monitor with your consoles or with buying a similar monitor for your console gaming area.

Assuming that you want a bigger screen than your computer monitor, you should next examine the space where you'll be gaming and think about what would be an optimal size. Being close to a screen that is too large impedes your play because of the amount of screen surface you have to view at any given time.

TIP

The easiest rule to use in gauging the best screen size is whether you need to move your head to comfortably see all parts of the screen. If you can't comfortably track the full screen just by moving your eyes, the display is too large. If you prefer to think about it mathematically, measure your gaming space and buy a television that will be roughly the same size diagonally as the distance you plan to sit from the screen. So, for example, if your TV will be 5 feet from where you sit when you play, you should look for a 60- to 65-inch TV.

Other elements can come into play as well. For example, if you tend to have issues with vision from a distance, you might want to go with a bit larger screen.

Although you should consider a number of technical factors when choosing a TV for gaming, many people forget to factor in the environment in which the TV will sit. Keep in mind these three aspects of your environment to help you have a better gaming experience:

» **Direct light sources:** Think about the light in the area. Try to avoid putting your TV right in front of or across from a window. If you must position near a window, make sure to have a curtain or blind that can block as much light as possible during the day. Many places sell curtains and blinds called "black out" for this specific purpose. Position the TV so that it isn't directly under or next to a light source that you plan to keep on when you are playing. Ideally, you will turn off all the lights other than potential bias lighting (explained shortly) while you play.

» **Screen height:** Think carefully about the height of the screen. This aspect isn't as easy to determine as the size versus distance issue mentioned earlier because you need to factor in the height at which you sit as you play. You should be able to see the screen comfortably while sitting up straight on whatever furniture you will use as you play. Think this issue through carefully before picking a TV stand or wall mounting for your screen. A common mistake is mounting a screen high on the wall. Needing to look up to see the screen is likely to result in neck stress and a less enjoyable experience.

» **Bias lighting:** Setting up bias lighting helps your viewing experience as well. In the first point in this list, I suggest avoiding light pollution, but doing so leads to a second problem with human vision. Our eyes strain from the darkness of a room if the only light is from a single bright source such as a TV. You avoid this eye strain by applying lighting to the back of the TV, projecting it onto the wall. This light source gives the effect of the TV glowing from the back, which keeps your eyes from straining. It also gives the overall TV unit a cool, edgy look. Some high-end sets even provide bias lighting that adapts to the colors on the screen. TV manufacturers are numerous, and sets run the gamut from bargain to luxury pricing. For the recommendations in the following sections, I assume that you're looking at a 65-inch screen. You can look at the same brands and specs for smaller or larger sizes as needed. Other than the absolute largest sizes, you should find that across brands, the prices stay proportional.

Considering a right option

If your goal is to find quality without having to spend a premium price, beating the color quality of Vizio's sets would be difficult. A good, starter-level esports gaming TV from Vizio is the Vizio D-Series D65-F3 (https://www.vizio.com/d65e0.html). For around $800, this set offers HDR and all the elements you might need for a starter TV. The built-in speakers are generally viewed as low quality, leading most people to buy external speakers, and although the picture is high quality, the image processor isn't as good as a high-end unit. For the price, however, you get everything you need. Many teams use these screens for game video review in their esports arenas.

Looking at the midrange TV

If you want to go with a TV that has a bit more punch than the bargain level offers, the LG OLED (https://www.lg.com/us/tvs/lg-OLED65C9PUA-oled-4k-tv) 65-inch offers more future-proof elements than the Vizio described in the previous section. It also offers a better image processor, better speakers, and some bells and whistles that you might not need for gaming but that will enhance other aspects of your TV use, like Amazon's Alexa functionality (voice command) and the ability to run apps like Netflix and Hulu. The price for this TV is significantly higher than the Vizio, however, retailing for around $2,500. A major consideration here is how much you want to invest and how often you want to replace or upgrade your TV. Although the LG should last you twice as long as the Vizio, the price-to-life-of-use equation isn't favorable. If you have the money to spend, though, you will enjoy noticeably higher quality.

Going for a true luxury set

If you have another $1,000 dollars to spend on top of the LG TV, you'd be hard-pressed to find a better set than Sony's Bravia A9G (https://www.sony.com/electronics/televisions/xbr-a9g-series/buy/xbr65a9g).

Sony has, for years, been the industry leader for image processing, and this Bravia tests at the top of the market in terms of color reproduction, refresh rate, and image clarity. Sony's built-in sound is such that you might not need external speakers, which is a plus. If you're trying to maximize your value for the money, you probably can't justify the price difference between the $3,500 Sony and the LG, but you will absolutely see a quality difference.

REMEMBER

Other than that of the Sony described in this section, the sound provided by a TV isn't likely to meet the expectations of most gamers. Myriad soundbars and speakers are available for you to consider if you buy a different set. In contrast to other peripherals, however, choosing the right soundbar depends on how loud and clear you want the sound to be in the room you're playing in. For competitions, you will be much more concerned with the quality of your headset because you will almost always be wearing it when playing competitively, which will be the sound source that matters for gameplay.

Picking Your Peripherals

When you compete in esports, computers and consoles are often provided at the competitions. The items to bring with you are in the category called peripherals. These include:

>> Keyboard

>> Mouse

>> Mouse pad

>> Headset

>> Controller

A number of factors influence how gamers select each of these key items. Some players favor a particular brand across the board; others have a favorite company for each type of peripheral. Some players prefer a specific model of a specific item and seek out that same device when their current one gets old. I often explain this to people who are new to esports by making the comparison to traditional sports. Certain items are issued to everyone in sports (uniforms, for example), but the other gear, such as a basketball player's or runner's shoes, a football player's helmet, or a baseball player's glove or bat, tend to be highly personal. When I was a basketball player a lifetime ago, I always wore Air Jordan sneakers. I was particularly partial to the Jordan 11. I had roughly ten pairs of them over a three-year period because they were all I would wear. As an esports player, I have the same preference with my Razer keyboard. I need to have the response of its green switches to feel as though I'm playing my way. (More on switches later in this chapter.)

This section offers some key elements to consider and some recommendations of where to start as you look for your peripherals, but the key takeaway is that you need to go to a store where you can touch and tinker with these devices before you buy. The tactile qualities as well as the look of your equipment are critical determining factors in choosing your peripherals. No one, not even the best professional esports player, can tell you what your best option will be for each piece of equipment.

Choosing a keyboard

One of the most important connections that computer users have to their machine is their choice of keyboard. For some, using whatever keyboard came with their PC is fine. Others have no problem with a simple off-the-shelf, store-brand replacement. Most esports players, however, swear by mechanical keyboards, which I explain in the next section.

Considering two ways to play (but don't pick the membrane)

Basically keyboard construction comes in two types: the common (and economical) method of creating a keyboard that uses a rubber membrane for resistance as the keys are pressed; and a mechanical method wherein each key has its own button mechanism.

Some games that are not keyboard-input intensive can be played competitively with a membrane keyboard, but in almost 99 percent of cases, a competitive gamer wants a mechanical keyboard. Mechanical keyboards offer three benefits over membrane keyboards:

>> **Each key has its own individual input.** This type of input eliminates *ghosting*, which occurs when the keyboard reads multiple inputs when you tap a key. For example, on a membrane keyboard, a quick depression of the *G* key could be read as the user having hit the *G*, the *F*, and the *H*. Likewise, three quick taps of the *G* key could be read as three taps of that array of keys, or as only two taps, or, in an extreme case, as one tap. Some esports require an intense actions-per-minute (APM) count. A typical user or beginning player hovers around 50 APM, meaning that it takes more than a second to register an action. High-level professionals, particularly with games like *StarCraft*, can approach 400 APM, which means that the player is averaging just over six and a half inputs per second. Such intense play requires a quick response from the keyboard or imput device. A membrane keyboard would struggle to register those individual keystrokes, likely keeping the player from completing any cluster of actions within the game. (The ghosting on a membrane keyboard is irregular and unpredictable.)

>> **Mechanical keys last longer.** A typical mechanical key is rated for 50 million keystrokes. A membrane keyboard — even the most expensive, well-made ones — maxes out at around 5 million keystrokes. Many high-end mechanical keyboards also allow for individual replacement of switches and keys, which means that a gamer who heavily uses the *W, A, S,* and *D* keys — a typical movement cluster of keys — could replace those keys to lengthen the life of the keyboard.

>> **Mechanical switches, and the keycaps, can be customized so that a player gets a specific feel from the keyboard.** This feel would theoretically port to other keyboards because the switches are standardized, and any keyboard with cherry-red switches, for example, should offer the same response as another. This capability is important for gamers because it means that they have a level of control over the response rate, sound, and feel of their keys. It also means that after a player picks a switch type, buying a new keyboard with the same switches should result in the same key response.

Making the switch to switches

Selecting the right type of mechanical switch depends on how you answer the following:

» **Do you want linear or tactile switches?** A linear switch requires a full depression of the keycap to register an input. In contrast, a tactile switch requires the key to be depressed only about halfway, at which point it emits a click and you will feel a bit of feedback in your finger. You can continue to push a tactile switch without activating it further, but you can also stop when the key has registered and then move to your next input. Neither key type has an advantage for competition, but one will almost certainly suit you the best. Try both to determine which one literally feels better.

» **How much resistance do you want before a keystroke registers?** You can select switches that are stiffer or less resistant. You can also select shorter switches, meaning that the actual height and hence the amount of time needed to depress them lessens.

» **How loud do you want your keys to be?** Mechanical keys range from performing silently to clacking like an old typewriter, so you can play noise-lessly or on a keyboard so loud that your roommate (or in my case, wife) slowly loses her mind from the incessant clicking. This might seem like a trivial element to you if you haven't played with a mechanical keyboard, but in addition to people either loving or loathing the noise, those audible clicks can become an important part of gameplay timing as the clicks register the keys activating.

You might have noticed that earlier in the chapter I mention my preference for Razer green switches. Razer greens are tactile, require 50g of weight to activate, and emit a distinct clicking noise. They stack up as average for loud, mechanical, tactile keys, and are a solid starting point for someone who is new to mechanical keyboards.

Trying some recommendations

Keeping in mind that your choice of keyboard is a highly personal thing, you might find a board like the Razer Huntsman (https://www.razer.com/gaming-keyboards-keypads/razer-huntsman-elite) to be a great starting point. It will set you back $150–$200, depending on the configuration you choose, but it should last you ten years. The Huntsman has an Opto-Mechnical switch, which is unlike any of the switches mentioned in this section. The switch uses a light beam instead of a metal-on-metal connection, allowing for key activation with more speed and accuracy than other keyboards on the market. It is available in both a loud "clicky" version and a silent version.

In addition to its interesting and effective switches, the Huntsman, like most of Razer's products, has a wide range of color lighting options that you can control through software. The Elite version also has a wrist rest with illumination. The lighting doesn't add much in terms of function, but it looks cool sitting on your desk and adds a level of gamer credibility if you take it to a competition.

A cheaper potential starter mechanical keyboard is the Corsair K66 (go to `https://www.corsair.com` and search **K66**). The K66 lacks the visual bells and whistles, but the construction is solid. It comes with a variety of switch options. For $70 as of this writing, this is an ideal budget mechanical keyboard. If you choose to shop for something cheaper, make sure to investigate the switch quality. Googling the model number should yield you all the information you need.

Looking at the price difference in those two recommended keyboards brings up the perpetual final element that you need to consider as a gamer: How do you want your gear to look? The lighting options and styling of the Razer keyboard make it an attractive option, but in terms of performance alone, it probably isn't worth the extra $100. The cosmetics, though, often make the gear.

TIP

Remember to try before you buy if at all possible. Mechanical keys are something to test drive before investing. If you go to a big box retailer like Best Buy or Fry's, you find that most mechanical keyboard boxes have a small open space on the front so that you can tap a few of the keys. Many stores also have display units sitting out so that you can type a few sentences.

Of mice and mousepads: Picking your input device

Older readers will remember the days when mice contained a rubber-coated metal ball that rolled to indicate the movement of the pointer or element onscreen. Gamers of this generation and in the future are spared the horror of having to open the mouse and clean the pet hair and snack crumbs from the ball to regain precision, but the same principle guides the most important elements of mouse selection: dots per inch (DPI) and polling rate.

TECHNICAL
STUFF

DPI is a term used in various forms of digital media to refer to the density of the pixels in an image. For a mouse, it indicates how much of your screen it can traverse in a single movement. In contrast to photographs or video, higher DPI for a mouse isn't automatically better, though the capacity for it is. *Polling rate*, the other key technical element involved in mouse design, refers to how often the mouse communicates to the computer, measured in hertz, or Hz. In the case of polling rate, higher is always better, although a delicate balance exists between a polling rate so high that the mouse starts to hog resources and a polling rate that results in lag: 500 Hz is a good ceiling for polling rate.

Knowing the key factors for choosing your mouse

In the discussion about keyboards in the preceding section, speed is a critical factor. Movement speed, DPI, and response rate are all established through software, so your only concern about DPI and movement speed is to ensure that the mouse you're buying doesn't have a mechanical limit that could impact your configuration (likely to happen only if you're looking for a particularly obscure brand). Other aspects do matter, however. Here are the chief elements to think through when buying a mouse:

>> **Can you customize the mouse settings through software?** You can usually determine what you can do by looking at the manufacturer's website before buying. Typically, any company with a reputation for making quality peripherals will have a software suite that allows you all the customization you would ever need, so don't worry with brands like Corsair, Logitech, Razer, or SteelSeries. Other companies produce quality, but make sure that you can change settings as you desire.

>> **Is the mouse wired or wireless?** If you're serious about your gaming, the best answer is "wired" because a wireless mouse introduces a chance for another point of lag. If you're playing a game that doesn't need speed and pinpoint precision, however, wireless is an option. If you want both, look for a wireless mouse that also runs while connected through a USB. For most games, though, risking wireless mouse connectivity is a bad idea.

>> **How many buttons do you want or need?** Most high-end mice have numerous programmable buttons along with the scroll wheel that can serve as a button as well. Depending on the game you play and your gaming style, you probably have a preferred number of buttons. Some players thrive with just two buttons. Others use a mouse like the Logitech G600 (https://www. logitechg.com/en-us/products/gaming-mice/g600-mmo-gaming-mouse.html), which boasts a staggering 20 programmable buttons. In some cases, those buttons also have switches like the keyboard keys mentioned in the preceding section, thereby adding another element to consider.

>> **How much of an investment do you want to make?** In contrast to PCs, keyboards, consoles, and even TVs, mice tend to break down after intense use regardless of the quality of the build. That said, typically a $100 mouse lasts longer than a $30 one, but pro gamers will be quick to tell you that if you find a mouse that you love, you'd better buy a few of them before the model rotates out of production. Knowing that you might replace it after a year because of intense use, measure your mouse purchase according to that standard. Also look carefully at the construction of the mouse. Any soft rubber or loose parts on the chassis that might seem stylish will break down quicker.

>> **Related to all four previous points, how cool do you want your mouse to look?** Nifty lights and high-quality materials correlate directly with price, just as you might expect. My current mouse, for example, is a Razer Mamba Elite (https://www.razer.com/gaming-mice/razer-mamba-elite). For my gaming needs, I could have competed easily with a mouse that was half the cost, but given that I have a high-end Razer keyboard right next to my mouse, and the same lighting programming that runs my keyboard coordinates with the mouse, my gamer vanity made the Mamba a must-buy.

Trying some recommendations

If you decide to pick up a Razer Huntsman keyboard (described in the "Choosing a keyboard" section, earlier in the chapter), take a look at the Mamba Elite. It matches with the color programming of the Razer Huntsman and has the same level of polish and general feel. The buttons on it react like mechanical keyboard keys instead of typical buttons.

TIP

When looking at peripherals, people commonly look for the best fit regardless of brand, but you can benefit from choosing all your gear from the same company. A keyboard, mouse, and headset are typically controlled by a piece of software called a control panel. These control panels are often inclusive of all the items the company makes. This means that if you have a Razer keyboard, mouse, and headset, you can control all three of them with one piece of software. If you have a Razer, a Logitech, and a SteelSeries peripheral, you have to download and manage three different control panels. This necessity can become problematic when you travel to a competition and use someone else's computer. Gathering all that software and installing it before play can be difficult.

If you are concerned only about functionality, and lights and styling aren't a key element, you can easily compete with a mouse like the SteelSeries Rival 110 (https://steelseries.com/), an attractive mouse that you can find for $25–$30.

Padding your stats with a mouse pad

For about a decade, people thought that you didn't need a mouse pad for an optical mouse. That's not accurate. You need a mouse pad so that you have a consistent, efficient surface for your mouse to track. All that matters about the mouse pad is that it presents a good tracking surface for your mouse, though. Players often choose between small and incredibly large mousepads, some of which are so large that they look more like a desk blotter and sit below the keyboard, too, during play. Some swear by a harder, slick surface; others favor the classic fabric feel for their pad. Cosmetic options abound.

The type of mouse pad you have isn't likely to make a dramatic difference in your gaming, but you absolutely need an actual mouse pad. Tracking your mouse on a desk surface, or on the back of a magazine, loses valuable precision. It also wears out the surface of your desk unevenly.

Listen, hear: Picking the right headset

Gaming headsets are often a point of discussion and contention among players. I've watched professional players plug in a microphone to communicate and pop in cheap ear buds at tournaments. I've seen others pull out velvet drawstring bags that contain high-end, light-laden headsets that look as impressive as they sound.

When picking a headset, consider the following:

>> **How important is sound quality to you?** Just as you experience a difference between a pair of airplane freebie ear buds and a pair of Beats headphones, the speaker and microphone quality in headsets vary greatly. A big question to consider is whether you want to enjoy music and other media with this headset or if it's just for playing a game, and having a listening experience, such as with music, isn't a key element.

>> **Do you want an external microphone or one that's stuck to your headset?** With an external microphone, you can speak to people while you play; however, most people choose a headset with the microphone built in. If you choose a headset like that, you have to think about the quality of the speakers as well as the microphone, and sometimes those won't be created equal.

>> **Do you want to be able to use this headset with a console, too, or just with your PC?** Although all platforms have their own headsets, some sets can move between devices.

>> **Do you want wired or wireless?** As with mice, response time is quicker with the wired version than with wireless. The issue isn't as critical with sound as it is with the mouse simply because milliseconds won't matter as much with sound response. When hundredths of a second matter, the wiring is critical. With sound, it's not as big of a deal. Still, the general recommendation is to go with something wired.

The best advice anyone can offer you about a headset is to test listen if you can. Many factors go into choosing headphones for listening. From a gaming perspective, liking the sound of a headset at whatever level you typically play is key. Some headsets have more bass than others. Some can produce more sound, some have better vocal clarity, and some stand out in other ways. More expensive headsets offer better sound all the way around.

I currently use a SteelSeries Arctis Pro (`https://steelseries.com/gaming-headsets/arctis-pro`) headset. It's a high-end headset with a solid microphone and amazing speakers. I based my choice on the fact that when I'm not gaming, I'm listening to music while I work, and because I travel frequently, having a good-quality headset is useful. I also own a pair of Beats Pro (`https://www.beatsbydre.com/headphones/pro`) headphones, and the Arctis sounds almost identical. The Beats has a stronger bass, though not by much. If you want a great headset, the Arctis is a good choice.

If you're just looking for a good headset for gaming and aren't concerned about content-production quality from your microphone or expensive, headphone-caliber audio, you may do well with the HyperX Cloud Stinger (`https://www.hyperxgaming.com/us/headsets/cloud-stinger-gaming-headset`), which many players swear by. It's a $50 or less unit that will perform well in any esport. The Cloud Stinger is also compatible with consoles.

Taking control: Controllers that rule the game

Given the importance of controllers to gaming, there isn't nearly the competition among providers for high-end controllers in the esports world as there is for mice and keyboards. Few people use controllers for PC-based games. So few, in fact, that buying a controller for your PC isn't recommended. If you need a controller for a PC game and have consoles around, those controllers will work.

The Xbox controller

The Xbox One controller shows up frequently in various esports spaces because it's easy to use with Windows computers, but if you're serious about competition, you should consider only one controller for the Xbox One: the Xbox Elite Controller (`https://www.xbox.com/en-US/xbox-one/accessories/controllers/elite-wireless-controller-series-2`). For $180, you should expect quality, and that's exactly what you get. Microsoft worked closely with professional gamers to determine exactly what players want and need, and this controller is the resulting design. I rarely gush over a gaming item, but I've had my version one Xbox Elite Controller since it launched in October 2015, and it has made a clear difference in my console play. I favor the controller so much that I often try to avoid playing PS4 games in competition just because Sony doesn't have a controller that comes close. If you play on Xbox One, invest in the Elite Controller.

Sony PlayStation 4 controller

In contrast to what happened with Microsoft's Xbox (that is, players didn't like the original controller), the PlayStation's DualShock 4 controller is beloved by many gamers. The controller comes with the console and is comfortable and efficient. DualShock 4 controllers don't wear particularly well, however.

Two other options are favored by most competitive gamers who move away from the DS4. The first is a controller made by a company named Scuf. The Scuf Vantage (https://scufgaming.com/playstation-vantage-controller) is popular because of the level of customization available and its rugged construction. The controller has received complaints regarding calibration, however, which turns some gamers off. The Vantage 2 is now available as well.

The other PS4 option is the Razer Raiju (https://www.razer.com/gb-en/gaming-controllers/razer-raiju-tournament-edition), a well-built controller that integrates some of the technology that Razer uses in its mice and keyboards. This particular controller is used less in North America than in Europe, but at the same price point as the Scuf controller, it's feature rich and more durably built. Some models of the Raiju allow for moving the directional pads as well, which let a PS4 player play with an Xbox control style configuration. That configuration situates the primary directional pad on the upper left of the controller, as opposed to being in the lower-left-central position, where it sits on a DualShock.

Switch gaming controllers and other controller considerations

Of the wide variety of controllers available for the Switch, the Switch Pro Controller, made by Nintendo, is one of the few contemporary controllers that serious players use. Many *Smash Ultimate* players opt for modified original GameCube controllers, also manufactured by Nintendo. Players can use those controllers with the Switch through a converter dongle that you can easily obtain from numerous vendors and manufacturers online.

TIP

The one key factor to keep in mind above all others is that if you plan to compete in major tournaments, you need to have a tourney-approved controller. All the models recommended in this section are viable at major tournaments, but if you go exploring for controllers, make sure to think about whether it will be scrutinized when you go to compete. If you plan to simply play at home, this issue isn't a factor, but if you choose to seek out local competitions or larger semipro or professional events, don't show up with a controller by an unknown manufacturer, or with one that looks bizarre or has clearly been tampered with. If you're unsure, ask the vendor. If the vendor doesn't know whether the controller is usually competition compliant, that's a good sign to proceed with caution and do your homework. Remember that Google is your friend, and with an accurate model number, you can most likely find all the information you need about a device in a matter of minutes.

A final controller consideration is whether to buy a fight stick. A fight stick is a controller with a large base that contains an arcade-style joystick and a series of precise calibrated buttons. This choice depends largely on the games you choose to play. You can find more details about fight sticks in Chapter 5, in the discussion of fighting games. In most cases, a fight stick would be inefficient for any other esports-related titles because the size of the stick and configuration of the buttons work against the design of having shoulder buttons and triggers.

2

The Games You'll Play

Learn about the MOBA genre and games like *League of Legends*.

Discover key first-person shooter titles like *Counter-Strike: Global Offensive*.

Take a closer look at fighting games like *Mortal Kombat* and *Street Fighter*.

Explore the vast options for sports simulations like *Madden NFL*.

Check out the rise of battle royale games like *Fortnite*.

Shuffle through the world of virtual card games like *Hearthstone*.

Chapter **3**

Playing RTS Games and MOBAs

I n November of 1994, a relatively unknown studio by the name of Blizzard released a real-time strategy (RTS) game called *Warcraft: Orcs & Humans*. Primarily a one-player game, the original *Warcraft* is worlds away from the current offerings from esports giant Blizzard, but at the time of its release, *Warcraft: Orcs & Humans* was one of the first RTS games to capture the imagination of players, leading Blizzard to develop two sequels as well as a sci-fi-themed companion title, *StarCraft*. Esports competition as it exists today began with *StarCraft*.

In this chapter, you see how modding *SCII* and *Warcraft III* led to the birth of a new genre called the MOBA, and you find out the key games in the MOBA genre. I also touch briefly on playing professional esports on phones.

Grasping the RTS Genre

The real-time-strategy (RTS) genre emerged from the older turn-based tradition in which one player completed a set of moves or actions for a turn; then the next player likewise completed a turn, and so on until all players had a turn. A new round of play then started with the original first player until that round was completed in the same fashion. In RTS, the game speeds up because all the involved players can act in real time.

RTS games consist of maps, with each player (or artificial intelligence computer opponent) possessing a base and a series of buildings or other structures. The goal is to gather resources and build units — such as soldiers or vehicles — that the players eventually deploy to attempt to destroy any other players' bases.

The best way to understand an RTS in action is to look at how the one that is still currently played as an esport works. Here are the steps involved in playing *StarCraft II*:

1. **Select your faction.**

   You can select from three factions: Protoss, Terran, or Zerg. Each faction has its own specific gameplay criteria, but the three are almost perfectly balanced, leading to even matches across skill levels.

2. **Spend a period of time building and exploring.**

   You can build bases, barracks, and other needed resources while sending some early units out to explore the map, looking for the opponents.

3. **Approach "fog of war" areas carefully.**

   The map has a mechanism called "the fog of war," which obscures from view any area a player hasn't entered yet. This fog necessitates and rewards exploration but also reinforces the need for caution.

4. **Advance and attempt to destroy other players' units and bases.**

   You start this battle phase after you have developed what you consider to be a large enough number of offensive units. During this period, you must preserve and maintain some resources or your defenses (and offensive ability) will dissolve.

5. **Keep playing until all players but one surrender.**

   The game ends when only one player's base remains or all other players surrender.

StarCraft became an esports hit in South Korea, and in the minds of many, it was responsible for creating the esports competitions we see and understand today. *StarCraft* sometimes had major issues with game balancing (which helps each faction have equal powers and abilities), however, and worldwide enthusiasm for the game didn't arise until the release of *StarCraft II* in 2010. *StarCraft II* is still played competitively by several competitive bodies, including Intel Extreme Masters (IEM) and Global *StarCraft II* League (GSL), though the majority of that competition happens in South Korea. Blizzard has sponsored a *StarCraft II* World Championship

Series (WCS) since 2012, with the finals happening at BlizzCon, Blizzard's Annual Fan Conference and gathering in Anaheim, CA (https://wcs.starcraft2.com/en-us/news/22945358/). In 2019, the prize pool for the WCS was $700,000.

Understanding the staying power of *StarCraft II*

StarCraft II is one of the oldest games currently offering regular publisher-supported world championship competitions. Almost a decade after its release, *StarCraft II* maintains its position because of its massive popularity in South Korea and by being one of the most balanced esports. In addition, being a single-player game — also rare for esports — and free to play (Blizzard made it that way in November 2017) have helped the game retain players and gain new users.

Perhaps the biggest reason that *StarCraft II* persists is that it has one of the highest skill ceilings. The top players in the world average 600 actions per minute, as noted in the article "StarCraft 2 and the quest for the highest APM," by Kevin James Wong at www.engadget.com. That speed equates to 10 actions per second, and to watch the hands of a player who operates that fast is fascinating. In addition to creating that many inputs, the player has to be able to strategize and organize at the same time. That level of input speed and volume is unheard of in other current top-tier esports games.

Getting why *StarCraft II* (and RTSs) are fading, though

The free-to-play change by Blizzard gave *StarCraft II* a small resurgence in North America, but RTS games haven't had the staying power outside of South Korea because of the desires of esports players and the available titles. A *StarCraft II* match moves slowly from the start and can be less enjoyable to watch as a spectator. In contrast, games like *Overwatch* (a first-person shooter) open with almost instant action and draw in players and viewers alike.

The single biggest reason that RTS games lost ground is that the RTS itself, through the inclusion of game and map editors, spawned its own replacement. With the release of *Warcraft III: The Frozen Throne,* map editors were able to create a modified game called *Defense of the Ancients* (or *DotA*). *DotA* was the first MOBA game and is to this day the only esports game genre to be created by fans and later turned into not just a single game but many titles with different features based on the basic premise of *DotA.* The short answer to why *StarCraft II* lost popularity in most parts of the world is that the player base that was interested in *SC* and *SCII* moved on to MOBAs. Right now, *League of Legends* and *Dota 2* are both in the top-five most popular esports titles worldwide.

DEFENSE OF THE ANCIENTS: FROM FAN MOD TO THREE TRIPLE-A TITLES

In 2003, a player named Eul (Kyle Sommer) developed a substantial mod — that is, a modified version of the game made with editing software — to *Warcraft III* that he called *Defense of the Ancients (DotA)*. Eul's goal was to make a quicker playing version of *WCIII* that would allow players to focus more on the combat and attack strategies and less on the building and resource management. The result was a version of the game in which players took on the role of a hero, a unit with specialized abilities. Players in the game form two teams of five heroes each, with the goal being to destroy the opposing base.

DotA went through a number of revisions, along the way gaining a number of community assistant developers. The open source project was headed first by Eul and then by Steve "Guinsoo" Feak before being taken over by IceFrog, the developer who balances *Dota 2* to this day. A wonderfully detailed history of *DotA*'s development can be found online at Liquipedia (`https://liquipedia.net/dota2/Dota_History/Part_1`).

For years, Blizzard allowed *DotA* to be played in tournaments, going so far as to sponsor some of those events. But eventually, Blizzard became concerned about the use of its intellectual property. This concern caused a three-way split in how development proceeded:

- Blizzard asserted control of the property and started developing a game. It had numerous names during development (including *Blizzard AllStars*) but was eventually published in June 2015 as *Heroes of the Storm (HotS)*. Although *HotS* still exists and has a decent player base, in late 2018 Blizzard announced that it wouldn't be continuing its competitive esports support for the title, thereby ending its popular collegiate *Heroes of the Dorm* tournament and the *Heroes of the Storm* Global Championship professional event.

- IceFrog asserted that *DotA* was his. He formed a team with the publisher Valve and created the stand-alone game that was released in July 2013 as *Dota 2*. *Dota 2* — which is not *Defense of the Ancients 2* but is the spiritual successor to the mod — is one of the largest esports titles in the world. The *Dota 2* International, their world championship, annually has the largest tournament purse in all of esports. The 2019 International prize pool was $34 million.

- Steve Feak, meanwhile, teamed up with newcomer Riot Games to develop a game bringing what Feak felt was all of what made *DotA* great. The resulting title, 2009's *League of Legends*, became the most popular esports in the world based on viewership. At one point, *League of Legends'* 100-million-active player base dwarfed any other game on the market. *The League of Legends* World Championship (often called "Worlds" by fans), meanwhile, remains an esports viewership juggernaut. In 2018, Worlds had almost 100 million viewers, second among major sporting events to only the Super Bowl. More people watched the *League* World finals than the NBA Finals, the World Series, the Olympics, or the Masters of Golf!

Understanding the Basics of a MOBA

A Multiplayer Online Battle Arena (MOBA) is a team-versus-team competition in which the goal is to destroy the opponent's base. Strategically, it is similar to Capture the Flag if the goal after the capture were to destroy the flag, too. The vast majority of MOBAs are five-versus-five competitions, though modes exist in some games with teams of three players each, two players each, and even one player each. Although map format and layout can change, the two bases are typically positioned in opposing corners with a top lane, a middle lane, and a bottom lane connecting the two sides. Figure 3-1 shows this positioning.

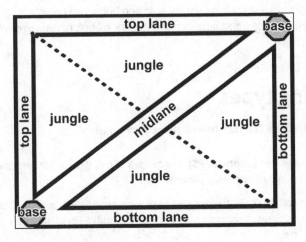

FIGURE 3-1: The most basic form of a MOBA map.

With some variation, MOBAs contain the criteria explained in the following sections.

Playing characters and roles

Player characters have basic attacks and special skills. Characters have role-playing game-style progression and gain experience within each match but reset to level 1 to start the next match. This approach varies from the more conventional RPG method of having the character retain levels after each play session. The new build in every match is part of the appeal of MOBA gaming. Players can select skills as the character levels up, allowing for the player to customize play style.

Typically, players have one of the following roles, which are defined by their position on the map:

>> **Solo laner:** Takes the shortest lane from their team's first tower to the other team's first tower

>> **Mid laner:** Plays the middle lane on the map and should excel in destroying groups of opposing creeps as they approach in waves

>> **Duo laner:** Either a support character or someone who can absorb damage; plays the lane with the longer distance between friendly and enemy towers

>> **Jungler:** Roams the area between the lanes and destroys as many things as possible to level quickly, gather gold and buffs, and be able to "gank," which means to slide into a lane to make a quick kill before returning to working the jungle

Playing types

Most characters fall into one of three play types:

>> **Damage Per Second (DPS):** Characters of this type are meant specifically to do damage to opposing players.

>> **Support:** Typically, these types of players are healers or characters who can create shields. A support player's role is to make sure that other characters don't die.

>> **Tank:** These characters absorb damage so that others can do damage. The primary goal of a tank is to occupy enemies while not dying.

Playing in the lanes

Most activity occurs in three of the "lanes":

>> **Top lane:** Typically, this is the lane with the shorter distance between towers or the solo lane.

>> **Mid lane:** This is the large lane that runs across the middle of the map, typically where the most creep wave — the automated minion characters — clearance is needed.

>> **Bottom lane:** This is typically the lane with the longer distance between towers; also called the duo lane.

Acquiring gold and skills

MOBAs have a variety of other standard characteristics as well. They have a series of "jungle" areas in which players can kill nonplayer characters (NPCs) for experience, to earn gold, and to gain skill "buffs," or temporary upgrades to their skills. Creeps, or waves of AI NPCs that fight for the player, deploy at timed intervals in each of the lanes. Some type of currency — usually gold — can be earned by killing enemies. Players can purchase pieces for an equipment system over the course of the game. Towers serve as base defense and are positioned in each of the lanes; usually, each lane has multiple towers along with several within the base area. A main "base" unit — called "core" or "nexus" in different games — represents the win condition of the game. It's the flag that players need to destroy.

Most MOBAs are third person and presented in isometric 3-D, which means that the graphics exist in an environment with an x, y and z axis, but the camera is fixed at an angle over the player character's shoulder.

Knowing the popular MOBAs

Numerous MOBAs have had their moments of popularity, but here are the most popular and longest-lasting esports MOBA titles:

>> *League of Legends (LoL)*

>> *Dota 2*

>> *Heroes of the Storm (HotS)*

>> *Arena of Valor/Honor of Kings (AoV)*

>> *SMITE*

With the recent decision by Blizzard to discontinue esports support for *HotS*, *LoL* and *Dota 2* are far and away the top-two MOBAs in terms of worldwide competition. Not to be overlooked, however, is Tencent's mobile (and Nintendo Switch's) MOBA *Arena of Valor* (*Honor of Kings* in China), which boasts more than 200 million users and generated $4.5 billion in revenue as of 2019 (`https://sensortower.com/blog/honor-of-kings-revenue-4-billion`). Although mobile esports haven't taken off in North America or Europe, *AoV* is positioned for major growth. Rounding out the MOBAs of note is Hi-Rez Studios' *SMITE*, a MOBA based on various mythologies that differs from the competition in that it is presented in third person with an over-the-shoulder camera that is more reminiscent of *World of Warcraft* or a third-person shooting game than of its competitors.

Although Tencent had made no official announcement as of this writing, rumors have circulated that Tencent might halt support of the North American and European releases of *Arena of Valor*, though the game would continue to be supported in China and Indonesia. These rumors run parallel to the announcement of Riot's *League of Legends: Wild Rift*, an *LoL* mobile title. Tencent owns Riot, so maintaining a competitor to Riot's new *LoL* mobile version in the Americas wouldn't make strategic sense.

Getting in the League (of Legends)

Release date: October 2009

Publisher: Riot Games

Number of players: 80 million

Major professional events:

- *League of Legends* World Championship
- *League of Legends* Mid-Season Invitational
- *League of Legends* All-Star Event
- *League of Legends* Championship Series (North America)
- *League of Legends* European Championship
- *League of Legends* Champions Korea
- *League of Legends* Pro League (China)

If *Defense of the Ancients* laid the groundwork for what a MOBA is, *League of Legends* is the evolved form. Although it's not as complex in places as *Dota 2*, *LoL* balances everything that is typical of a MOBA in a way that both makes for a pleasant gaming experience and maps perfectly to the claim that a game should be "easy to play, hard to master." As a result, *LoL*'s popularity surged upon release, and at one point, the 100 million active players seemed like an impossible number to match. Although *StarCraft II* might have brought the idea of professional esports to the world, *LoL* is the current standard bearer, the game that even people who don't play esports have heard of or seen in action. Figure 3-2 shows a moment of gameplay in *League of Legends*.

FIGURE 3-2:
League of Legends
in action.

WARNING

As I mention elsewhere, some members of the *LoL* community are what gamers refer to as "toxic." This term refers to rude players, often including a few people who are just trying to elicit a response. The *LoL* community is one of the more notorious ones in terms of not being super welcoming to new players. This reputation doesn't reflect on the game or even the majority of *LoL* players. During one period, the bad element among *LoL* players was extremely loud, and Riot couldn't move quickly enough to develop ways to control the trolling issues. Riot has since caught up, and the overall game experience is much better. Still, you're wise to remember that if someone is being rude or otherwise insulting to you, you can just leave the game and find another match. Do not fall into the belief that the community is "just like that."

Starting with the basics

In the previous section, "Understanding the Basics of a MOBA," I talk about MOBA basics. If you skipped that, flip back a couple of pages and read that description. *LoL* exhibits the best of that MOBA structure. In this section, I describe some game basics that are specific to *LoL*. (If you need help installing and setting up *LoL*, check out Chapter 9.)

LoL player characters are called champions. The "creeps" that are not under the player's control are called minions. The game has three types of structures that players must attack to invade the enemy base:

>> **Turrets:** These stand within lanes and attack from a distance.

>> **Inhibitors:** These are positioned where lanes intersect with the base area at the end of the map. Destroying the inhibitor releases a super minion for the other team. Inhibitors can regenerate after 5 minutes.

>> **Nexus:** This is the actual "base" at the core of the base area. It generates the waves of minions and is what champions must destroy to win the game.

Killing opponents, opposing minions, and using Non-Player Characters (NPCs) is how players gain experience and gold. You can use gold at the shop near your base to buy items. Items are extremely important to the character build because they grant buffs for skills, abilities, and armor.

Each champion is typically suited for one role more than others. Champions have a mix of the three common traits: dealing damage, tanking, and healing or buffing.

Team composition depends on selecting five champions that can cover all needed roles. At the professional level, this fact makes drafting a team critical.

Picking play modes and sides

LoL offers multiple game modes and maps, but the standard for competition is the five-versus-five map *Summoner's Rift*. *Summoner's Rift* follows the prototypical MOBA format wherein the two team bases are at opposing corners of a square with a top lane, a bottom lane, a middle lane, and two jungle regions. The square is cut across the opposite corners by an area called the river, though it is dry in most spots.

Another map and play mode is the *Twisted Treeline*, which is a scaled-down three-versus-three map with a single lane. The *Howling Abyss* map and play mode uses *LoL*'s *All Random, All Mid (ARAM)* map, a five-versus-five competition with a focus on mid-map team fights. In nonranked play, players can choose to compete against the artificial intelligence instead of playing live opponents.

For the competitive scene, players must play in ranked mode. Ranked mode almost always takes place on *Summoner's Rift*, but the method of selecting teams and players can vary. Almost all major competitions use a specific format, referred to as pro draft. For a pro draft, one team is assigned the blue side and the other the red side before the game.

Picking and banning players

After each team in a MOBA competition has been assigned its side, as explained in the preceding section, the following phases occur:

- **Ban phase one:** Starting with the blue teams, the two teams take turns banning one champion each. This phase proceeds until each team has banned three (meaning that six champions are now banned from that game).

- **Pick phase one:** The blue team picks a champion and then the red team picks two champions; next, the blue team picks two, and the red team ends the phase by picking a third. At this point, each team has three champions.

- **Ban phase two:** The red team starts this time, making one ban, and then the blue team makes a ban. Then the two repeat. This phase results in four more bans and leaves a total of ten champions banned from play.

- **Pick phase two:** The red team picks a champion and then the blue team picks two champions. Next, the red team picks its final champion. This process leaves each team with five champions for the match.

The pick/ban phases of *LoL* competition is critical to the strategy because they can have a profound impact on an event. Teams have to weigh the following options as they consider which champions to ban:

- What are the strongest champions in the current meta of the game?
  - Do you pick first? If so, do you want to try to make sure one of those champions is available?
  - Can you risk leaving multiple top tier champions on the board?
  - Are you confident in your team if all the top choices are eliminated before picking? This can be a moment where play is leveled.

- What are the main choices of your opponents?
  - Can you remove the main choices of three of the opposing players without missing an obvious top-tier ban?
  - How many of the opposing team's main champions are also main champions for your team? Is it wiser to remove them via ban or to fight it out to see who picks which ones first?
  - If your opponent has a star player that is vastly superior to the others, can you remove all their practiced champions via the initial ban? Removing three of the same type of champion is risky, but it could leave an opposing player scrambling.

» Can you use the draft to shape your opponent's selections through banning so many champions that are well equipped for a certain role that early picks must be used a certain way out of a sense of preservation?

» Can you develop a strategy for team composition that will survive the entire pick/ban process? The deeper into the process, the more likely circumstances are to change, and sometimes targeting one specific composition can be catastrophic if the final piece or pieces are not available.

Because of the format of the pro draft, most competitive players practice a pool of champions that is at least three, and often even four or five, deep. The odds that an opponent would choose to ban more than three champions of a single type is unlikely because doing so would leave the top choice in at least one type available for players to select. By the same token, having players on a team who are comfortable and competitive playing a champion that is four or five slots down from the top-tier meta pick makes drafting much easier. If your team has a jungler, for example, who practices a number of champions that are outside the top five or six chosen, your team will have the flexibility to pick up a powerful champion in another position as your opponent jockeys to get the best jungler champion that isn't banned.

An important part of understanding all the dynamics of the pick/ban process is the meta — or the best possible choices and most powerful characters and strategies in the current game — and understanding tier lists. A tier list (see Figure 3-3) is a list compiled by the competitive community that shows which characters are the best choices at any given time. These characters are typically updated by patch, and ones that rank the entire 148 champion pool are visually complex and can be overwhelming. To help with this problem, the lists are broken into tiers that indicate quality. The tier rankings range from S for superior to D (and sometimes F), following an A, B, C, D structure like course grades. For most competitive tier lists, however, the rankings are cut at B because champions below B level are rarely if ever viable in competition.

In Figure 3-3, the image is limited to the S tier (or God Tier) champions in each typical role, with their level within the tier reading from left, or most powerful, to right, or least powerful. Although this tier list in Figure 3-3 will likely be out of date by the time you read this, it can still offer an example of how to interpret the list. In a match in which scouting hadn't indicated that the opposing team had a superstar player who played off the meta with characters not considered the best at their role, the first six bans from this list would be Volibear, Dr. Mundo, Garen, Malzahar, Jinx, and Soraka. This ban removes the two best jungle champions and the top choice in each other slot. The blue team would then most likely pick Master Yi, because having a high-quality jungler is critical to the early game. Picking Master Yi would, of course, be a situation in which all the players are considered equal, so it's not likely to go down exactly like that in many cases. But this sense of ranking is how the tier list is meant to function; it should offer a guide as to what champions are most valuable. Seeing the very top-tier champion make it through the pick/ban process would be a true rarity. The blue team would be wise to try to let that champion slide so that they can draft it, but the red team is unlikely to play into that strategy.

FIGURE 3-3:
League of Legends patch 9.21 tier list by Mobalytics.

Strategizing to win

After the match starts, the win condition occurs from destroying the opponent's nexus within that opponent's base. This way of winning is consistent for all MOBAs. Rushing forward to secure the objective isn't the best strategy, though. *LoL* involves both patience and aggressive play. Balancing both makes you an elite player. Here are some tips to keep in mind:

>> **Hold back:** Pushing a lane (to kill the minions coming at you and attempt to move forward up the lane) is not wise in the early game. You can earn just as much gold and experience by staying at your turret and killing the minions as they come. Advancing puts your minions in greater danger and opens you to being attacked from behind. Don't push until you have a teammate with you, and remember that pushing early has no real benefit in *LoL*.

>> **Build your resources:** In the early game, farm as efficiently as possible, even if doing so means skipping chances to go for player kills. Although farming is not as vital in a MOBA as it is in an RTS, you do need resources and levels to get to your maximum potential. The sooner you level up and acquire gear, the better you'll be able to help your teammates.

>> **Work efficiently:** If you're the jungler, kill efficiently and engage in early-match combat only if you clearly have an advantage. If you're not the jungler, resist the urge to "help" the jungler clear the jungle. You have plenty of stuff to kill, and stopping the jungler's early progression could hurt your whole team. Keep these ideas about the jungler in mind:

- The jungler's job is to "snowball," or to gain levels as quickly as possible. In a competitive game, the jungler should be several levels ahead of all the other champions in the early game.

- If your team's jungler falls behind in the early game and is out-leveled by the opposing team, the game is almost certainly over.

>> **Know when to resist helping:** This point can be difficult to manage as a teammate, but if you see an uneven team fight starting, learn to know when it is a lost cause and don't pile on. If three of your teammates are losing a three-versus-five fight, you might feel instinctively as though you can even the numbers by jumping in, but losing you as well will mean that only one member of your team is left. The smarter move is to fall back on defense and rally under a turret than to give in to the desire to help when the odds are out of your favor. Here are two related issues that can help you remember to resist helping out in an uneven fight:

- MOBAs like *LoL* include a much-debated activity called feeding. *Feeding* refers to the death of a player within a situation that appeared to be hopeless, giving experience and gold to the other team. Some players call any death to uneven odds feeding, whereas others use that term only when a player wound up that way by making bad choices, but either way, feeding will put your team at a major disadvantage.

- A problem related to feeding is called *spiralling,* which occurs when a player dies in a fight and rushes back to the fight only to die again after respawning (and sometimes does the same a third time). Respawn timers in the game are such that if you die in a fight, your team would have to have incredible luck and skill for you to respawn and get back to the location of the fight without a change in the situation. If the situation is worse and you charge in, you could die instantly.

>> **Isolate opposing players:** You have to communicate with your team, and as a group, you should all constantly be looking for your chance to isolate members of the other team. With relatively evenly matched teams, the team that sees the opening to take out an opponent or two in mid- to late game is often the one that scores the win.

>> **Avoid tunnel vision and keep adapting to change:** *Tunneling,* or having tunnel vision, happens most commonly with players who do not communicate well. To *tunnel* is to become so focused on your one role in the game that you don't actively adapt to the changing circumstances. For example, if a team battle is raging in the middle lane but you, as the top laner, don't leave your spot in the top lane, your team will lose a five-versus-four battle because you're not there to help. Worse still, if the winners of that fight don't choose to advance on your base, they're all coming for you and no one on your team can help because they just died.

League of Legends persists a decade after its launch because Riot built its game on the premise of making one game and keeping it updated and balanced, supporting its fan base, and constantly pushing out new content. Although the strategy of having a free-to-play game with purchasable cosmetics might have seemed unwise as a business choice in 2009, Riot and Tencent have built a game with a massive player base, a strong economy, and the largest viewership of any professional championship. They also offer the Collegiate *League of Legends* (CLoL), arguably the most reputable collegiate tournament in esports. For more on CLoL, check out Chapter 11.

RIOT TAKES ON EVERYONE

Riot Games was founded on the principle of doing one game and doing it right. A decade later, Riot has done well with *League of Legends,* but in late 2019, Riot announced potential competitors for almost every esports space. New Riot titles in production include:

- *League of Legends: Wild Rift:* A mobile version of Riot's five-versus-five MOBA

- *Legends of Runeterra:* A Combat Card Game in the spirit of *Hearthstone* or *Magic: The Gathering Arena,* based on the *LoL* universe

- *League of Legends: Teamfight Tactics:* An auto-chess/battle royale mix

- *Project L:* An *LoL*-based fighting game

- *Project F:* An *LoL*-based open-world game in the spirit of *Diablo*

- *Project A:* A tactical shooter, and the only game on the list not housed in the *LoL* universe

Riot is also at work on an animated film set in the *LoL* universe. Although it is far too early to know how any or all of these games will turn out, Riot has moved quickly from being known just for the *LoL* MOBA to having the potential to offer games in each of the major esports areas. Only time will tell how successful its plans will be, but if early fan reaction is any indication, big things lie ahead for Riot.

Counting on Dota 2

Release date: July 2013

Publisher: Valve Corporation

Number of players: 422,000

Major professional events:

- The International *Dota 2* Championships
- *DotA* Summit
- DreamLeague
- World Cyber Games
- ESL One

Dota 2 occupies an interesting space in esports competition: It has never had the following in America that it has in other regions. Though *Dota 2* was released after *League of Legends,* most people consider it to be the true evolution of the original *Defense of the Ancients* because of the centrality of IceFrog to *Dota 2*'s development. In fact, IceFrog, who has never revealed his (or her?) true identity publically, balances *Dota 2* himself. This fact marks a departure from a game like *League of Legends,* which has an entire portion of the development team devoted to balancing and changes, and it gives *Dota 2* a different feel and challenge curve. Figure 3-4 shows a *Dota 2* game in action.

The level of challenge (or frustration, depending on the player) is what people most often credit for the fact that *Dota 2* never came close to the popularity of *LoL* in North America. The other major factor in play is, of course, that *LoL* had a four-year head start, giving it a significant installed base.

Playing the game

The basics of *Dota 2* are extremely similar to *LoL,* so if you skipped the "Getting in the League (of Legends)" section, earlier in the chapter, you want to read the basic rules there before continuing. Although both *Dota 2* and *LoL* are isometric 3-D MOBAs that derive much of their play style and options from the original *DotA,* four aspects truly distinguish *Dota 2* from *LoL:*

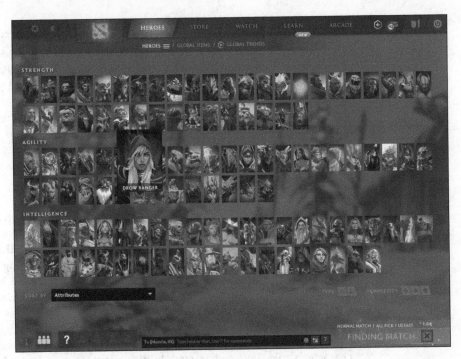

FIGURE 3-4:
Dota 2 gameplay.

>> **The name of the player character:** In *LoL,* the player's character is a "champion," whereas in *Dota 2,* the player character is a "hero." These names may simply be branding differentiators, but they also indicate the difference between the two philosophies of character design. Whereas *LoL* depends on the deep skill sets woven into champions, *Dota 2* depends more on the flexibility to customize a hero to perform varied tasks. *Dota 2* heroes are less likely to conform to the standard of being a Damage, Tank, or Support because of the level of complex development customization the game allows.

>> **Role diversity:** Diversity of character expands to diversity of role. In almost every game of *LoL,* the players choose their role at the beginning. In fact, this choice of role is so ingrained within gameplay that it governs how the character selection or game draft works, with roles assigned to each respective champion as it is selected. In *Dota 2,* roles can be much more easily swapped based on build (skills and gear chosen for the hero), and although the meta of the game often dictates that some heroes fulfill certain roles, you don't have to have one hero in each specific role at the start of the match.

>> **Better-behaved players:** Because of *Dota 2*'s steeper learning curve, the *Dota 2* community also seems to have less of the sort of toxic behavior that at times mars the experience for *LoL* gamers. *Dota 2* players remember how difficult the game was when they started and tend to be more forgiving when dealing with new players.

>> **More complexity:** *Dota 2* adds complexity beyond what *LoL* offers. In *LoL*, the max level for a character is 18, but in *Dota 2* it is 25, which adds to the complexity of building your character because seven additional level-up moments occur in which you must choose skills. Also, in *Dota 2*, you can engage in friendly fire, killing your own creeps or killing a teammate that is afflicted with a massive debuff, or reduction in skill, power, or health (or sometimes all three). This capability allows you to deny the other team experience and gold for the kills. And finally, in *Dota 2*, the player can not only hide in but also manipulate the environment of a level by removing trees or other obstacles.

As mentioned previously, *Dota 2* has a steep learning curve. When considering it as an esport to participate in, that learning curve is the number one thing to keep in mind. For several years, people thought that *Dota 2* offered the most complex gameplay, *LoL* offered the most streamlined but still challenging experience, and *HotS* served up the most user-friendly experience, with *SMITE* hovering around the edges as a different sort of experience from the others because of its camera.

Dota 2 heroes typically have three regular abilities and one ultimate ability that is significantly more powerful. In contrast to *LoL*, in which the abilities define the character's role, *Dota 2* character abilities allow for more customization and can cater to different potential outcomes. Some play modes even let a hero have other heroes' abilities. Each ability has a timer associated with the period between uses — a cool down (CD). Ultimate abilities often have a significant CD.

Playing *Dota 2* requires a particular tolerance for learning through failure. On the positive side of that aspect, the game can be incredibly rewarding after you master a few key elements, and compared to other games, the player base is generally more forgiving of people who are learning or who might be struggling with a new character.

Understanding the play modes

Dota 2 offers a host of play modes that focus primarily on how player characters are chosen along with other slight variations. The modes fall into two categories: ranked and unranked. The ranked modes include the following:

>> **Captains Mode:** This mode is the standard competitive mode. Captains for each team go through the pick/ban process until each team has five players. The individual players then pick from their team's five and begin competition. Pick/ban here is nearly identical to pick/ban for *LoL*, as described in the "Getting in the League (of Legends)" section, earlier in the chapter.

>> **All Pick:** This mode is similar to Captains Mode, but in this case, players go through a ban round in which each player can ban a hero. They then go through a round selecting directly from the pool of heroes remaining.

>> **Random Draft:** In this mode, 50 heroes are placed in the pool and players must then select one to play with.

Now for the unranked modes:

>> **Captains Mode:** Works the same as in the ranked category.

>> **All Pick:** Same as in the ranked category.

>> **All Random:** The game assigns each player a random hero.

>> **Single Draft:** The game assigns each player a unique group of three heroes, from which the player selects one.

>> **Least Played:** This mode functions like All Pick, but players cannot select any of their 40 most-played heroes.

>> **Ability Draft:** The player receives a random hero and then a pool is created that includes all the abilities of all the heroes selected for the match. Each player may draft three normal abilities and one ultimate ability.

>> **1 versus 1 Solo Mid:** This mode involves a one-on-one match with a single lane.

>> **All Random Deathmatch (ARDM):** Players are given a random hero, and when it dies, it respawns as a different random hero. This game mode's victory condition adds running through a team total of 40 respawns (which means that the team loses), achieving 45 kills (which is a win), or destroying the Ancient or base (win).

Dota 2 is a game to play if you're looking for a major challenge and a potential major payday. Despite being smaller in terms of participants and viewers than *LoL* Worlds, the *Dota 2* International's 2019 prize pool of $34 million is the largest ever for a single esports event. The International has set the standard for prize pools every year, and the professionals who play at that highest level have such parity that no team repeated as International champs until 2018 and 2019. That honor went to European powerhouse OG.

Earning Valor in the Arena (*AoV*)

Release date: November 2016

Publisher: Tencent Games

Number of players: More than 200 million

Major professional events:

- *Arena of Valor* World Cup
- *Arena of Valor* International Championship
- King Pro League (China)
- Garena Championship Series (Taiwan)
- Arena of Glory (Vietnam)

Longtime players of *League of Legends* no doubt recognize the art style of *Arena of Valor (AoV)*, Tencent's mobile device MOBA. Because Tencent owns Riot, the maker of *LoL*, the two properties share a number of the resources and asset creation teams. *AoV* is a five-versus-five full-map MOBA, though it is scaled back a bit for the mobile platform. Although *AoV* hasn't reached major popularity in North America or Europe, it is hugely popular in China, Thailand, Taiwan, and Vietnam. The game boasts 200 million peak monthly players, which is 20 times that of *Dota 2* and more than twice that of *LoL*. Figure 3-5 shows an action shot of *AoV*.

FIGURE 3-5:
Arena of Valor
gameplay.

To make the MOBA format work for mobile, a game called *Vainglory* attempted to switch to a three-versus-three format. Although *Vainglory* found some footing, it was blown out of the water when *AoV* was released with full five-versus-five competition (as opposed to three-versus-three) and a map that looks almost exactly like that of *LoL*. In fact, *AoV* feels like *LoL* with the following alterations:

- In the early game, player characters (heroes) level much faster, gaining access to all their abilities as early as level 5.

- Players can make purchases with gold to upgrade gear and materials from any place on the screen.

- Damage done by players, as well as the health of towers, bases, and creeps, are scaled so that the sweet spot, or average time, for a competitive match is 15 minutes. This keeps the game in line with other mobile games and is well short of the 45 minutes to an hour average time for an *LoL* match.

- The graphics and graphic effects, although attractive, are targeted to mobile device standards.

AoV has two other major selling points that make it unique among top esports MOBAs:

- It is available on the Nintendo Switch. It is the only isometric 3-D, traditional MOBA available for the Switch or any console.

- It includes several DC Comics properties among the heroes, including Batman, the Joker, Superman, and Wonder Woman.

In spite of having a complexity level similar to *LoL*, *AoV* has struggled to take hold in the West, presumably because of bias against mobile gaming. In other parts of the world, however, *AoV* conducts major professional tournaments in the United States, a region in which players are not overly interested in mobile esports, with $1 million prize pools. *Honor of Kings*, the version of *AoV* played in China and Korea (and technically the original, though *HoK* is, again technically, based on *LoL*), had a prize pool of $2.3 million in 2019 (https://esportsobserver.com/honor-of-kings-world-champion-cup/).

In late 2019, Riot Games announced that it would continue development of a game called *League of Legends: Wild Rift*, a mobile version of Riot's PC game. People expect the arrival of *Wild Rift* to mean the end of *AoV* in North America, but *AoV*'s international audience is less likely to abandon the game. Only time will tell as to whether mobile esports become a "thing" worldwide, but *AoV* shows that the complexity and level of competition, as well as the support of major publishers, is there.

AoV's game modes include a ranked mode complete with a series of placement games to start each season and a rotating set of casual modes that include the five-versus-five base mode, a three-versus-three mode, a one-versus-one mode, and varying event games like soccer and a battle — style game. The true focus of *AoV* is the ladder (or ranking levels that players can climb as they win and gain experience), however, because most players engage in the casual modes only to practice a hero or to complete daily missions to earn in-game rewards.

GAMING PHONES

In November 2017, Razer Inc., the company famed for mice, keyboards, and headsets (as well as striking laptops), released the Razer Phone. Touted as the first phone developed specifically for gamers, the Razer Phone runs the Android OS and sports a 5.7-inch, 1440p, 120 Hz display. The display makes all the difference, because the refresh rate makes a mobile device capable of allowing for ultra-low latency. (Razer claims "virtually no latency.") The phone also features stronger built-in speakers than almost any other phone to allow for immersive gameplay.

A Razer Phone 2 was released a year later with upgraded hardware and the inclusion of Razer's trademarked Razer Chroma lighting effects. The phone is favored by many in the *AoV* professional world.

The question that quickly arises is whether you need a phone just for gaming. I own an original Razer Phone, and although the refresh and the screen are fantastic — easily the best among the Android phones I've used — I still find myself looking to a tablet to play mobile games. To this point, no one has made a tablet that is more comfortable for *AoV* than the Apple iPad Pro, though if Razer applied the exact same tech from its phone to a tablet form, it would be an amazing device. For now, it's hard to imagine a gaming phone being worth the price. If you're an Android user and it's time to upgrade, though, you could do much worse than the Razer Phone 2, particularly if your other interests are video related. The Razer Phone 2 retails for around $400 and can be found on sites like Amazon and Newegg (though at the time of this writing, Razer itself was sold out online). The original MSRP was $699.

Smiting Your Enemies with *SMITE*

Release Date: March 2014

Publisher: Hi-Rez Studios

Number of players: 20 million (estimated by publisher) across all platforms (PC, MacOS, Xbox One, PlayStation 4, Switch)

Major professional events:

- *SMITE* Pro League (https://esports.smitegame.com/)
- *SMITE* Minor League
- *SMITE* Console League

SMITE is very much the little MOBA that could. With a radically different look and feel from other MOBAs because of how it is graphically presented, *SMITE* is also a product of a much smaller studio than the other titles here, so it has a smaller professional footprint. Also, some people dispute how many of the reported players of *SMITE* are actually active; many online communities have regular discussions about the health of the game that start with the ominous question, "Is *SMITE* dying?"

Professional competition in *SMITE* is almost all part of the large network that Hi-Rez Studios has built for its playbase. Hi-Rez presents a *SMITE* Pro League that is capped yearly with a *SMITE* World Championship. Hi-Rez also hosts a *SMITE* Minor League that resembles the challenger leagues for other major esports, allowing amateur talents to display their skills and attempt to fight their way onto top-tier teams. Another league hosted by Hi-Rez is a *SMITE* Console League, which is specifically for players who compete on PlayStation 4 and Xbox One.

The *SMITE* World Championship is typically held in Atlanta, GA, during the DreamHack event. The tournament has had six champions, the latest of which is Splyce Esports. The most recent prize pool for the *SMITE* World Championship, in 2019, was $1 million, up from $785,000 in 2018, but down from an all-time peak of $2.6 million.

SMITE has a pool of 100-plus gods available for player use in competition. Although almost all competitions are played in Conquest mode, a total of six gameplay modes are available in *SMITE*:

>> **Arena:** A five-versus-five competition that happens in a round arena similar to a coliseum. This mode is reminiscent of *World of Warcraft*'s Arena mode.

>> **Assault:** An all-random, all-middle (ARAM) mode in which players are assigned a god at random and must attempt to defeat their opponents on a single-lane map that is much smaller than the map in other game modes like Conquest.

>> **Conquest:** The standard MOBA five-versus-five competition that uses three lanes and a jungle version of *SMITE*.

>> **Clash:** A more casual version of *SMITE* that emphasizes team fights and has only two lanes. The game itself encourages the use of this mode as a tutorial or learning mode.

>> **Domination:** Teams must battle to maintain control of three Sand Guardians (unmoving spots on the map).

>> **Joust:** A single-lane, one-versus-one or three-versus-three mode.

Although *SMITE* has a decent-sized installed base and offers multiple platforms for play, it deviates too dramatically from the standard MOBA camera to keep up with the elite titles *League of Legends* and *Dota 2*. MOBA purists are generally turned off by the major differences the camera positioning makes in understanding map position and teammate positioning. The online assertions that *SMITE* is dying appear to be premature, but there are also no indicators that the *SMITE* player base is growing. It is a title worth watching, but if you're interested in the MOBA genre, you can find more popular and more populous games to play.

Figure 3-6 shows a scene from a *SMITE* game.

FIGURE 3-6:
SMITE in action.

The Future of the MOBA

The MOBA standard-bearer *League of Legends* is a decade old, but MOBAs show no sign of rotating out of the esports elite. Although some might debate whether *SMITE* is growing or dying (see the preceding section), and the mobile market might not be playing MOBAs in North America, *LoL* and *Dota 2* both remain in the top-five most watched games on Twitch.tv on a daily basis. *LoL Worlds* is still the most watched esports event (though *Fortnite* is creeping up from behind it), and *Dota 2*'s The International remains the highest prize pool in esports. The future still looks bright.

Riot, or Valve, or both may choose at some point to release an *LoL 2* or a *Dota 3*, respectively, but beyond giving their games face-lifts and adding some basic improvements, there's no reason to believe that ten years from now The International won't still have a massive prize pool or that *LoL Worlds* won't eventually become a viable ratings challenge to the NFL. MOBAs are a part of the DNA of esports.

Chapter **4**

Taking Aim at First-Person Shooters

In 1992, a company named id Software released a game called *Wolfenstein 3D* wherein the main character adventured through a pseudo-3-D castle shooting Nazis. The company followed up a year later with *Doom*, a similar shooting game in which the protagonist, a space marine in the style of the heroes of the *Alien* movie franchise, fought demons. id's games differed from those of most competitors in that id presented them in first-person point of view. That is, the player looks out on the world of the game through the camera's perspective, as though it were the player's head. Players can see their character's hands or what they are holding but no other parts of the player model. These two games, *Wolfenstein 3D* and *Doom*, created one of the most popular genres in gaming: the first-person shooter (FPS).

In this chapter, you find out about the basics of the FPS genre and explore key games like *Counter Strike: Global Offensive, Call of Duty,* and *Overwatch.*

Understanding the First-Person Shooter (FPS)

If you remember your English classes from school, the idea of first and third person in the gaming world could confuse you. In writing, first person refers to the use of "I"; the narrative is from the perspective of the writer. Third person is an external narrator's description of events. In gaming, first person versus third person relates the position of the camera for the game. In a first-person game, the camera is positioned as if it is the eyes of the player character. In first person, aside from seeing the events occurring in the game, you can see only your hands (and maybe your feet, if you move the camera around) as well as items you hold in your hands. In a third-person game, the camera is positioned so that players can see their character. In esports, most games are in third person. The fact that shooter games usually use the first-person perspective makes them unique.

FPS games were at the center of the early era of local area network (LAN) parties, events to which people brought their computers together to create an ad-hoc network in some location to play against each other. In those days, in the mid- to late 1990s, LANs were necessary because playing competitive games over a dialup network connection resulted in latency nightmares that made the games almost unplayable. A generation of gamers cut their teeth playing *Quake*, id Software's follow-up to the *Doom* series and the first of its games to feature real-time 3-D rendering. With *Quake*, many of the conventions of the FPS started to take full form.

REMEMBER

In addition to the possible confusion over the meaning of first- and third-person games, the use of the labels 2-D, *pseudo-3-D*, and 3-D might be hard to understand as well. These are descriptions of the graphics in the game themselves and not about presentation. A 3-D FPS doesn't react to 3-D classes or visually extend past the screen. The term 3-D in this context means that the art is rendered using an x, y, and z axis. Before rendering FPS in full 3-D, developers used an effect called *pseudo-3-D*, which used digital sprites and visual tricks with background textures to give the impression of a third axis without actually having one. The easiest way to remember it is that *sprite animation* (which is drawn using pixels or manually like a cartoon) is 2-D and has no third dimension; the third dimension is simulated through perspectives in the art. 3-D modeled art can be turned and looked at from multiple sides.

Qualifying as an FPS game

For a game to be considered an FPS, the following criteria must be true:

>> The player must view the game in first person for the majority of gameplay.

- The primary weapons in the game must be ranged, meaning that they fire some sort of projectile (guns, bows, tossed spears).

- The game has some manner of heads-up display (HUD) that includes key health, weapon, and map information so that the player can interpret what is happening in-game.

- Competition must happen in a map that exists in three dimensions within the game.

Additionally, in many cases the following are true of esports FPS games:

- Weapons, ammunition, and healing items exist on the maps and must be found by the player.

- Esports FPS games are almost always team based.

Beyond these criteria, two types of FPS dominate the current esports space. The first type are what people refer to as standard FPS titles, meaning games like CS:GO in which the individual player can carry different weapons but all player characters have the same abilities. The second type of FPS is called a *hero shooter*. An example of a hero shooter is *Overwatch*, in which the players select a specific character (or hero), which results in having different skills from those of other players within the game. Hero shooters offer more variety and require more strategy than the standard FPS, but much can be said for the even playing field of a game like CS:GO, in which player talent and not available skills is the major differentiator between competitors.

Honing the skills to pay the (virtual) bills

FPS games are among the most demanding esports in terms of skill set and learning curve. Most FPS games move quickly, and although the maps are not tiny, they are rarely sprawling, so players have few places to seek cover while planning strategy or finding teammates. Maintaining awareness is key. The first-person perspective of these games can also present a new challenge to some players because spatial awareness within a game changes when you cannot see your avatar. For example, my teams often find that I'm not completely hidden because I don't think about the position of my player character's virtual body and as a result I get shot in the butt. For some reason, it's always my butt that is sticking out from cover.

Here are the key skills you need to succeed in FPS games:

» **Staying aware of your physical position:** If you're in the open, you get taken out by the opponent. Knowing where you're standing at all times is a must.

» **Maintaining map awareness:** You need to know all the hiding places, the key routes to and from certain locations, and multiple ways out of whatever position you've placed yourself in.

» **Aiming:** In most current FPS games, the absolute key to your success as an offensive player is how well you can aim. This requirement makes transitioning from console to PC difficult for players of FPS games. On a console, you aim with the analog sticks, but on a computer, you aim with the mouse. The sensitivity difference is dramatic. PC players using a controller feel as though they are moving in mud; console players using a mouse for the first time find that they have far more control over their aim speed and can move much faster, but that speed can be overwhelming.

» **Understanding different map and mission types:** Some FPS games don't have multiple mission types, but most esports FPS titles have goals beyond just getting the most opponent kills. A game might have a bomb to diffuse (or set), a payload to escort, or various flags (or locations) to capture. Knowing how to utilize the maps to maximize the mission is a key to high-level success.

» **Knowing the differences among weapons or hero skills:** Depending on the game type, knowing what different items do and what different skills the various characters have is critical to being able to compete at the highest levels. Knowing what your character can do is not enough. You need to know what others might do and how to react to them.

» **Keeping your game sound turned up and listening carefully:** Because you need to have spatial awareness of your opponents, use the in-game sound to help you locate people and judge when they're moving.

» **Learning to be stingy with your shots:** You may be tempted to just keep firing when you see an opponent, but remember that the more noise you make with your weapon, the more easily you can be found. Plus, in some games, you can run out of ammo quickly and find yourself trying to survive with just a knife. Shooting should be about precision.

If you develop all the skills in the preceding list, you should be able to find success in any of a number of FPS games.

Although many of the skills required to play FPS games are interchangeable, if you want to play at the highest possible level, you should select one game and stick with it. As mentioned elsewhere in the book, the reason for this recommendation is muscle memory. You want aiming and moving around the map to become second nature —something you just do without having to think about it. If you play multiple games that move at different speeds or have different aiming standards, you can't develop the instinctive reactions that someone who focuses on one specific game has.

Navigating FPS Esports Titles

The variety of FPS titles is second only to the variety of fighting games in the esports world. (See Chapter 5 for more about fighting games.) Currently, six FPS games are played in regular competition, each with a world championship at the very least. Table 4-1 lays out the full slate of games that appear regularly in competition and lists their major events.

TABLE 4-1   **Major FPS Esports Titles and Their Biggest Annual Event**

Game	Style of Shooter	Major Annual Event(s)
CS:GO	Five-versus-five player, standard, objective-based FPS	ESL Pro Tour
Call of Duty: Modern Warfare	Five-versus-five standard FPS	*Call of Duty* League
Overwatch	Six-versus-six objective-based hero shooter	*Overwatch* League, *Overwatch* World Cup
Rainbow Six Siege	Five-versus-five objective-based hero shooter	The Six Invitational
Halo Infinite (2020 release)	Standard FPS	*Halo* Championship Series (no official *Halo Infinite* dates have been set); HCS support for *Halo V* ended in 2019
Paladins	Five-versus-five objective-based hero shooter	*Paladins* World Championship

Countering opponents in *CS:GO*

Counter Strike: Global Offensive, known as CS:GO, is the longest-running esports FPS, having been in competition since 2013. CS:GO's popularity is so high that it was featured on the TBS network in the first season of its esports series *ELEAGUE*. Many FPS purists are drawn to CS:GO because of its tried-and-true gameplay.

All player characters in CS:GO are the same, with the only real variation appearing through weapons and equipment. Each stage of the competitive games has an objective, such as diffusing a bomb or rescuing a hostage, and the primary win condition is achieving that objective. Along the way, of course, players pick up kills of the opponents and can die themselves.

Valve, *CS:GO*'s developer, is one of the few companies that doesn't devote a great deal of its resources to hosting a major tournament. The big event for the *CS:GO* year is the Intel Extreme Masters, a tournament held by computer processor giant Intel in partnership with major tournament operator ESL. IEM events take place all over the world, with the most recent ones being in Beijing, China, and Chicago, IL, United States. You can see the final bracket from the Beijing event in Figure 4-1.

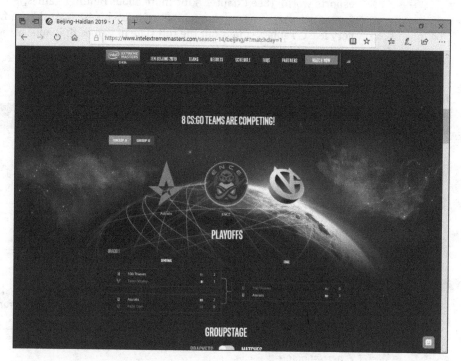

FIGURE 4-1:
The IEM Beijing 2019 *CS:GO* final bracket.

CS:GO is available through Steam for Mac and PC. It has moved to the free-to-play model with in-game purchases from its most recent $14.99 retail price. It was available on the previous generation of consoles (PS3, Xbox 360) but is not available on any current consoles.

Hearing the *Call of Duty*

Call of Duty (*CoD*) has lived an interesting life as an esports title. It's currently a standard FPS on the rise with the release of *CoD: Modern Warfare* in 2019 and the launch of *CoD* League 2020. The previous release in the series, *CoD Black Ops 4*, attempted to add a mode that stepped into the battle royale space (Black Out) but met with little success.

The *CoD* League is only the second esports league (after the *Overwatch* League, which you can read about later in this chapter) to follow the professional sports method of having franchised teams that exist in specific cities around the world. This approach differs from the methods other esports use, in which teams qualify for tournaments and work through a bracket. The *CoD* League will almost assuredly have at least these founding teams because each team has a franchise within the league. Unlike other tournaments in which a team must earn a bid, the *CoD* League teams are already part of the league's competition without a need for placement. You can see the *CoD* League's website in Figure 4-2.

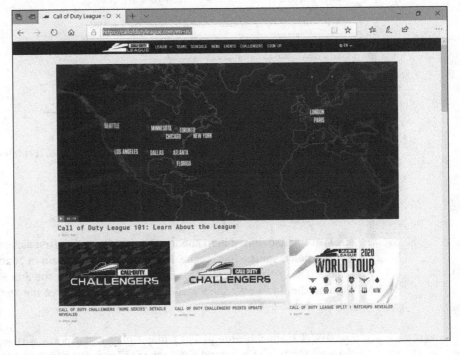

FIGURE 4-2 The *Call of Duty* League website with the map of the locations of the initial 12 teams.

The *Call of Duty* League started with 12 teams. You can find the names of those teams and their cities in Table 4-2. As of this writing, it's too soon to know how well the league will fare, but if it has the same success as *Overwatch* League, you can expect major expansion in subsequent years.

TABLE 4-2   ## The Founding *Call of Duty* League Teams

Team Name	City
Atlanta FaZe	Atlanta, GA, USA
Chicago Huntsmen	Chicago, IL, USA
Dallas Empire	Dallas, TX, USA
Florida Mutineers	Miami, FL, USA
London Royal Ravens	London, England, UK
Los Angeles Guerrillas	Los Angeles, CA, USA
Minnesota RØKKR	Minneapolis, MN, USA
New York Subliners	New York, NY, USA
OpTic Gaming Los Angeles	Los Angeles, CA, USA
Paris Legion	Paris, France
Seattle Surge	Seattle, WA, USA
Toronto Ultra	Toronto, Ontario, Canada

CoD: Modern Warfare is available on PC, PS4, and Xbox One. It retails for $59.99 and features in-game purchasing.

Taking over with *Overwatch*

Blizzard's squad-based hero shooter *Overwatch* was the first esports game to form a professional sports-like league. Entering its third season in 2020, the *Overwatch* League (OWL) had 20 teams for its 2019 season, with the San Francisco Shock winning the finals over the Vancouver Titans. You can see the 20 teams and their cities in Table 4-3.

The OWL has quickly emerged as a major player in esports. Although the league's championship is still behind the *League of Legends* League Championship Series (LCS) and The International (for *Dota 2*) in viewership, it is climbing fast, and investors are excited about the OWL. According to ESPN, 2019 expansion franchises for the league cost ownership groups $30–$60 million, with most informal sources claiming the total to be around $50 million (per https://www.espn.com/esports/story/_/id/23464637/overwatch-league-expansion-slots-expected-30-60-million). Given the OWL's $5 million prize pool, the franchise fee indicates that investors expect massive growth and potential.

TABLE 4-3

The Current *Overwatch* League Teams

Team Name	City/Division/Conference
Boston Uprising	Boston, MA, USA/North/Atlantic
London Spitfire	London, England, UK/North/Atlantic
New York Excelsior	New York, NY, USA/North/Atlantic
Paris Eternal	Paris, France/North/Atlantic
Toronto Defiant	Toronto, Ontario, Canada/North/Atlantic
Atlanta Reign	Atlanta, GA, USA/South/Atlantic
Florida Mayhem	Miami, FL, USA/South/Atlantic
Houston Outlaws	Houston, TX, USA/South/Atlantic
Philadelphia Fusion	Philadelphia, PA, USA/South/Atlantic
Washington Justice	Washington, DC, USA/South/Atlantic
Chengdu Hunters	Chengdu, China/East/Pacific
Guangzhou Charge	Guangzhou, China/East/Pacific
Hangzhou Spark	Hangzhou, China/East/Pacific
Seoul Dynasty	Seoul, South Korea/East/Pacific
Shanghai Dragons	Shanghai, China/East/Pacific
Dallas Fuel	Dallas, TX, USA/West/Pacific
Los Angeles Gladiators	Los Angeles, CA, USA/West/Pacific
Los Angeles Valiant	Los Angeles, CA, USA/West/Pacific
San Francisco Shock	San Francisco, CA, USA/West/Pacific
Vancouver Titans	Vancouver, BC, Canada/West/Pacific

Seeing why *Overwatch* is different from other FPS events

Among current FPS games, *Overwatch* departs from the norm. Alongside *Paladins*, a game I discuss later in the chapter, *Overwatch* adopts a fantasy and sci-fi style that makes few attempts to seem realistic (see Figure 4-3). Unlike *CS:GO* and *Call of Duty*, whose makers pride themselves on their games' realism, *Overwatch* thrives on creativity and interesting mechanics, such as those of the hero Doomfist who uses melee and fighting-game style attacks — a true anomaly in a game genre that calls itself a shooter.

FIGURE 4-3:
Early in an *Overwatch* match, a player tries to track the opponents from across the map.

The other major difference between *Overwatch* and other FPS games is that teams consist of six players and not the usual five. Although no definitive reason has been given for including an extra player on each team, professionals believe that the three roles in the game should be balanced (two of each, though that isn't the only strategy used). Unlike a game such as *CS:GO*, in which all players have the same skills, in *Overwatch*, players take on one of three roles based on their hero skills:

>> **Damage per second, or DPS:** The players who focus on attacking enemies and goals

>> **Support:** The players who heal or offer beneficial "buff" effects that grant teammates bonuses (or sometimes do both)

>> **Tank:** The players who absorb damage and distract the opposition from the DPS and supports

The meta of *Overwatch* has shown that having two players in each role is standard but has been subverted at multiple times as part of the ever-changing meta that results from gameplay patches and new characters being added. Players also have the ability to switch heroes when they die within a match, so some strategies depend on a player's ability to shift between roles.

The pace of *Overwatch* is also much faster than many of the other esports FPS games. Some of the game missions involve needing to protect a payload that is moving from one location to another, and those sorts of missions lead to fast, frequent team fighting. Also, some *Overwatch* heroes aren't as dependent on the player's ability to aim, which means that players who excel at positioning and map knowledge can contribute to a match in ways they couldn't in a game like *CS:GO*.

Checking in with the OWL

The OWL is unique in that it operates like the NFL or NBA, with franchised teams connected to cities around the world. Although I mention this method earlier in this chapter when discussing the *CoD* League, OWL was the first esports league to adopt this method of play.

Events like LCS for *League of Legends* and the International for *Dota 2* operate through a series of qualifiers. Professional teams from organizations like Team Liquid and Cloud9 earn their place in their respective tournaments. In the OWL, the competing teams are known at the start of competitive play. They are connected to cities and exist in divisions and conferences. Instead of playing for the right to be in a tournament, the OWL teams play for seeding in the playoffs.

In the 2020 season, the OWL is being divided into two conferences, Atlantic and Pacific, and each conference has two divisions (Atlantic has north and south; Pacific has east and west). The year 2020 is the first year when teams play home and away games in the actual cities they represent; previous seasons leaned heavily on the use of the Blizzard Studio in Los Angeles. Competitors in the league play on identical computers that are set up before competition, and OWL games happen on a server that's separate from other *Overwatch* gaming. Also of note is that both leagues are owned and run by Activision Blizzard, Inc., and the *CoD* League is modeled largely according to the OWL. Some of the teams will likely share facilities across the two leagues.

Overwatch competitions are played almost entirely on a PC through the Battle.net app, but the game is also available on Xbox One and PS4, and was recently released for the Nintendo Switch. It retails for $49.99 and features in-game purchasing.

Fighting fire with fire with *Rainbow Six Siege*

Few games in esports have seen the sort of bounce that *Rainbow Six Siege* (known as *Siege*) has. Part of the extensive *Rainbow Six* universe based on the work of Tom Clancy, *Siege* was released in 2015 for PC, PS4, and Xbox One. It experienced an initial popularity spike and then faded quickly, as many games in the esports space do.

In late 2017, *Siege* developer Ubisoft chose to adopt the philosophy that helped Riot so much with *League of Legends*. Instead of developing a new game to replace *Siege*, Ubisoft worked to develop new content for the game. Slowly, the game experienced a resurgence. In a recent discussion I had with a colleague who is working with high school esports programs, he said to me, "You'll never guess what game is the most popular with [students]," and gave me a knowing smile when I said "*Siege*, right?" I saw the same thing with the 2019 Miami Esports Summer Camp. Young players, ages 13–17, have a strong interest in *Siege*.

Siege merges the realistic style of *CS:GO* and *CoD* with the hero shooter style of *Overwatch*, resulting in a complex and interesting hybrid. Game modes are objective based, and although the player characters — called operators — are not outlandish or fantasy based, each has a unique set of skills that adds depth to the game. You can see an example of an operator's select screen with the data about the operator's unique skills in Figure 4-4.

FIGURE 4-4:
The Maverick operator with numerous icons to indicate abilities from *Rainbow Six Siege*.

Siege's multiple modes of play also offer interesting variations. Those modes include:

» **Hostage:** One team must hold and defend a hostage while the other team must try to recover the hostage.

» **Bomb:** One team must attempt to locate and diffuse bombs while the opposing team must attempt to eliminate their opponents and preserve the bombs.

» **Secure area:** One team must hold control of a facility while the other team tries to invade and take control.

The growth of *Siege* is such that the 2020 edition of the Six Invitational will crown a world champion and award winners from what could total more than $3 million, depending on the volume of in-game purchases made. Those in-game purchases are used to partly crowdfund the event. *Siege* is available on PC, PS4, and Xbox One. It retails for $29.99 and features in-game purchasing.

Shooting with all the rest

In addition to the six prominent games in this chapter, other FPS games rotate in and out of major competition as well. Although some of these games, like *Quake Arena*, don't have major staying power on the highest levels, others, such as *Paladins*, keep their status through the efforts of their publishers and efforts at the grassroots level. A simple Google search can put you on the path to finding events.

Mastering the Chief with *Halo Infinite*

One of the most hotly anticipated games of 2020 is 343 Studios' *Halo Infinite*, also known as *Halo 6*. Although no one knows how *Halo 6* will be handled in competition because the game hasn't released yet, *Halo 5: Guardians* had a solid several years of competition through the *Halo* Championship Series (HCS). In anticipation of *Halo Infinite*, HCS halted support of *Halo 5* in late 2019.

Halo Infinite will be available for PC, as was *Halo 5*, but one of the things the *Halo* series is known for is its close association with the Xbox console. The original *Halo* games (*Halo*–*Halo 3*) were Xbox-exclusive titles. *Halo Infinite* will still be an Xbox console exclusive, available only on the Xbox One and the new Xbox Series X, releasing in 2020, and on Windows PC. *Halo* features space marines and is a sci-fi combat shooter. In the single-player campaign of the game, players adopt the role of a soldier named Master Chief who wears hulking green armor and has a special relationship with an AI called Cortana (the same name that Windows uses for its virtual assistant).

Playing the hero with *Paladins*

Paladins, a five-versus-five hero shooter from Hi-Rez Studios, is often dubbed an *Overwatch* clone. In truth, the games were developed at roughly the same time, and *Overwatch* likely didn't have as much impact on *Paladins* as some fans believe. In the most general sense, though, this coincidence makes *Paladins* easy to describe. It is a five-versus-five hero shooter that operates in ways that are very similar to *Overwatch*.

Paladins has a few major benefits going for it. It's available on a wide range of platforms and is free to play. It can be downloaded on PC, PS4, Nintendo Switch, and Xbox One. It's also one of the few games that supports console-only competitions as well as PC competitions, holding Hi-Rez–sponsored leagues on each (go to `www.esports.paladins.com`). *Paladins* also has an annual collegiate tournament through the National Association of Collegiate Esports. Because *Paladins* is free to play and can be downloaded through Steam or the console app stores, new players can easily pick it up and try it. There's even a version of the game called *Paladins Strike* available on Android and iOS.

A THIRD-PERSON SHOOTER: *GEARS 5*

Almost all competitive esports shooters are FPS. Almost. One title that maintains a spot in competition is the *Gears of War* series, including 2019's *Gears 5*. What makes *Gears 5*, and all the *Gears* games, different is that they are third-person shooters. This means that as you play, you can see your player character. This seemingly small change makes for major differences in how players hide, interact with the environment, and aim their weapons.

The *Gears* series is post-apocalyptic, based on a version of Earth that has been invaded by aliens. The core characters are Marines who serve a global government's army, including the iconic *Gears* lead character Marcus Fenix. The game has also included interesting celebrity cameos: *Gears of War 4* includes rap duo Run the Jewels, and *Gears 5* has professional wrestler and actor Dave Batista. *Gears 5* is available for PC and for the Xbox One and retails for $59.99.

Shaking things up with *Quake Champions*

In the early days of FPS, id Software's *Quake* was the first to use real-time 3-D rendering and quite literally changed the game. Although *Quake* isn't among the absolute top-tier shooters as of early 2020, Bethesda Game Studios maintains a strong presence with its *Quake* Pro League playing *Quake Champions*. You can find more information on the league online at `https://quake.bethesda.net/en/esports`.

An interesting aspect of *Quake* esports is that *Quake* Pro League has solo competitors. Some smaller *Quake* tournaments also include duos competition. *Quake* doesn't adopt the large team structure that other FPS games adopt, though, which changes the game strategy significantly, making it similar to but not the same as a battle royale game. You can read more about battle royale games in Chapter 7. *Quake Champions* is free to play on PC through Steam.

Chapter **5**

Finish Him! Playing Fighting Games

O f all the esports game genres, fighting games are the oldest. The first fighting game, as such games are currently understood, was 1984's *Karate Champ*. Although the combat in *Karate Champ* simply involved kicking and punching, it had all the essential elements: two players, buttons for attacks, and the need to understand the battle space. Three years after *Karate Champ* appeared, Capcom released the first *Street Fighter* game. It was the start of fighting games as we've come to know them.

In this chapter, you discover how fighting games function as a genre and learn about the differences in their visual and spatial presentation (2-D, 2.5-D, and 3-D). I also tell you about the major titles and competitions that make up the fighting-games esports community. More than other games, fighting games are most often played with two competitors in the same physical space, so in this chapter, you also see how that aspect causes the fighting-game esports scene to differ from games like the Multiplayer Online Battle Arena and first-person shooters of the previous two chapters.

Fighting One on One: The Basics of the Fighting-Game Genre

Fighting games have a fascinating ecosystem. A massive number of titles have been created, and modifications and advancements have been introduced in various games during the 30-plus years that fighting games have been a part of the gaming world. The following criteria are essential to competition and are true of almost every fighting game:

>> Two characters appear on the screen, each controlled by a single player.

>> The characters engage in combat based on button presses and joystick inputs, often including complex combinations of buttons and gestures.

>> In-game characters have different moves and attacks, creating variety.

>> Combat takes place on a "stage" or "map" that is a defined space. The edges of that space become important in that a player can be stuck in a corner or, in some more rare cases, can lose by being forced out of a level.

>> A match consists of rounds (typically best of three) with victory coming by bringing the opponent's health level to zero or by having more remaining health when the round clock expires (in games with timed rounds).

In the current esports world, you see essentially four types of fighting games:

>> **2-D fighters:** Two-dimensional games have characters that appear as pixel sprites or hand-drawn, cartoon-style characters. In this style of fighting game, the characters can move only left, right, up, and down on an x and y axis. Characters can't move in or out of the frame/screen (because there is no third dimension).

>> **2.5-D fighters:** The graphics of these games are 3-D–rendered but the game still moves on the two-dimensional axis, giving the appearance of 3-D but not actually using a third axis.

>> **3-D fighters:** The graphics are three dimensional and the player characters can move on a z axis, crossing each other, moving into and out of the screen, and so on.

>> **Platform brawlers:** These are 2-D or 2.5-D games in which one of the primary goals is specifically to knock the opponent off a platform or off the screen.

Each of the preceding styles of game has at least one popular representative in the fighting-games community, and many have great longevity or are parts of a multi-title series. In fact, at Evolution Championship Series (EVO) 2019, the nine-game slate hit on each style relatively evenly with long-time title representation, as shown in Table 5-1.

TABLE 5-1   **EVO 2019 Titles**

Game	Style	Years in Competition
BlazBlue: Cross Tag Battle	2-D	Two, with previous *BlazBlue* title the year prior
Dragon Ball Fighter Z	2.5-D	Two (since release)
Mortal Kombat 11	2.5-D	One (an *MK* game has appeared at eight of the last nine EVOs)
Samurai Shodown	2.5-D	One (2019)
Soulcalibur VI	3-D	One (five other years feature an *SC* game)
Street Fighter V: Arcade Edition	2.5-D	Four (an *SF* game has been a part of every EVO)
Super Smash Bros. Ultimate	Platform brawler	One (an *SSB* game has appeared at nine EVOs, including the last six)
Tekken 7	3-D	Four (a *Tekken* game has appeared at all but one EVO since 2003)
Under Night In-Birth Exe: Late[st]	2-D	One (considered a surprise tournament pick)

Among the nine games on the biggest fighting game stage at EVO were two 2-D titles, four 2.5-D titles, two 3-D titles, and one platform brawler (with the last not a surprise because only two major platform brawler games exist).

Flattening the field with 2-D fighting games

To state it as simply as possible, a 2-D fighting game has two-dimensional graphics and moves on a two-dimensional axis. This relationship is shown in Figure 5-1, which is the start of a match in *BlazBlue: Cross Tag Battle*. Almost every 2-D fighter exists on a stage that works like a cartoon's background. The player characters can move left and right through the stage, but at some point on each side, the stage ends. This boundary means that a character can be pushed up against a sort of invisible wall that is formed by the edge of the stage.

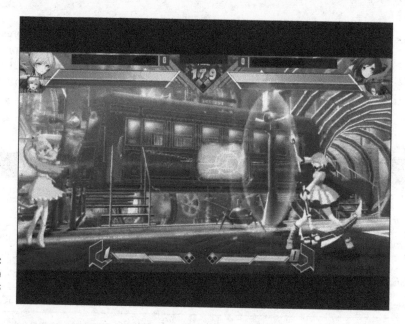

Many fighting-game purists favor 2-D fighters. In terms of gameplay, the two-dimensional play axis is still maintained by many fighting games, but keeping the older-looking, two-dimensional graphics lends a certain charm. It also results in sprite-based animations that opponents can read and anticipate in ways that that they can't do sometimes with the motions of a 3-D model. More important, those sprite-based animations have to finish before new ones can start, meaning that a move that has a long animation has to happen and end before more actions can be input and completed, at least in most cases. This might seem like an unnecessary or minor detail to the casual player, but for pros, it can be the difference between perfectly blocking a powerful attack or taking a match-ending assault to the face.

2-D fighters also represent the origin point of the fighting game genre. *Karate Champ* was a 2-D fighter, as was *Street Fighter* (and *Street Fighter II*). In that sense, all fighting games that exist now borrow from the 2-D style and mechanics, and in fact a number of fighting-game innovations happened first in 2-D.

Seeing 2-D go 2.5-D with *Samurai Shodown*

In 2019, SNK released an updated 2.5-D version of its 1993 hit *Samurai Shodown* (or *Samurai Spirits* in its native country of Japan). The original game was 2-D with pixel-art sprites, as you can see in Figure 5-2. Mechanically, the game features fighters who almost all brandish weapons, primarily swords, and fight by charging forward and falling back in a 2-D side-scrolling environment. One of the worst possible things that can happen to a player is to be forced to the edge of the screen and up against the edge, which works like a wall. A player stuck there can be "juggled" by repeated attacks, with the edge of the screen allowing the opponent to essentially bounce the other player.

FIGURE 5-2:
Two combatants about to fight in 1993's *Samurai Shodown.*

The 2019 release of *Samurai Shodown* features 3-D graphics. That is, essentially, the only major difference in the two versions of the game. Other updates have occurred, of course — the game can be played online and will provide for downloadable characters and post-release balance that didn't exist for the original — but the major update made the graphics and player models appear in a 3-D art style, as shown in Figure 5-3. The combat itself still happens on a two-dimensional plane moving left and right, and many of the characters have the same basic look and move sets. The merger of 2-D gameplay with 3-D art is the hallmark of a 2.5-D game.

The major advantages of 2.5-D are all about visuals. 3-D models take longer to create, but more parts can be reused and animations can be shared across multiple models. In the old 2-D sprite design style, a new sprite had to be created for each character and each potential motion. 3-D art also allows for higher resolutions and more realistic characters; sprite animation of photographs remains choppy and unnatural looking. In terms of gameplay mechanics, 2-D and 2.5-D are remarkably similar.

FIGURE 5-3:
Two combatants about to fight in the 2019 update of *Samurai Shodown.*

Stepping forward with the 3-D fighter

With the advent of 3-D game art and 3-D rendering, many games began allowing three-dimensional movement, with characters moving into and out of the screen.

TIP

Remember that 3-D in a game is not the same as a 3-D movie or picture. The third axis in these games doesn't literally jump out of the screen. But the presence of a third axis does mean that actions can happen in directions other than left and right and up and down.

The first 3-D fighter was Sega's *Virtua Fighter (VF),* which released in arcades in 1993 and later on the Sega Saturn console. The series was revolutionary in that it allowed for the characters to move at all manner of angles across a fighting arena that allowed the player to spin 360 degrees to view the entire space. Many versions of *VF* came about, and the series extended to a fifth installment with several mini-updates along the way. Though rarely seen in competitive play now, *VF* even had its day at EVO in the mid- to late 2000s.

Knocking people off the platform (brawler)

The final type of fighting game comes with a little bit of controversy. Among die-hard fighting-game fans, the titles that fit the classification of platform brawler would not be considered fighting games. Their audiences and competitive player bases would disagree, however, and EVO has recognized Nintendo's *Super Smash Bros. (SSB)* — the game that created the genre — for years.

What makes games like the *SSB* series different from other fighting games is that in addition to doing damage to each other, characters can win by knocking their opponent off the various platforms, or areas where players can stand, on the screen. These work in essence the same way a platform works in a game like *Super Mario Brothers*, in which missing a jump or being knocked off means that a player character falls to its death. Although the *SSB* series is by far the most popular platform brawler, a free-to-play game called *Brawlhalla* has formed a rather large audience as well, particularly with fan-favorite events that include World Wrestling Entertainment superstars in the game, as shown in Figure 5-4.

BRAWLING WITH *SUPER SMASH BROS.*

Nintendo's *SSB* series gave birth to a subgenre of games that follow its platform-based combat principles, but that's far from the only selling point for this series. Nintendo's winning formula is much more about giving gamers a high-speed, beginner-friendly-but-hard-to-master, visually stunning (and at times overwhelming) game that features almost every one of its properties as well as some guests. In the original *SSB*, for the first time Link from the *Legend of Zelda* could fight with Mario or Donkey Kong. Samus Aran from *Metroid* could try her hand at besting Luigi. In fact, the most recent entry in the series, *SSB Ultimate* on the Nintendo Switch, boasts a roster of more than 80 fighters.

SSB also holds one of the most interesting distinctions in esports: The Nintendo GameCube game *SSB Melee*, released in 2001, is still played frequently in competition, particularly on college campuses. Although some games near that age still see play, *SSB Melee* is the only game played in competitions on a console that was discontinued in 2007. Competition GameCube consoles are at least a decade old, and the *SSB Melee* game discs are almost as old as the college students who play them. Avid *SSB Melee* fans even have to find old CRT televisions to get the proper refresh rate and resolution because the game isn't competition quality if it is upsampled or emulated.

Grappling with the Major Fighting Games

Unlike some other esports genres that have relatively few titles, the fighting-game genre includes literally hundreds of titles. Not all of them see regular competition in the esports world, though in the most technical sense, any fighting game could be an esport. This section takes a look at the big names so that you know what to expect if you want to dive into the most popular esports fighting-game titles.

Taking it to the street *(SF V)*

The longest running and arguably most successful fighting-game series is Capcom's *Street Fighter* (*SF*) series. Although the original *SF* didn't make quite the major splash that the sequel did, every version of the game from 1992's *SF II* forward has been a mainstay in fighting-game competition and was once the quarter-gulping center point of many arcades across the world.

The current competition edition of *SF* is *SF V: Arcade Edition*, and it features nearly 40 fighters including downloadable content. It has been a featured game at EVO and other major tournaments since its launch in 2016. An updated edition called *SF V: Championship Edition* added a 40th character when it was released on February 14, 2020. It is expected to become the competition standard, though it's too early to know for certain.

SF V is a 2.5-D fighting game with a deep combo system and a series of regular characters like Ryu, Chun-Li, and Akuma. It is a console-exclusive title for the PlayStation 4 but also appears on Windows PC.

Fighting with *Capcom vs. [Everyone]*

Not a company to sit back and enjoy the success of a single title, Capcom created a number of other fighting games to complement *SF*. Some of the *Capcom vs.* titles were crossovers with other game companies like SNK, which created games like *King of Fighters* and *Samurai Shodown*. Entries in the series pitted fighters from various games. At times, games in the Vs series include characters from nonfighting games as well.

The series blossomed into a true esports hit when Capcom started to cross over with the Marvel comics universe. The first of these games was *X-Men vs. Street Fighter*, a 1996 arcade release, and it later spawned the popular *Marvel vs. Capcom* series, which has spanned four entries to date. The most recent game in the series, *Marvel vs. Capcom Infinite*, was released in 2017. Although *Marvel vs. Capcom* wasn't featured at EVO in 2019, it is still a game with a healthy competition base.

Killing it with *Mortal Kombat*

Often thought of as "the other" major fighting-game series, *Mortal Kombat* has been around since 1992, sharing arcades and consoles with *SF* as the other heavy hitter. Known for being far more bloody than other fighting games, one of *MK*'s signature features is the ability to finish an opponent with a brutal move at the end of the match that would all but certainly kill the opponent. Such moves, which often have complicated combo inputs required to execute, are called *fatalities*.

MK attempted to use photo-realistic sprites, which in the original games looked quirky and rough but worked. The style morphed over time into a 3-D photo-realistic take on fantasy characters. The series dabbled with full 3-D combat, but returned to 2.5-D for the last several releases. The current game in the series, *MK11*, was so highly anticipated that it was announced for EVO 2019 before it had been released.

Originally owned by Midway, the *MK* team eventually spun out from the bankruptcy and closure of Midway Games, and NetherRealm is now owned by Warner Bros. Interactive Entertainment. *MK* appears on Xbox One, PS4, Switch, PC, and mobile.

MK isn't as fast-paced as *SF*, and at times the combat is all about punishing an opponent for leaving himself open to a particularly strong attack. The series is dominated by a recurrent set of ninja characters including Scorpion and Sub Zero, two of the most famous fighting-game characters of all time. You can see those two characters squaring off in Figure 5-5.

FIGURE 5-5:
Scorpion and Sub
Zero go head to
head in *Mortal
Kombat 11*.

Tipping the scales with *Injustice*

Just as Capcom partnered with Marvel comics, so Midway partnered with the
other comic book giant, DC. Initially following the Capcom format, *Mortal Kombat
vs. DC Universe* released in 2008. Although the game didn't fare poorly, it was not
embraced by the community because DC wouldn't license its characters to be
killed, and without the signature fatality moves, *MK* fans didn't feel that the game
was truly *MK*.

Even though *MK vs. DC* wasn't a huge esports hit, the idea of a fighting game with
DC heavy hitters like Superman, Batman, and Wonder Woman still struck the MK
team as a viable competitor to the *Capcom vs.* series. The answer to making the
game work was removing *MK* and the need for fatalities. The resulting game was
Injustice: Gods Among Us.

Based in an alternative universe in which Superman is evil, *Injustice* featured some
of DC's most popular characters along with the mechanics that fans loved from
MK. In the place of fatalities, the *Injustice* series includes supermoves, which are
short cinematic moves that do heavy damage and feature the character's super-
powers. Watching the Flash run someone through time into the past and bounce
the character off a dinosaur, or watching Batman call in his Batmobile or Batwing,
gave the series something to replace the gory fatality finishes from *MK*.

UNCOVERING FIVE MORTAL KOMBAT SECRETS

Mortal Kombat, with its penchant for gore and constant replacement of the letter *c* with the letter *k*, is an iconic fighting-game series with some interesting history. Here are five secrets you might not have known about the *MK* series:

- The original *Mortal Kombat* is the reason that the Entertainment Software Ratings Board (ESRB) exists and rates games. The blood and violence in *MK* prompted a discussion in the U.S. Congress!

- No manual or other source existed to reveal the original *MK* fatality moves. Players had to discover them via experimentation or by finding people who knew them. There wasn't even a Reddit for people to go to and ask!

- One of the series' most famous characters, the ninja Ermac, was created because eagle-eyed fans noticed the phrase *ERMACS* in the first game. The phrase was a shortened form of *error macros* and indicated a macro in the boot code meant to catch errors. The phrase was never meant to have anything to do with the actual game, but through fan rumors, Ermac grew into such an urban myth that the *MK* team couldn't resist creating him.

- *MK* character Scorpion shouts a gravelly taunt of "get over here" before using one of his signature moves, a thrown grappling hook or spear that pulls the opponent over to him. This iconic vocal was recorded by *MK* co-creator Ed Boon, and the menacing sound comes from Boon's having yelled himself hoarse at a football game the day before he recorded the famous line that has appeared in every *MK* game.

- Over the years, *MK* has hosted a series of celebrity guest fighters, including Jason Voorhees from *Friday the 13th*; the xenomorph from *Alien*, the *Predator*; Arnold Schwarzenegger's *Terminator*; DC's *Joker*; and the Image Comics character *Spawn*.

The current game in the series, *Injustice 2*, is still frequently played in competition. The art style and animations are based heavily on *MK*, making the play style familiar to *MK* players, but there is an obvious appeal to being able to play as a character like Batman (see Figure 5-6).

Fighting in three dimensions with *Tekken*

In the "Stepping forward with the 3-D fighter" section, earlier in this chapter, I mention *Virtua Fighter*. Although Sega's *VF* created the foundation for the 3-D fighting game, the *Tekken* series took the concept and fashioned it into a massive arcade and console success. First released to arcades in 1994, Bandai Namco's *Tekken* began a long lineage of games based on hand-to-hand combat and a slower, less jumping-based fighting style.

FIGURE 5-6:
A NetherRealm-
styled Batman
prepares for
battle in
Injustice 2.

Tekken has been so successful that it has released nine installments (the seven *Tekken* titles and two in the series called *Tekken Tag Tournament*) and has presented versions of its game on arcade cabinets, Android, Game Boy Advance, iOS, Windows, PlayStations 1–4, the PlayStation Portable, Wii U, Nintendo 3DS, and Xbox 360/Xbox One. The *Tekken* series has also been an EVO mainstay.

The current title, *Tekken* 7, includes a roster of 52 fighters, including guests like *Street Fighter*'s Akuma, and Negan from *The Walking Dead* (shown in Figure 5-7). Because *Tekken* 7 is the premiere 3-D fighter, you can easily find tournament play for the game on every level, from local to international events.

One of the most dramatic shifts to *Tekken* from the 2.5-D fighting games mentioned previously is that in *SF, MK,* and similar games, jumping is frequently used to cover space, whether to create separation or to close in on a target. In *Tekken,* jumping is rarely the right choice, and the more realistic gravity aspect of game physics results in jumps that cover a relatively small amount of space, leaving a player open to multiple attacks. This situation can frustrate new players who are familiar with other fighting games as they attempt to use their preexisting skills within the *Tekken* system.

FIGURE 5-7:
Fan-favorite villain Negan from *The Walking Dead* brings his bat Lucille to *Tekken 7.*

Who are you?

Accessing the Fighting-Game World

Fighting games differ from major esports titles like *League of Legends* and *Overwatch* in that they are almost exclusively matches of one on one. This aspect comes from their origins in arcade culture. In contrast to all esports other than the early high-scoring competitions and speed runs, fighting games owe their popularity and the origins of their competition style to having been distributed not as PC games but as games housed in arcade cabinets with a pair of controllers on the front. Early fighting gamers didn't challenge each other through matchmaking or ladder rankings but rather through whoever put their quarter in the machine to play next.

Dropping quarters at the arcade

The arcade culture of the 1980s in many ways predicted today's online gaming culture. The arcade was where gamers went to play and socialize with other gamers just as online games, forums, and Discord servers are now. But arcade gaming had another important impact on the development of gaming and esports as well. Arcades made video games accessible to people without the income to afford high-end PCs. For a quarter, or in the case of most fighting games, 50 cents, a person could play on a competitive machine with a quality controller.

Bringing home consoles

As arcades died out, the sort of gaming that happened in arcades moved to the console market. By the era of the PlayStation 2 and the Xbox, home consoles were capable of replicating arcade quality games in the home. A market emerged for competition-level controllers, some of which you can read about in Chapter 2.

Just as arcades had made games more accessible to more people, so consoles gave more people access to fighting-game competition. Although consoles aren't cheap, they're far cheaper than a high-end PC. In fact, the majority of fighting game competition to this day happens on PS4, Xbox One, and Switch consoles, with competitors bringing their own controllers to events. Fighting games are the only genre of esports for which this console-centered play is true, though games like *Fortnite* and *Rocket League* allow for console play though high-level competition happens on PC, and the games *SMITE* and *Paladins* from Hi-Rez Studios have console-specific competitions separate from their PC events.

Going Out to Pick a Competitive Fight

Fighting-game esports happen at multiple levels. The single biggest event is EVO, the annual Las Vegas summer mega-tournament that serves as a sort of fighting games Super Bowl. Other large events occur as well, like DreamHack and the Capcom Cup. More important, though, is the massive network of smaller competitions that range from as small and casual as a local fighting-games night at a game shop in a small town to much larger regional events like University of Michigan's *Super Smash Bros.* community's Big House, an event so large that it requires Detroit's Cobo Center to house all the competitors.

Getting started as a fighting-games player is as easy as going to your local game store or talking to the esports club at your closest university. Moreso than other esports, you can build your reputation by simply showing up and playing. You don't need a team or have to learn team tactics. You can pick up a console, choose a game, practice, and then get out there and join in the action!

TIP

With fighting games, the natural desire is to play as many of them as possible. Doing so isn't a bad strategy if you just want to play and have fun. To be a top-level competitor, though, you should pick a primary game and practice that game as much as possible. Although fighting games might seem similar, you build muscle memory based on the game you play, making what at first seems like a complicated combo or gesture second nature. These muscle-memory moves will last for years as you hone them. For example, I've played the character Sub Zero in every *MK* entry since the first eponymous version, and in every edition of the game, his core mechanics are the same. The muscle memory I developed 20 years ago still kicks in when I play a competitive match. With other games, not so much.

Chapter **6**

It's *Madden* Season! Playing Sports Simulations

n 2014, EA Sports launched its annual NFL game, *Madden NFL 15*, with a series of commercials starring comedian Kevin Hart and actor Dave Franco. The commercials declared that it was "Madden Season" and showed the two friends and rivals elevating their *Madden* competition while treating the game's launch as a holiday.

When most people unfamiliar with esports enter discussion about the esports scene, most often the title they think of is *Madden Football*. It might sound like I'm elevating it to an obnoxious level, but I don't think a week has gone by in the last four years without someone saying to me, "Esports? You mean like *Madden*?"

When looking at games like *Madden*, *NBA 2K*, *FIFA*, and their ilk, you have to consider a nearly paradoxical truth. If esports means competitive gaming, then *Madden* and *NBA 2K* are clearly esports. If you stress the word *sports* in *esports*, games that simulate real sports are esports. But when discussing esports in the sense of contemporary competition, sports simulation games fall far, far behind genres like the FPS, the MOBA, and squad-based shooters, as well as card-based games like *Hearthstone* or *Magic: The Gathering Arena*. So the seemingly easy question, "Is *Madden* an esport?" can get confusing.

This chapter helps you to understand the esports scenes surrounding video games that simulate real-world sports. You learn the key titles and the real-world games they correspond to, plus you explore the competitions for each respective title.

Simulating Sports: Making Physical Games into Video Games

The major difference between sports simulation games and the games discussed in the other chapters of this book are that sports sims, at their core, attempt to replicate real-world games complete with the stadiums, the uniforms, and the individual players and their abilities. In a game like *Overwatch*, you can play as Reaper, a defined character with a specific look and specific skills. But Reaper, as he exists in the game, isn't a real person. By contrast, in *Madden NFL 20*, if you select to play as the Kansas City Chiefs, you control Patrick Mahomes, an in-game character who is supposed to represent and replicate the skills of Patrick Mahomes the actual human being, who is the quarterback for the Chiefs.

Most sports simulation games follow these basic parameters:

>> The game replicates a series of real-world spaces in which the game is played.

>> The game strives to replicate realistic movement, realistic speed, and realistic physics.

>> The game features one league from the respective sport and has a licensing agreement that allows for the use of logos, team names, player names, and player likenesses.

>> The game is usually bound to a specific year or season of the sport, and successful titles are updated yearly even if the core gameplay isn't dramatically changed. Although most sports games update during the year, updates cease after the next entry in the game series is announced.

>> In addition to having a robust player-versus-player element, most sports simulations also have a season or tournament mode that replicates how the real-world organization operates. For example, *Madden* football has a franchise mode in which the player manages the team from the preseason through the season and playoffs (if they perform well enough). Then the player goes through the off-season of contract signings, trades, and a draft before starting the next season of the game.

TIP

Unlike most other games, older versions of sports sims are rarely collectible and are almost never played competitively after the new edition of the game is released. Copies of *Madden* football have been sold every year since 1988, but except for the higher prices of the first releases from 1988 and 1989 (owing to nostalgia), you can purchase the older editions of the game for less than $5 each. If you want to play competitively, you need to upgrade the game every year. A pro tip to keep in mind: Every year, major retailers like GameStop offer a special trade-in discount if you trade in the previous year's version of a sports game. Unless you prefer to hang on to all versions, trading in your previous year's version then is best because older versions of sports games will never have a higher value.

Differentiating Esports Gamers and Sports Gamers

Competitive esports as people know them in the 2020s emerged from gaming communities. And gaming communities, as studies by Nielsen, Twitch, and other outlets have recently shown, don't overlap with traditional sports audiences in significant ways. If I spend a Sunday with my esports players, they seem perplexed as to why I'm checking scores or why I have the Indianapolis Colts game playing on my screen. The sports world for their generation(s) belonged to athletes, and the gamers who built *Blizzard* and *Riot*, or who dreamed up *Fortnite* or *Apex Legends*, were not athletes. That's not to say that they were stereotypically not athletic. They simply didn't choose to play sports. Also, in contrast to previous generations, gamers who didn't play sports tend to not watch sports nearly as much as their parents or grandparents do. They watch esports instead, because they can. Likewise, people who don't play or watch sports don't tend to be attracted to sports-based games. All of which is just to say that a distinct divide exists between the "typical" esports scene and the sports simulation esports scene.

An enormous community exists, however, of people who play games like *Madden*, *NBA 2K*, and their ilk. In fact, the Madden Bowl, a *Madden* tournament that started in 1995 as part of the NFL's Super Bowl Championship Weekend, was one of the first esports events to gain widespread media coverage, and ESPN's 2005 series *Madden Nation* was the first time that esports competition was covered regularly by a television network.

Although many influencers, players, and organizations in the esports world make moves to distance what they do and what they play from professional sports and real-life sports simulations, pro sports teams grow more active daily in the professional esports scene. 2K Sports and the NBA's 2K League is one of the three currently operating esports leagues in America that has a franchise system linked to ownership groups and cities. Another is the *Overwatch* League, discussed in detail in Chapter 4, and Activision launched the *Call of Duty* League in 2020.

REMEMBER

At various points in the book, I offer the reminder that in spite of the generally good nature of gamers and games communities, toxic behavior sometimes occurs. The small but vocal minority of esports players and fans who don't want to make space for sports simulations can create the impression of a huge chasm existing between "esports" and any esport that might be similar to "real" sports. That certainly isn't the case, but remember that you are more than likely to meet people in the esports world who don't think of *Madden* or *NBA 2K* as esports games. No one owns the term "esports," so such discussions will pop up. If you want to compete in one of these titles, don't let the sentiment that sports games aren't esports dissuade you. You will have no trouble finding competitions and communities that embrace you.

Madden Football: Tackling a Gaming Juggernaut

John Madden Football debuted in 1988 as an Apple IIe game (see Figure 6-1). The game didn't gain wide recognition until 1990, when *John Madden Football* was released for the Sega Genesis and Super Nintendo consoles. In 1990, the *Madden* game for Genesis was considered the first "killer app" for that generation of the console wars, ranking as one of the highest-rated and highest-selling titles for the life of that console (https://www.gamespot.com/articles/madden-nfl-19-has-strong-first-weekend-franchise-h/1100-6461144/).

FIGURE 6-1:
John Madden Football (1988) compared with *Madden NFL 20*.

Madden rose to the top of the football gaming pile for two reasons. First, it was fully licensed with the NFL; second, John Madden, a Super Bowl–winning coach and well-known sports commentator, gave the game not only a celebrity name but also access to his understanding of how football playbooks worked, helping to implement that knowledge in video game form. The *Madden* series became the football game that could simulate real football, though the 1990 version was nowhere near the level of the game's artificial intelligence and the mechanical polish that the 2019 version offers.

Having the only license in town

In 2020, *Madden NFL 20* is the only title that has the NFL and NFL Players Association (NFLPA) license. Having this license means that although other companies might try to make a football game, *Madden* is the only one that can have the actual NFL teams, players, and stadiums. It makes *Madden* and EA Sports the only game in town.

WHO IS JOHN MADDEN?

Although his last name has become synonymous with the *EA Sports* football game, contemporary fans might not know much about John Madden, the man behind the initial game. From a game-design standpoint, he pushed the field by insisting that programmers find a way to expand their early game prototype of 7-versus-7 players to 11 versus 11 so that it would look like real football, and he pushed for years to get realistic commentary — originally delivered by Madden himself — into the game so that it would, again, feel like real football. Here are some interesting facts about John Madden (https://sports.jrank.org/pages/2957/Madden-John.html):

- He was college player at California Polytechnic State University (Cal-Poly U) and was drafted by the Philadelphia Eagles, though he was injured in training camp and never played in an NFL game.

- He coached the Oakland Raiders from 1969–1978, achieving a Super Bowl win in 1976.

- He worked as an NFL commentator from 1979–2008. Over that span, he worked for every major network. He ended his career working Monday Night Football with Al Michaels.

- He refused to fly, and instead drove from game to game as a commentator on a tour bus called the Madden Cruiser.

- The only regular NFL event Madden never covered was the Pro Bowl, because during his tenure as an announcer, it always happened in Hawaii and he didn't want to charter a boat.

Possessing this license also highlights a way that *Madden* competition differs from other esports. In a *Madden* competition, you play as an NFL team with an accurate roster. Although the game has a creation suite, competitions don't welcome customized players or rosters. To compete, you need to understand the real-life counterparts to your in-game team, at least to some degree, because everyone that you use in-game is meant to perform in a way that corresponds to the way the players perform on the field. *Madden* even updates after each week of the season to tweak the ratings of players, move any player who was traded, and rotate injured players out of the play rotation.

Understanding *Madden* esports

You can find local tournaments for *Madden* that have their own house rules, but the primary mode of competition for *Madden* is the standard mode in which each player picks an NFL team. Rosters update weekly during the actual NFL season and then lock, barring some major change that might result in an off-season update. From August through January, the game updates regularly, but from February through July, rosters remain generally unchanged.

The other popular competitive mode for *Madden* is the Madden Ultimate Team (MUT). This mode uses virtual card packs and allows players to collect and build teams in a style similar to deck building in a collectible card game like *Magic: The Gathering* or *Hearthstone*. This mode has a highly competitive online ladder mode and community, but using MUT as a drafting tool to build teams for competitions is also common. MUT has pay-to-win issues, though, because paying for packs will get a player better players, so no official tournaments utilize it as their actual competition mode.

You can find a number of EA Sports-sponsored *Madden* tournament events (the *Madden* Championship Series) through the web page at ea.com/compete. Here you will find events like the following:

» **The Madden Classic:** A classic-style, head-to-head, on-ground tournament with several regional qualifiers.

» **The Madden Club Championship:** A bracket-style tournament in which one esports competitor is selected to represent every real-life NFL franchise. Each NFL team runs its own qualifier.

» **The Madden Challenge:** A 16-player tournament that uses *Madden Ultimate Team* drafting to build teams.

» **Madden Bowl:** The culmination of all the other events here, with players who rank in the top two of each various event coming together along with players from the top six of the last-chance qualifier (LCQ) offered online. The winner can boast to be the champion of the annual *Madden* Championship Series.

The *Madden NFL* Championship series is one of the largest sports simulation esports events in the world, largely as a result of the sponsorship of the event and EA Sports and the NFL's partnership. The prize pool has exceeded $1 million each of the last two years, and major sponsors include Pizza Hut, Snickers, Starbucks, and Bose (: https://www.ea.com/games/madden-nfl/madden-nfl-20/compete/).

Sadly, a *Madden 19* video game tournament at a bar in Jacksonville Landing, Jacksonville, FL, was the scene of what has been the only mass shooting associated with an esports event as of this writing. See the sidebar "The Jacksonville Landing shooting" for more information.

THE JACKSONVILLE LANDING SHOOTING

On August 26, 2018, a solo gunman opened fire during a *Madden 19* video game tournament at GLHF (Good Luck, Have Fun) Bar in Jacksonville Landing, Jacksonville, FL. Three people died, including the shooter, who killed himself. Another 11 were injured. It was, to date, the only mass shooting associated with an esports event.

Two things make the incident particularly chilling. The first is that the shooter was a participant in the tournament, and after losing, he refused to shake the hand of his opponent and left the bar. He would return later, we now know, having retrieved a handgun from his vehicle. Witnesses say that he specifically targeted his first victim from a distance. Other participants claim to have seen the red dot of a laser scope on the chest of the first victim.

The other chilling element of the shooting is that it was witnessed live on the Twitch.tv streaming service because someone was streaming the tournament when the shooting took place. Although nothing of the shooting can be seen because the stream shows the game itself, the gunshots can be heard, as can the panicked reactions of several people before the feed cuts.

In the days, weeks, and months following the Jacksonville Landing shooting, numerous esports organizations and tournament organizers reconsidered security at events. As a result, most major events now include metal detectors, and participants have their bags searched before entering venues.

Hooping It Up in *NBA 2K:* Starting Your Career as a Baller

In contrast to football esports, several games have the full license of the National Basketball Association (NBA) and NBPA to produce video games. Amid the sea of titles that include EA's *NBA Live* and an arcade-style two-versus-two-game called *NBA Playgrounds,* no basketball game has found the following and competitive dedication of the *NBA 2K* series by 2K. Currently on *NBA 2K20,* with new Los Angeles Laker Anthony Davis on the cover (see Figure 6-2), *NBA 2K20* has sold between seven and ten million copies each in the last five years.

FIGURE 6-2:
Anthony Davis and LeBron James in *NBA 2K20.*

The 2K series gained popularity after 2K made a profound effort to make the game feel like a simulation. In contrast to more arcade-style basketball games, in which almost every basket is a slam dunk and players fly back and forth at seemingly unrealistic speeds, passing and setting up an offense matter in 2K, as do blocking out and getting back on defense.

Letting you be you — as a player

Many people play *NBA 2K* the same way they play *Madden.* That is, they pick a team and play that team to get better, look for local competitions, and try to win as LeBron or Giannis. Unlike *Madden,* however, the most powerful built-in competition mode in *NBA 2K* asks you to create your own player. Although that player doesn't need to be you, most people replicate themselves in the game because of the robust editing mode and a companion app, MyNBA2K20, that lets you to take a photo of your face and upload it. (You can see mine in Figure 6-3.) It's not perfect, though, so in some cases getting a likeness is difficult to impossible, depending on a person's features. Also, you can't create a female player even though the *NBA 2K* League now has a professional female player.

FIGURE 6-3:
Your pal Phill
in *NBA 2K*
thanks to the
MyNBA2K20 app.

After you create your own player, you may select from a set of player archetypes that map to the five key positions in basketball: center, power forward, small forward, shooting guard, and point guard. In a number of play modes, you can use your created player to earn experience and climb the ladder. The two most important ones are Playground, in which you can find three-versus-three online games that work like a real-life pick-up game on a huge virtual playground; and Pro-Am, in which you can take your created player online and join a five-on-five team to compete against other players.

These modes are of particular importance because the route to elite competition in *NBA 2K* runs through them. In concert with the NBA itself, *NBA 2K* runs an *NBA 2K* League, which is a professional *NBA 2K* esports league with 23 teams owned and operated by 22 of the NBA's teams (and one team managed by a professional esports organization).

Playing in the *NBA 2K* League

Founded in 2017, the *NBA 2K* League is owned by the National Basketball Association and Take-Two Interactive, the producers of the *NBA 2K* video game. In league play, two teams play each other in the 2K Pro-Am mode, with each player choosing an in-game archetype. The league started with 17 teams in 2018 but expanded to 21 for 2019. Two more teams have been approved to join in 2020. You can see the list of teams and their affiliations in Table 6-1.

TABLE 6-1

NBA 2K League Teams, Cities, and Affiliations

Team	City	NBA Affiliation
76ers Gaming Club (GC)	Philadelphia, PA	Philadelphia 76ers
Blazers Gaming	Portland, OR	Portland Trailblazers
Bucks Gaming	Milwaukee, WI	Milwaukee Bucks
Cavs Legion GC	Cleveland, OH	Cleveland Cavaliers
Celtics Crossover Gaming	Boston, MA	Boston Celtics
Gen. G Tigers	Shanghai, China	Non-NBA owners, Generation Gaming (Gen. G)
Grizz Gaming	Memphis, TN	Memphis Grizzlies
Hawks Talon GC	Atlanta, GA	Atlanta Hawks
Heat Check Gaming	Miami, FL	Miami Heat
Hornets Venom GT	Charlotte, NC	Charlotte Hornets
Jazz Gaming	Salt Lake City, UT	Utah Jazz
Kings Guard Gaming	Sacramento, CA	Sacramento Kings
Knicks Gaming	New York, NY	New York Knicks
Lakers Gaming	Los Angeles, CA	Los Angeles Lakers
Magic Gaming	Orlando, FL	Orlando Magic
Mavs Gaming	Dallas, TX	Dallas Mavericks
NETSGC	Brooklyn, NY	Brooklyn Nets
Pacers Gaming	Indianapolis, IN	Indiana Pacers
Pistons GT	Detroit, MI	Detroit Pistons
Raptors Uprising GC	Toronto, Ontario, CA	Toronto Raptors
T-Wolves Gaming	Minneapolis, MN	Minnesota Timberwolves
Warriors Gaming Squad	San Francisco, CA	Golden State Warriors
Wizards District Gaming	Washington, D.C.	Washington Wizards

Why the *NBA 2K* League matters

The NBA 2K League is of particular importance to the esports landscape for three key reasons:

» Alongside the *Overwatch* League and *Call of Duty* League, the *NBA 2K* League is one of the few esports leagues that attempts to mirror traditional sports in that it has franchises based in cities. Those teams are also directly connected to professional NBA teams. The major significance of this method of organizing franchises is that it allows for local teams and an entryway for new fans to get involved.

» The *NBA 2K* League is the first esports league to be directly connected to professional sports. Although many professional sports teams have started to enter the esports space, the *NBA 2K* League is partly owned by a professional sports league, and the teams are connected to the owners of the NBA franchises they represent.

» The *NBA 2K* League was the first esports league that contained the ability of a player to try out entirely within the game.

How to Join the *NBA 2K* League

You obviously need to be quite good at *NBA 2K* to make it into the *NBA 2K* League. But to take your chance, all you need is a copy of the most recent *NBA 2K* title and an Xbox One or PlayStation 4 console. Each year, the *NBA 2K* League sets a period during which you can qualify for the 2K League Combine. To do that, you send in an application and then win 100 Pro-Am or Playground mode games within the qualifier period, as well as at least 50 percent of your matches. In other words, if you play 190 games and win 100 of them, you qualify.

After the qualifiers, all players who fulfill the requirements are invited to the online combine. In the combine round, a player must compete in five-versus-five games with other people in the combine pool. While watching and analyzing the play in this round, the *NBA 2K* League selects 150 players to take part in the 2K League draft. Those players move on to the live draft and have a chance to be picked up by one of the 23 2K League teams to start their careers as professional players.

REMEMBER

You can find all the details on the qualifying process on the 2K League website at 2kleague.nba.com/ (https://2kleague.nba.com/), under Qualifier Information.

CHIQUITA EVANS: THE FIRST WOMAN IN NBA 2K LEAGUE

During its first draft, the *NBA 2K* League was surprised to find that only a single woman made it into its combine pool and did not make it in to the draft. The league wouldn't have to wait long for that problem to resolve itself, however, because in the second combine and draft, a star emerged in Chiquitae126.

A 30-year-old who worked at Foot Locker while grinding her way into the qualifier pool, Chiquita Evans became the first woman to be drafted into the *NBA 2K* League. She was picked as 56th overall by Warriors Gaming, the Golden State Warriors–owned *2K* League team. Evans made it in to the draft pool in spite of facing moments in the process in which other players wouldn't pass her the ball, forcing her to prove her skills through defensive moves and rebounding.

In her first season, Evans was a star on and off the virtual court. Because of her high visibility and sincere candor about the lack of women in esports, many believe that Chiquita will encourage other women to aspire to the highest levels of professional esports. In addition to being the only female player in the *NBA 2K* League, Evans is 30, which is also inspiring. Although 30 is far from old, in professional esports years, being in your 30s usually signals the end, not the start, of a career.

Checking In with Other Sports Sims

At the risk of sounding repetitive, some games qualify as esports, but most people in the esports world don't think of them as being prime titles. Some of these games don't even have organized tournaments; instead, they depend on local gatherings and small-scale tourneys to offer competitions. So you shouldn't regard the games described in this section as ways into professional esports. If you're fond of these other major professional sports (hockey, soccer, and base-ball), however, these are the most competitive titles in those sports.

Getting your hockey fix

Hockey fans will want to check out the EA Sports title *NHL 20*. As with many sports games, it updates each year, with the last two numbers of the year becoming part of the title. *NHL 20* is the most advanced hockey game on the market, and EA Sports has partnered with the NHL to bring the best possible esports competition. NHL is played exclusively on consoles.

NHL has a single major tournament, and it's enormous. The *NHL* Gaming World Championship brings together players from around the world through a series of weekends offering single-elimination qualification. These qualifications lead to a series of regional finals and a final championship. You can find more information on the structure of the event at `https://www.nhl.com/fans/gaming`. Beyond this one tournament, the *NHL* esports scene is almost nonexistent. It's a small community.

Playing soccer

Another of EA Sports' top-selling titles is its *FIFA* game. It has the same naming standard as EA Sports' *NHL* title: Each version consists of the *FIFA* name followed by the last two numbers of a year. The newest edition of the game is *FIFA 20*.

FIFA is played primarily on a console, as *Madden* is, but its worldwide appeal means that even though it has only one major tournament, it's a major tournament. You can find information about it at `www.fifa.com/fifaeworldcup`. The structure of the *FIFA* tournament is similar to what EA Sports does with *Madden*, with a number of qualifier opportunities being provided for online play, all building toward a Grand Final. There, the top 32 *FIFA* players in the world battle for the trophy.

Because of the international appeal of soccer, *FIFA* esports is considerably larger than hockey or baseball. It is one of the few sports sims with a truly international world championship. It is also one of the stronger esports console games. In spite of that, it still lags far behind esports giants like *League of Legends* and *Dota 2*.

Hitting with the only baseball game in town

Major League Baseball hasn't locked in its MLB and Major League Baseball Players Association (MLBPA) rights to a single publisher, but the only truly updated, current-generation MLB game is Sony's *MLB: The Show*. Made by Sony Interactive Entertainment's San Diego Studio, the game is a PlayStation 4 exclusive, which limits its overall audience. *MLB: The Show* doesn't have an active competitive scene in the United States, but in June 2019, MLB launched the *MLB* China Esports League, offering competitive *MLB: The Show* matches in seven cities.

Playing Esports with Cars: Racing Games and *Rocket League*

Historically thought of as highly competitive games, racing games have little representation in the esports landscape. Players mark this as a commentary on the skill-to-luck ratio in playing racing games, and most manufacturers still see racing games as suitable for living room play, and not as much for major competitions.

Running a good race

Some competitive events are supported by the *Forza* game series, which you can learn more about at the Forza Motor Sports website at orzamotorsports.net/en-us/frc. A few other scattered events involve titles like *Formula 1 Racing* and *Gran Turismo*. Racing in esports is more of a casual gaming experience, though. Game developers are working on games and competitions that might make racing esports relevant, but right now, that's a far-off goal. Just as sports simulations in general have had mixed results entering the esports ecosystem, so have racing games found the terrain difficult, keeping their wheels spinning.

The most popular racing game is the Nintendo Switch title, *Mario Kart 8 Deluxe.* This title hasn't gained traction in the esports world because of the way the game is structured. It is meant to be a party game, and as a result, it is not at all balanced because of random power-ups that change player abilities during matches. The game tries to help those who are behind to win, and a randomly occurring power-up such as an item that increases speed or causes an opponent to crash can negate the skill of any individual player. Nintendo continues its attempts to spread *Mario Kart* to the masses with its new mobile game, *Mario Kart Tour,* which you can play on iOS and Android devices (see Figure 6-4). Although the mobile game is unlikely to catch fire in North America, it could gain esports traction in China and Korea, where mobile games like *Clash Royale* and *Arena of Valor* have major tournaments.

Only time will tell if racing games eventually take on a larger role in the esports world, but for now, few organized events and leagues focus on racing.

The one place where racing games have a solid foothold is the *Formula 1 Esports Series* (https://f1esports.com/). One of the largest esports leagues that few people are aware of, the *F1 Esports Series* has an esports team for each of the ten actual Formula 1 racing teams, and in 2020, the league is attempting to expand into China. With a 2019 prize pool of $500,000, the *F1 Esports Series* is the place to go for esports players interested in racing.

Playing soccer with cars

Perhaps the most surprising game to see exponential esports growth over the last few years is Psyonix LLC's *Rocket League*. Although the game has an astounding level of strategy and depth, describing it is simple. It's soccer, but you drive a car. The cars hit a huge ball and try to score goals in their respective nets.

Rocket League, shown in Figure 6-5, has grown so quickly that in May of 2019, Psyonix was purchased by Epic, the makers of *Fortnite*. With a robust esports scene that you can check out at www.rocketleagueesports.com, the major appeal of *Rocket League* comes from the following:

>> Psyonix went to its fans who were making grassroots efforts and helped those fans grow their community and competitions.

>> *Rocket League* is the classic "easy to learn, hard to master" game that almost every gamer feels able to pick up and go with. The strategy at first can be as simple as "hit that ball with your car."

>> *Rocket League* is a game that lets you play on multiple platforms without demanding different skills or skill levels. Although you can play games like *Overwatch, SMITE,* and *Call of Duty* on a PC and on consoles, those two platforms present massive differences in speed and aiming ability. Someone who plays *Rocket League* on a console can, however, have the same experience as someone playing *Rocket League* on PC. In fact, *Rocket League* is one of the few PC games for which most players opt to use a controller.

FIGURE 6-5:
Rocket League
in action.

With *Rocket League* now falling under the Epic Games umbrella, support for the game and exposure to the enormous *Fortnite* audience should only help as the game looks to expand and take on a greater role in the esports landscape.

Rocket League is a high-profile esport as the game heads into the ninth season of the *Rocket League* Championship Series, an event held in partnership with NBC, ESPN, ELEAGUE (on TBS television), and the gaming event DreamHack. Recent season prize pools totaled approximately $1 million. You can read more about *Rocket League* competitions in Chapter 11.

Chapter **7**

Playing Battle Royale Games

The newest genre in esports is also currently the most popular. With 250 million players (according to Statistica, courtesy of _Fortnite Insider_ at www.fortniteinsider.com), _Fortnite_ was, as of March 2019, the largest esport in the world. This feat is particularly astonishing because _Fortnite_ was launched in July 2017, making it not even two years old when it arrived at 250 million active users.

In this chapter, you discover the battle royale style of game, take a look at a few key active titles, and find out about _Fortnite_ esports competition. Although the battle royale seemed to emerge from nothing, its origins are shockingly similar to the MOBA (described in Chapter 3), and based on the early popularity of key titles, reasons abound to assume that it will have the same longevity as _League of Legends_ and _Dota 2_.

Watching Fans Make Esports History: _Minecraft Hunger Games_

Few game genres make tracing their origins in a straight line easy, but the name _battle royale_ comes from a 1996 novel by Koushun Takami and a 2000 film of the same name. The novel and movie had a simple premise. It was set in a middle school where the students had to battle to the death, with one winner. Everyone else loses. This same basic concept with some stylistic modifications makes up the base storyline for the novels and movies of the *Hunger Games* franchise, in which various competitors battle until only one survives.

In 2012, users Cliff Jameston and mlamascese52 created *Minecraft Hunger Games*, a modification of the famous building/exploration game *Minecraft*, in which players spawn into play near boxes of gear. The players need to quickly collect what they can and run before the hunting begins. Although the mode was simple, it still retains popularity among players. It's not an esport in the classic sense, though, because different versions of the modified game have too much variability and therefore lack the required balance to be highly competitive.

In 2015, Daybreak Game Company released a game called *H1Z1*. The game was well received in spite of being incredibly buggy, but it gained wide acclaim and built a fan base thanks to a mod by a developer named Brendan "PlayerUnknown" Greene. His mod, *HI1Z King of the Kill*, was such a hit that he eventually teamed up with Bluehole Studios to build a new game. That game was *PlayerUnknown's Battlegrounds* (PUBG).

Going 1 versus 99 with *PUBG*

PUBG cemented what would become the standard mode of play for the battle royale genre. Released in 2017, *PUBG* is still extremely popular in Korea and China, but in North America, it has lost significant ground to *Fortnite*. At the time of its release, however, *PUBG* set the standard by building the following set of rules for the battle royale:

>> Each standard match has up to 100 players. There are also modes with teams of 2 or 3, and a match can have far fewer than 100 players.

>> The goal is to be the last person standing.

>> The gameplay is based on a shooter but includes melee combat.

>> At the start of the game, all players parachute into the map, as you can see in Figure 7-1. Gliding during this part of the game can let players have some small measure of control over where they start the game, but it is mostly random.

>> Items are generated at random and placed around the map. Players must search for supplies like guns, health packs, and so on.

» The outside edges of the map constrict every few minutes (an effect called "the storm" by players). As this constriction happens, the center of the map remains "safe" while anyone outside the constricting circle dies almost instantly. This constriction forces the map to become smaller and means that players can hide for only so long before no space remains.

» The game ends when only one player is left alive.

FIGURE 7-1:
A player skydiving into a *PUBG* match.

PUBG has a professional global league that's organized by its publisher. You can find the full information on that league at www.pubgesports.com. Although the competition is vibrant, *PUBG* doesn't have nearly the popularity as other battle royale games among young people in America. Most esports experts consider *PUBG* to be "in decline," but it is still a wildly successful game. Much of its success is because of its mobile client and its ability to catch on in large regions without a strong esports presence, such as India. According to the *Esports Observer* (https://esportsobserver.com/pubg-mobile-india-esports-primer/), *PUBG Mobile* is the top game in India and is building an entire esports ecosystem there.

In spite of the relative decline of *PUBG*, the 2019 *PUBG* Global Championship was still a massive esports event, with 32 teams gathering in Oakland, CA, to battle for $4 million in prize money. In 2020, *PUBG* will present a Global Series, with four major events around the world leading to a major championship in November.

In America, however, to discuss battle royale games is to tackle one specific title above all others: *Fortnite*.

Spending a Couple of Weeks with *Fortnite*

Few video games have ever exploded onto the scene in the way that Epic Games' *Fortnite* did. Originally announced in 2011, the original single player mode of the game was not well received. *Fortnite Battle Royale* didn't see public release until 2017, but by the end of its first day, it had 1 million players. After a month, it had 17 million players. In the first year, it passed 100 million players. One of the chief reasons for this rapid growth is that the base mode of the current *Fortnite*, the Battle Royale mode, is free to play, whereas *PUBG* is a retail game. People can install *Fortnite* without committing to buy anything, which resulted in a massive early player base.

Fortnite makes a few small but significant changes from the formula for *PUBG*. The first change is with *Fortnite*'s stylized character models. They don't try to be photo-realistic, as you can see in Figure 7-2. Initially, the player receives a randomly generated character that has a random gender and race, but skins and outfits within the game allow for customization. Players can choose from appearances similar to the iconic John Wick, or their characters can wear a mascot rabbit costume, with outlandish options that include NFL football uniforms. For a brief period, players could even claim the Infinity Gauntlet and play as Marvel's Thanos.

The other major addition that *Fortnite* made to the battle royale genre involves allowing players to build structures. Although the structures aren't particularly complex, having the ability to build a wall or a small tower radically alters how the game is played, and that small addition makes *Fortnite* a far more complicated early game. Players can choose to go to the center of the map and focus on creating a scenario that gives them the high ground, or they can roam the map, building resources and trying to get the drop on other players until the map constricts.

Crossing platforms to maximize *Fortnite* access

Whereas *PUBG* exists on Windows, PS4, Xbox One, Android, and MacOS, *Fortnite* appears on all those platforms as well as Nintendo Switch and Macintosh. As a result, gamers can play *Fortnite* on almost any device they might choose, and Epic has developed a cross-platform play system that allows most gamers to play with people on most other platforms. The exception to this versatility is that the Nintendo Switch version of *Fortnite* runs at only 30 frames per second (fps), as compared with the 60 fps of the PC, Mac, PS4, and Xbox One versions. Epic is still tinkering with ways to make cross-device play with the Switch fair. Still, it's impressive to be able to play the same game with the same audience on so many different platforms and consoles.

This cross-platform compatibility made the game extremely popular with young people because a group of friends could all play together without having the same type of device. A PS4 owner and an Xbox One owner could play with their friend who has a PC. Because many younger gamers have a computer or a single console, *Fortnite* became the game through which they could all gather.

Dancing the *Fortnite* away

Fortnite's popularity is also tied to the game's various taunt dances. These are dances that players can do in-game, typically after a kill or while waiting in a lobby. Moves like the floss and Turk's dance quickly penetrated popular culture, with children around the world posting their versions of the dances on social media. The dances meld with the outlandish characters to give *Fortnite* a distinct vibe, a certain cool factor that hit perfectly with the young gamer demographic.

Walking into a match with Drake and a ninja

Fortnite is also the game of choice of the most popular esports influencer, Tyler "Ninja" Blevins. Ninja's streams on Twitch were so popular that he more than doubled the number of followers of the second most-followed streamer with a stunning 14 million followers. This popularity enabled Blevins to earn $500,000 a month, and in mid-2019, his popularity was so high that Twitch's rival, Microsoft's Mixer streaming service, signed Ninja to an exclusive deal. On Mixer, Ninja has already garnered more than a million followers in just a few months.

Although Ninja is certainly no slouch when it comes to competition, he represents a different facet of professional esports. He's an influencer in the style of social media or celebrity figures like Kylie Jenner or Jamie Oliver. In short, Ninja is cool, and having him play your game, use your gear, drink your energy drink, or show up at your event means that his followers want to do all those things, too.

When Ninja was on Twitch, he made a staggering amount of money from his followers' contributions to his streams (giving him money through the site in return for his streaming). At one point in 2018, Ninja was making $500,000 a month from his Twitch subscribers. Subscribers pay $5 a month to subscribe to a channel on Twitch. The streamer gets half of that money. Streamers can also get random tips and make money when people buy a currency called "bits" that they can spend in Twitch chat. No public accounting of how much Ninja made from those revenue streams is available.

Ninja doesn't make as much now from his Mixer followers, but Microsoft presumably made a huge financial commitment to lure him away from Twitch. Although no definitive number has been announced to the public, sites like Geekwire have reported that Microsoft made an offer of $20–$30 million a year (https://www.geekwire.com/2020/heres-much-microsoft-reportedly-paid-game-streaming-star-ninja-defect-amazons-twitch/).

A colleague of mine who works at Twitch spoke with me once about securing a guest speaker for one of my classes. I jokingly mentioned Ninja. My friend said he was sure Ninja would speak to my class if I could cover the subscription money he would lose from not streaming that hour. My friend's napkin math for that hour of Ninja's earnings was $50,000. Obviously, Ninja wasn't the guest speaker in my class that night. But the takeaway is that being a popular streamer is highly lucrative and can allow a gamer to build a financial empire.

Just how famous is Ninja? He has been on the *Tonight Show* more than once, teaching Jimmy Fallon how to play *Fortnite*. Red Bull built Ninja a full-streaming studio for him to use in his capacity as a brand ambassador. But in April 2018, Ninja made a jaw-dropping pop-culture crossover by playing *Fortnite* duos as the partner of Drake, rapper, actor, and noted Toronto Raptors fan. After a win, Drake gave Ninja a $5,000 tip. That amount was far from the most money that Ninja had received from a single fan.

Ninja's popularity paired with *Fortnite*'s explosive growth gave the game tremendous exposure on Twitch.tv and in the media, as Ninja participated in events like Ninja Las Vegas, where Ninja played matches against any and all comers. Each match provided a cash bounty on Ninja's head, with the prize to be awarded to anyone who could eliminate the flamboyant streamer.

Competing in *Fortnite* esports

In the summer of 2019, Kyle "Bugha" Giersdorf, who was 16 years old at the time, won $3 million in the *Fortnite* World Cup by besting 99 other players in the finals of this tournament of 40 million total entrants. The prize turned heads, and the age of the champion established that *Fortnite* is a young person's game.

The 2019 *Fortnite* World Cup was the first of what will presumably be many major events run by Epic. Prior to the World Cup, however, professional *Fortnite* competitions were rare and hadn't been centralized. One of the major issues facing *Fortnite* competition is the fact that so much of professional esports is about teams and strategies, but even though *Fortnite* offers competition with duos and trios, the chosen format for almost all players is 1 versus 99. That format doesn't allow for teams, other than in the way that drivers on racing teams practice and train together but ultimately must compete against each other.

Epic's strategy for *Fortnite* competitions had been to utilize the in-game system as opposed to any sort of external tournament organizing body, not just to create a ladder but to build the competitive scene. Players can play arena games to earn points that allow them to register for tournaments. They can play in weekly open events to gain points as well. Those points lead to chances to enter the *Fortnite* Champion Series. That Champion Series can lead to the next World Cup and a chance to win millions in a single, high-stakes match.

Climbing to the Top of *Apex Legends*

The other rising battle royale title is *Apex Legends,* by Electronic Arts Inc. (EA). *Apex Legends* takes a slant on the battle royale formula that is more esports friendly. Instead of the 1-versus-99 format, *Apex Legends* involves up to 60 players in teams of three who are dropped onto an island.

In addition to the squad-based default mode, *Apex Legends* also borrows from the hero shooter genre made most famous by *Overwatch.* Players select from characters with specific skills, meaning that teamwork is key because some skill sets held by "legends" (in-game characters) may work well only in tandem with other characters. In the most popular mode in *Fortnite,* the literal Battle Royale, only one person can win. (*Fortnite* also offers duos and a trios mode called "squad," but these lag behind the 1-versus-99 mode in terms of popularity.) *Apex Legends,* however, rewards those who know their teammates and collaborate well. An example of one of the individual "legends" or in-game characters is shown in Figure 7-3.

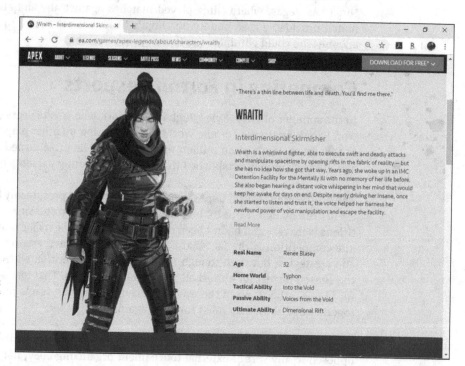

FIGURE 7-3:
The profile for
Apex Legends
character Wraith
from EA's *Apex
Legends* site.

SPINNING CUBES WITH *TETRIS 99*

In early 2019, Nintendo released a surprise hit for its Switch console. Although no one would have doubted that Nintendo could strike big with another entry in the *Tetris* game franchise, no one expected what was delivered with *Tetris 99.* The concept seems crazy: *Tetris 99* is a battle royale game.

In *Tetris 99,* the player takes on 99 other players who are also playing *Tetris.* An algorithm directs the action as each player clears rows and sends problematic blocks to other players, just as they would in a standard one-versus-one *Tetris* match. One by one, players drop from the massive 99-game background behind the player's active window. In the end of what is a frantic 15–30 minutes depending on player skill, a single player reigns supreme as the sole survivor.

In many ways, *Apex Legends* plays more like *Overwatch* than like *Fortnite* or *PUBG,* but the appeal of mashing up the hero shooter with the battle royale genre is undeniable. In December 2019, EA announced the *Apex Legends* Global Series, a set of four major events that will culminate in a championship whose winners will split a $3 million prize pool. Each major will feature 100 teams of three, meaning that the field for the Series will include 1,200 players. To earn a spot, players have to win online qualifiers. You can find more info on the *Apex Legends* Global Series at `https://www.ea.com/games/apex-legends/compete`.

Although *Tetris 99* has yet to take off as an esports title, it has amazing potential. *Tetris* serves a different audience than most other esports titles do, and the chance to include players who come from different populations gives the game the chance to be a runaway hit in the coming years. That different audience includes older players, a more-female-than-male player base, and Switch owners who are starved for esports titles because Nintendo doesn't consider itself to be in the esports space, according to ESPN.com (`https://www.espn.com/esports/story/_/id/26857358/nintendo-aims-do-competitive-gaming-their-way`).

Running into issues in the 1-versus-99 Format

No one can deny the popularity of the battle royale genre. Although its scene isn't organized beyond what publishers offer, at least at this point, the potential for major esports events surrounding *Fortnite* and *Apex Legends* in the Americas and *PUBG* in China, India, and Korea is great. People love to play, influencers are building lucrative careers streaming and casting, and the game developers and publishers see the audience's desire for more content.

That said, the battle royale genre has one massive hurdle to clear: the nature of the game itself. Although EA works to eliminate some of the numbers issues for *Apex Legends*, and *Fortnite* can in theory be scaled down, a 100-player all-for-one esport presents some problems. Those issues include:

>> **Space for matches:** How do you organize the stage for a major match so that players can be seen and have ample space? Most events balance 10–12 players on stage at any given time, so *Fortnite* multiplies that by 10.

>> **Format for watching matches:** It's difficult to broadcast, too. The thing that makes *Fornite* fun to watch on stream, the ability to watch someone like Ninja play into the very end of a match, becomes a problem when you're trying to stream a match with 100 equal players. If you have 100 great *Fornite* players in a match, one of the really good players has to die first. Coverage, then, becomes sort of like a high-speed version of covering pro golf, where the broadcast jumps from player to player.

>> **Ability to keep tabs on players:** It's hard to know all 100 players and have a grasp on how the match might go. When watching games that are five-versus-five or six-versus-six (or card games or fighters that are one-versus-one), scouting the teams and knowing whom you're about to watch isn't difficult. Keeping 100 players straight is tough.

>> **Ensuring equal bandwidth:** If the event isn't in a single location, making sure that the network latency is fair for 100 people coming from 100 different places is difficult as well.

>> **Opportunity to scrimmage:** Although the option exists to play a great deal to prepare, how can professionals actually scrimmage at their skill level to prep for an event? Gathering 100 players to scrimmage would be difficult, if not impossible.

None of these issues mean that *Fortnite* and similar games won't have major esports success. If the last year is any indication, *Fortnite*'s 2020 World Cup will be even bigger than the one that saw Bugha walk away with 3 million reasons that he can afford to go to any college he'd like. Keep the points in the preceding list in mind as you think about where esports is headed. The industry has figured out how to handle one-versus-one games, as well as how to handle five- and six-team, squad-based games. Handling a game with 100 players, though, will require even more innovation in a field known for pushing the envelope. *Fornite* isn't going anywhere, and the ways in which it will change esports could be fascinating.

Chapter **8**

Playing *Hearthstone* and Other Digital Card Games

I n 1993, a company named Wizards of the Coast released a card game called *Magic: The Gathering* (MTG). *MTG* was a game that was played as one versus one, with decks built from cards that people could purchase in packs. The game was the start of a genre called the Collectible Card Game (CCG), a game style in which players collect cards the way people collect baseball cards from packs and then use those cards to assemble decks for competition.

Although CCGs still exist and thrive in the hobby circuit, the cost of buying packs and the need to carry the cards with you to be able to compete made it very much a diehard hobby with dwindling numbers. The game style, however, adapted well to the digital space. In 2014, Blizzard released a CCG based on its *Warcraft* universe, a game called *Hearthstone*. That same year, *Hearthstone* was a featured esports competition event at BlizzCon, Blizzard's annual fan convention.

This chapter gives you the basics of how collectible card games work. You also find out about the biggest current esports CCG titles, including *Hearthstone* and *Magic: The Gathering Arena*, and I tell you just a bit about the mobile device esports scene.

Collecting to Win with CCGs

CCGs operate under the following principles with some minor variations:

» **Each player builds a deck of cards.** For the esports version, these are virtual as opposed to physical cards, and players build the deck before play begins. Various rules govern what cards and decks players can use, as well as the types of competitions they can participate in, but players are made aware of all these rules before the decks are made.

» **The decks are shuffled and players receive initial cards to start their hand.** Amounts of cards vary from game to game.

» **Each card has a value printed on it.** That value corresponds to an amount of energy that a player gets to use during each turn. Many games call this energy "mana" or "land." On their turn, players can play cards adding up to the amount of energy they have.

» **The cards are aligned in rows, facing each other, on a virtual table.** Each round, the cards tell players to take whatever action is printed on them. For example, a card saying "draw another card" means that the player draws another card from the player's deck; a card saying "destroy an enemy card" allows the player to remove one card from the enemy's side of the board.

» **Each player begins with a certain amount of health.** For example, in *Hearthstone,* both players start with 30 health points. Cards can both do damage and heal, subtracting from or adding to that total of 30. Players lose when their health reaches zero.

CCGs are an interesting variation on typical esports in that reaction time and speed are not major factors; instead, strategy is key. The resulting gameplay is no less complex than it is for other esports, but it is much easier to watch and follow, and players who want or need a bit of extra time to consider their choices are not punished.

Hearthstone is by far the most popular esports CCG, offering the most competitions both locally and globally. I tell you more about *Hearthstone* a bit later in the chapter. Meanwhile, in the past year, three new titles have made their case for becoming a part of the esports landscape, with varying amounts of success. Those games are *Magic: The Gathering Arena*, from Wizards of the Coast; *Elder Scrolls: Legends*, from Bethesda; and *Legends of Runeterra*, from Riot. The following sections describe each of these three new games.

Recapturing the magic with *MTGA*

Magic: The Gathering Arena (MTGA) is a newcomer to the esports world, having been officially released in 2019. Styled to resemble the original *MTG*, the game has grown quickly in popularity and is already beginning to offer international competition.

MTGA banks largely on the installed fan base for *MTG*, and every aspect of the game looks to faithfully replicate the real-world card game in a digital medium, as shown in Figure 8-1. Many players consider the game to be deeper than *Hearthstone*, plus it has the potential for players to build far more decks than in *Hearthstone* (with variations for each class in the tens as opposed to the hundreds for *MTGA*), and for these reasons, *MTGA* has gained popularity. However, so far it has no mobile phone client, which has negatively impacted player-base growth. *MTGA* is highly likely to continue to grow over the coming years, with 2020 looking to be the first year for the game to have a full professional season. Wizards of the Coast (and parent company Hasbro) is banking on big esports success; its initial steps into the competitive esports world include a $10 million investment in building the professional scene.

FIGURE 8-1:
Early in a match of *Magic: The Gathering Arena.*

Reading the *Elder Scrolls: Legends*

Elder Scrolls: Legends is a CCG based on the popular *Elder Scrolls* universe from such games as *Skyrim* and *Morrowwind*. Originally planned to be available on multiple platforms including home consoles and PCs, *Elder Scrolls: Legends* was released only on Steam and on mobile platforms before production was halted in December of 2019. Although the game is still playable, it isn't likely to see future development. Without support from the publisher, only a grassroots fan community could keep the game alive as a competitive title. Such support does not seem likely from fans. Although Bethesda didn't offer a definitive reason for halting support for the game, many outlets like Techspot (https://www.techspot.com/news/83095-bethesda-puts-elder-scrolls-legends-indefinite-hold.html) attributed it to the low concurrent user numbers; the game often has fewer than 1,000 players online at any given time.

Rioting for a shot at the *Legends of Runeterra*

Riot Games, the developers of *League of Legends,* announced a slew of new upcoming games in late 2020. One of those is a card game based on the *League of Legends* universe called *Legends of Runeterra*. At the time of this writing, the game exists only in closed beta, but it is expected to release in 2020, and given Riot's esports successes, there is every reason to believe that *Runeterra* will be an esports hit. Make sure to check it out upon release. You can get updates on the release schedule for the game at www.playruneterra.com.

Gathering around the Hearth(Stone): The Standard for Esports CCGs

Blizzard's *Hearthstone* is far and away the most successful, and most often played, esports card game. The game is based around a tried-and-true system of card collecting and gameplay, and the borrowed story and art from *Warcraft* adds a level of polish to the game. To help you understand how a game of *Hearthstone* works, this section walks you through the standards from the first section of this chapter within the specific game. If you take a look at Figure 8-2, you can see what the screen looks like in the middle of a *Hearthstone* match. That view can help as you consider the following stages:

FIGURE 8-2:
The middle of a
Hearthstone
match, with
numerous cards
in play.

>> **Before playing against an opponent, players develop decks within the game's collection feature.** The game has nine classes of hero (or deck) type, and each of those classes has a "hero skill" that can be used along with their cards. You can see the classes, the default or classic hero for each, and their hero powers in Table 8-1.

>> **At the start of the match, players select a deck from their collection.** In Figure 8-2, I have chosen a hunter deck. The class of the deck determines the player's hero, the character that sits on his side of the board above his hand and represents his health.

>> **At the start of the match, the player who will go first is chosen at random.** That person receives three cards as her starting hand. The person who goes second will receive four cards as well as a coin that grants one mana crystal.

>> **After receiving your initial cards, you may choose to discard any or all your cards to receive new ones.** When this process is finished, the match begins.

TABLE 8-1

Hearthstone Classes, Hero, and Hero Powers

Class	Classic Hero	Hero Power
Druid	Malfurion Stormrage	Shapeshift (+1 attack, +1 armor for one round)
Hunter	Rexxar	Steady Shot (2 damage to opposing hero)
Mage	Jaina Proudmoore	Fireblast (1 damage)
Paladin	Uther Lightbringer	Reinforce (summon 1/1 recruit minion)
Priest	Arduin Wrynn	Lesser Heal (heal 2 points)
Rogue	Valeera Sanguinar	Dagger Mastery (equip a 1/2 dagger)
Shaman	Thrall	Totemic Call (summon a random totem)
Warlock	Gul'Dan	Life Tap (take 2 damage, draw a card)
Warrior	Garrosh Hellscream	Armor Up (add 2 armor)

» **The game is played in rounds, with one player going first, completing her turn, and then the other going and completing his turn.** In the first round, each player has one mana crystal, meaning that each player can play any card with a 1 in the upper-left corner. Each round until round ten adds one mana crystal, and the crystals refill on each turn. Mana crystals are not added after ten.

» **The lower-left of each card contains an attack value.** This refers to how much damage the card can do to another card or to the opposing hero. The lower-right corner contains the health value of each card, or the amount of damage it can take. When a card is played against another card, its health value is reduced by the other card's attack value, and vice versa.

» **Cards without those attack and health values are spell cards and cause an effect when played, as shown in Figure 8-3.** Note that the Arcane Missiles card reads "Deal 3 damage randomly split among all enemies." Playing that card results in three one-damage hits registering to random opponents.

» **Each hero starts with 30 health.** When the opposing hero reaches zero health, you've won.

» **Many cards have additional actions or effects.** These actions or effects are written on the cards themselves, similarly to how spell cards are structured. In Figure 8-3, the Daring Fire Eater has one of these conditions that occurs as a battle cry, which means that the action happens when the card is played and only that one time.

Although the game might seem too complex to try to understand from a quick overview and a couple of screenshots, *Hearthstone* has a relatively low learning curve. You can play it on a PC or Mac as well as on an Android or iOS mobile device. It is particularly popular on tablets like the iPad.

FIGURE 8-3:
A page from the *Hearthstone* collection, showing several cards and their details.

Keeping *Hearthstone* fresh

Because the gameplay is based on building decks, after a set period of time the game's meta, or most optimal decks, become common knowledge and competitive play can become stale. To keep this staleness from happening, Blizzard releases regular expansions with new cards and annually "retires" some cards from competitive play. This approach does keep the game fresh and make competition and strategy ever evolving, but it also can make for an expensive gameplay experience.

Bear in mind that although the base game of *Hearthstone* is free to play, players obtain cards through "packs" that they slowly earn in-game or by purchase. Each pack contains five cards. Table 8-2 shows the relative cost of keeping your decks up to date based on the 2019 releases if you don't choose to spend endless hours earning packs in-game and waiting for opportunities. Table 8-1 represents a sort of best-case scenario, assuming excess cards. You can have two of any non-epic card in your deck at any given time, but beyond two, extra copies of cards are useful only as fodder for crafting. You can use the dust produced from destroying extra cards to craft cards you don't have, but the expense to craft epic cards is high, meaning that the best method to get cards when you're starting out is through packs and not crafting. You're likely to need to spend even more than the number listed to get all the cards in the game.

The basic and classic sets are the only two standard sets that do not rotate out of competition, meaning that within two years, the other six sets of cards listed here will have been replaced by new expansions, with *The Witchwood*, the oldest here, likely to rotate out before this book sees print. When a new expansion launches, players can typically get 80 packs along with some bonuses for $79.99 or 50 packs for $49.99.

TABLE 8-2 ### The Cost of Building a Top-Tier Standard *Hearthstone* Deck in 2019

Cards	Number in Set	Best-Case Price to Get All Cards
Basic Set	133	Free (earned in game)
Classic Set	244	120 packs = $139.98
Witchwood (2018)	129	60 packs = $69.99
Boomsday Project	136	60 packs = $69.99
Rastakhan's Rumble	135	60 packs = $69.99
Rise of Shadows	136	60 packs = $69.99
Saviors of Uldum	135	60 packs = $69.99
Descent of Dragons	140	60 packs = $69.99
Total Price		$559.92

To give you a sense of how likely you are to get the entire set from 60 packs of cards, here are the results of my having opened 66 packs from the *Descent of Dragons* expansion launch. From those packs, I received 330 cards. Of those,

224 were duplicates. That means I received 106 of the 140 cards in the set, not accounting for how many of my doubles are useful in decks. That's not terrible odds, but if I were to continue at the same rate, I would need around 30 more packs to flesh things out. And because many of the cards I didn't receive are the more rare epic cards, the math probably wouldn't measure out exactly like that. You also have no mechanism for trading cards, so you have to either draw or craft the cards you need.

Taking heart with the Hearth

In the preceding section, I explain how expensive obtaining cards can be. Don't let my analysis scare you away from the game, though. You have several other aspects to bear in mind. The first is that you aren't likely to need every card to be competitive. Some people build four decks because that's what players typically use in tournament competition. At most tournaments, you submit four decks and play with three because your opponent for each round gets to ban one deck.

Another aspect of the game to keep in mind is that you need only the cards for your decks, so if you don't expect to tinker greatly, you can use any cards you don't plan to play with to make dust, and you can then construct cards to fill out the decks you want to use. There are some great web resources like HearthPwn (www.hearthpwn.com) and *Hearthstone Replay* (www.hsreplay.com/meta) that help you figure out the best decks at any given time and find out how much in-game dust you need to craft the cards.

Also, if you don't attempt to collect every card, you can play enough of the game to earn the cards to build the decks you need. This approach is just time consuming, and many players who are professional or aspire to be pro don't have the luxury of giving up the practice time to grind to get the cards. They need to play with those meta decks as soon and as often as possible.

Buying virtual cards

Although the pricing can also be off-putting, buying *Hearthstone* cards is much cheaper than buying physical CCGs, and moving your collection is much, much easier. As a frame of reference, I purchased two starter decks of 30 and two five-card character expansions for a real-world CCG called *SRG Supershow*. I received an event discount and still spent $40 on 70 cards. Fourteen *Hearthstone* packs would have cost me only $20, and I wouldn't have had to carry them around for the rest of the event.

The portability of *Hearthstone* cannot be ignored. As an esport, it is among the easiest to travel and compete with because you can use a single smartphone in any competition. The latency issues of Wi-Fi and cellular reception aren't a major factor because *Hearthstone* is turn based, and control precision isn't a major issue because the movements are simple. Being able to keep a collection on the cloud that you can access from a PC, phone, or tablet at any time makes a *Hearthstone* collection an interesting investment. Although you cannot physically play with the cards, you also can't damage or misplace them, nor will you ever end up playing in a competition with a grape soda stain on your best card. (Not that I ever did that with a CCG.)

Keeping it real with *Hearthstone* competition

The other CCGs mentioned in this chapter have yet to hit their stride as esports, but *Hearthstone*, although it might not receive the same press coverage as some of the other top-tier esports, has had major competitions since its launch. You can see the full slate of Blizzard-sponsored competitions at PlayHearthstone.com (https://playhearthstone.com/en-us/esports/), but to put it in perspective with some of the other major events, the 2019 *Hearthstone* Grandmasters Global champion, Chinese competitor Xiaomeng "VKLiooon" Li, took home $200,000. She was also the first female to win a championship at BlizzCon. It's not the $3 million that went to the winner of the *Fortnite* World Cup, but a $200,000 prize is still significant for a professional esport.

Beyond the Grandmasters tournaments held by Blizzard, a massive local and regional *Hearthstone* tournament community exists. This community is supported through the fact that as a game, *Hearthstone* allows for events called "Fireside Gatherings"; any approved community members with a reliable site can list their own events on the web at www.firesidegatherings.com and create a special competition space for their own tournaments, or even just gather people for casual games. Because you can play on your phone, you don't need to lug around a computer, or a console, or anything you wouldn't usually have with you.

PROTESTING IN ESPORTS: BLITZCHUNG AND *HEARTHSTONE*

On October 6, 2019, Hong Kong native and *Hearthstone* professional Ng Wai Chung, a.k.a. Blitzchung, sparked controversy at the *Hearthstone* Grandmasters event in Taiwan by placing a gas mask over his face and exclaiming "Liberate Hong Kong, the revolution of our times" while on the official event video stream. The stream was cut almost immediately.

The following day, Blizzard suspended Blitzchung from competition for one year and took away his prize money. Blizzard's reasoning was that Chung had violated its tournament rules by "offending the public or impugning Blizzard's image" (https://www.theverge.com/2019/10/8/20904308/hearthstone-player-blitzchung-hong-kong-protesters-ban-blizzard). Blizzard also fired the two casters, Virtual and Mr. Yee, who were running the interview in which Ching made the comment.

Blizzard faced backlash for the event, which extended into protests at its annual BlizzCon event in November, where one of the *Hearthstone* Grandmasters casters dropped out of the event, publically citing how the company handled the incident. Blizzard did soften its stance less than a week after the ban, however, reducing Blitzchung's ban to six months, reinstating his prize money, and reinstating Virtual and Mr. Yee with a six-month ban (as opposed to firing them).

The importance of the Blitzchung incident to esports overall remains to be seen. To date, it represents the first time that a player has been punished for a nonvulgar instance of free speech. Although most of the public protest of Blizzard's handling of the event has dissipated in 2020 as of this writing, it wouldn't be surprising if, upon Chung's return to play in April or May, the story makes another round as a hot topic for esports discussion.

Playing on Your Phone

Hearthstone is one of the few games in America to bridge the gap between mobile gaming and competitive esports. Although titles like *Honor of Kings* (*Arena of Valor*) and *PUBG Mobile* are big in other countries, those games are viewed more as social gaming than competitive games in the Americas.

A game that is right on the cusp of esports competition is Supercell's *Clash Royale* (*CR*). This game is based loosely on building a deck of units that you deploy to defend towers, as shown in Figure 8-4. *CR* has hosted tournaments with $400,000 prize pools, and Supercell hosts its own *Clash Royale* League (CRL), which awarded $1 million in prizes for its first two final events (in Tokyo in 2018 and Los Angeles in 2019). Although mobile games are just getting their footing, the potential for growth in mobile esports is massive.

It's astounding to consider how many people play mobile games that could eventually become esports. At one point, *Arena of Valor* had 200 million active players, and 128 million people play CR regularly. Some of that audience isn't yet esports minded, but by comparison, the *League of Legends* active player base is only 80 million and *Dota 2*'s player base is just over 10 million. The numbers exist for a mobile esports revolution in the coming years.

3
Community and College Gaming

Discover the places you can compete in esports online and in person.

Learn how, where, when, and why to get your name and face out there in the esports world.

Think about the opportunities to play, or study, esports in college.

Chapter **9**

Finding Online and Local Places to Play

Thanks to the Internet and high-speed connectivity, you can now play esports against high-level competition from the comfort of your own home. All you need is Internet connectivity, the right gear (see Chapter 2 for an overview of types of gear you might want and need), a physical space to play in, and all the right accounts. In this chapter, you look at setting up all those accounts as well as explore how you might find people in your local esports scene.

Starting the Process: What You Need

If you're reading this before reading Chapter 2, I strongly suggest that you go back and read over the information on computers, consoles, and gear there. I'll wait here while you check that out.

Here's a quick checklist of what you need to begin playing alongside the best:

>> **A computer or consoles:** Depending on your chosen game or games, you will need a capable PC or the proper console. You can find help in deciding on those purchases in Chapter 2.

>> **High-speed Internet:** For the highest level of play, you want to have your computer or console connected via an Ethernet cable to wherever your Internet service enters your home (usually a modem). Strong Wi-Fi will also work in most cases. You should look for an Internet plan that refers to itself as broadband Internet. With good latency (which, sadly, you can determine only by checking it after you have the service), any service rated as broadband should suffice to play any game at a competitive level. If your latency is high, meaning that it takes more time for your computer to reach the game server, you will suffer a time lag on your keyboard and mouse inputs, and your graphics could skip as your machine tries to compensate.

>> **A table or desk:** Depending on your choice between PC and console, you most likely want a desk, but if you expect to play in your living room or to always be in front of a big-screen TV, you're better served with an entertainment center or a coffee table. You should pick what works best for you, but you want something that can hold all your gear along with a bottle of water or your beverage of choice so that you don't get dehydrated while you play.

>> **A comfortable, ergonomic chair:** Whatever seating option you choose should offer good support and allow for proper posture because you're likely to spend several hours at a time in your gaming chair. Many excellent options are available from vendors like Dxracer.com, Vertagear.com, and Xrocker. com. Different gamers swear by different chairs, but as you will see on each of those sites, the traditional design is a chair similar to a race car seat, and any chair that follows that basic design will serve you well. Many console players choose to play from a couch, which is also viable, but remember that if you play for long hours on the couch, you should be attentive to how your body is positioned. Your body can tense up in a slouched position while playing, and the resulting stiffness can be problematic. Take it from a *Mortal Kombat* couch player who had a chronically stiff neck: It's better to sit up as you play.

>> **Plenty of electricity:** In most cases, if you have a single electrical socket and a six-plug surge strip, you'll be in good shape, but make sure that

- You have a surge protector in your power strip. You don't want a power spike to damage your expensive equipment.

- If you're in an old dwelling with old electrical wiring, make sure to test your power situation by turning everything on and checking for problems with your fuses or breakers before starting a long game session.

- Remember that the power converters for your electronics get hot during use. Try to position them so that they aren't sitting on the carpet and so that they can receive air flow. It's never a bad idea to get a small fan to point at your power supplies just to keep air moving.

>> **Soundproofing or a location away from bedrooms:** If you live with people and want them to be supportive or at least tolerant of your gaming, play in a location that won't be disturbing. If you find you are a loud gamer or if you choose to use speakers instead of a headset, make sure that you are in a place where your noise isn't disrupting your family and friends (or neighbors, if you live close to others).

Setting Up Your Accounts

After you obtain your equipment and prepare your space, all that remains to do before you can get started on your path to becoming a legendary esports star is to create the accounts needed to play your games of choice. To aid you in determining what you'll need to install and set up, look for your game of choice in Table 9-1. If you don't see your game of choice listed, you can determine what service or services it uses by doing a Google search for the name of the game and the word *platform*.

Each service listed in the table requires a specific setup process. Some of them are connected to the accounts on your consoles, whereas others require you to create an entirely new account.

TABLE 9-1   **Services Needed to Play Top Esports Titles**

Game	Service Needed	Other Options
League of Legends	League of Legends Launcher (`https://signup.na.leagueoflegends.com/`)	You can play *LoL* only with Riot's Launcher.
CS:GO, Dota 2	Steam (`http://www.steampowered.com`)	You can launch *Dota 2* only through the Steam client. *CS:GO* was supported on Xbox 360 and PlayStation 3 but is not on the current-generation consoles.
Overwatch, Hearthstone, and *StarCraft II, Call of Duty: Modern Warfare*	Battle.net client (`http://battle.net`)	All Blizzard.com games must be launched through Blizzard's Battle.net.
Fortnite	Epic launcher (`https://www.epicgames.com/fortnite/en-US/download`)	You can also play *Fortnite* on mobile platforms (Android and iOS) as well as on Xbox One, PS4, and Switch through their respective online platforms.

(continued)

TABLE 9-1 *(continued)*

Game	Service Needed	Other Options
Rocket League	Steam (http://www.steampowered.com)	You can also play *Rocket League* on Xbox One, PS4, and Switch through their respective online platforms.
Super Smash Bros. Ultimate	Switch Online (https://www.nintendo.com/switch/online-service/)	You can also configure Switch Online on the Nintendo Switch Console itself through the Nintendo Store.
Street Fighter V	No launcher; requires online connectivity through Windows or PS4	Online play on the PS4 requires PlayStation Plus (https://store.playstation.com/en-us/psplus).
Mortal Kombat 11	No launcher; requires online connection via platform of choice	PS4 requires PlayStation Plus. Switch online play requires Switch Online. Xbox One play requires Xbox Live (https://www.xbox.com/en-US/live).

Installing the *League of Legends* Launcher

If you've already installed *LoL*, you're all set to play. The *LoL* Launcher is installed with the game, and the account you generate to play is all you need. If you haven't yet installed *LoL* but want to, follow these steps:

1. **Go to** https://signup.na.leagueoflegends.com/.

    Under Your Legend Starts Here, you see an arrow pointing to a text entry box that says Enter Email Here.

2. **Type in your email address.**

    In previous chapters, I suggest creating a games-specific email to avoid losing game emails in a different account's Inbox. Use that email address here.

3. **Click Next.**

4. **In the window that appears,** use the drop-down lists to select your month, day, and year of birth.

    You must be 13 years old to play *LoL*. If you lie, it is a violation of the game's Terms of Service and your account will be suspended.

5. **Click Next below the entry of your date of birth.**

6. **Enter a username (remember to use your gamer tag!) and then a password you can remember; enter the password again to confirm.**

7. **Read the terms of service and select the box to agree.**

8. **Select the box if you want to receive emails (I usually choose not to) and then, at the bottom of the screen, click Next.**

9. **Complete the image captcha and then click Verify at the bottom right of the window.**

   The next screen displays a You're All Set message, which means that your account is officially set up.

Now you can download the software by clicking Download for Windows at the bottom of the screen. Make sure that you write down your username and password that you created through this process. You need them when you log in to play *LoL*.

Obtaining Battle.net to play Blizzard games

Blizzard has the advantage of offering several games through a single software launch package. After you've set it up, you just click new games to choose them because all your account information remains the same. To open your free Battle.net account, follow these steps:

1. **Go to** http://battle.net.

   In the upper-right corner, you see My Account on the page that appears.

2. **Click My Account and in the drop-down list that appears, click Create a Free Account.**

   The account creation page appears.

3. **To enter your account information, do one of the following:**

   - If you use Facebook, you can enter your Facebook credentials to start the account-generation process.

   - If you use Google, you can enter your Google account credentials to start your account-generation process,

   - Enter all your information yourself, as requested. (This is the recommended option because it keeps your account independent of your Facebook and Google accounts.)

4. **If you are entering all your info yourself, begin by selecting your country from the drop-down menu and then continue by entering your name, birth date, gaming email address, and password.**

   As with all online accounts you create, you need a password that you can remember. This site also asks you to select a security question and answer that you want to use.

5. **Click the Create a Free Account button.**

   The next screen that appears confirms your login email and prompts you to download the Battle.net app.

6. **Click Download and install the Battle.net app.**

   When you first run the app, you input your gamer tag.

Use the app to select your chosen games and install them by clicking their names and then clicking the Install button at the bottom of the screen. Remember that some games, like *Overwatch*, must be purchased, whereas others are free to play.

You can use the Battle.net app to install any Blizzard game, and the software will periodically check to see that your installed games are up to date. You don't need to install more than one game. You can also use the Battle.net app to chat with friends who are members of Battle.net.

Figure 9-1 shows the launch screen for *Hearthstone* within Battle.net. As you can see, the names of all the available games are in a menu on the left. Clicking any game's name takes you to the launch screen for that game. Because I've already installed *Hearthstone*, the large button at the bottom says Play. If I hadn't already installed *Hearthstone*, that button would say Install.

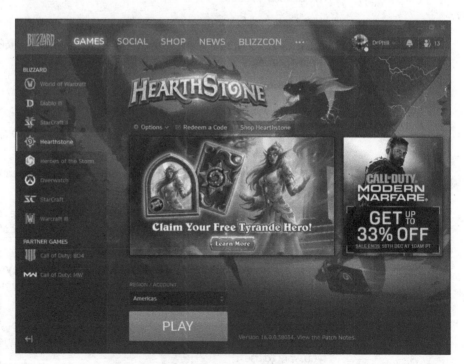

FIGURE 9-1:
The Battle.net launcher screen on the *Hearthstone* tab.

Also notice that the top right of the screen displays an icon along with my gamer tag (DrPhill). Next to that icon are a bell icon (for notifications) and a little stick figure with a number. Clicking the stick figure opens your Battle.net Friends menu and allows you to chat with anyone you know who is logged into the Battle.net client and playing any game.

TIP

When you join Battle.net, you can enter your gamer tag. The Battle.net system also assigns you a number, much the way services like Discord do. (You can learn more about Discord in Chapter 10.) You can find this number by clicking your username on the main menu. Mine, for example, is DrPhill11X3X. This is the number you give to your friends for them to add you to their Friend lists. Searching for just a gamer tag without the numbers doesn't work.

Creating your Steam account

Although it's used as a launcher for numerous esports games, Steam is also one of the largest repositories of PC games available. It's a highly useful program to have, and you're likely to end up having numerous non-esports games in your Steam Library. You need Steam to play *CS:GO*, *Dota 2*, or *Rocket League* on a PC. To download Steam and create an account, follow these steps:

1. **Go to** www.store.steampowered.com **and in the upper right of the page that appears, click the green Install Steam button.**

2. **On the screen that appears, click the blue button that says Install Steam.**

    The application file downloads.

3. **When the file finishes downloading, double-click it to install Steam.**

4. **Click the Steam icon to launch Steam.**

    The login screen should load.

5. **At the bottom of the login screen, click the Create a New Account button.**

    On the next screen, you are asked for your email address and country of residence, as well as to complete a captcha. You also need to read and agree to the user agreement and then click Continue.

6. **Verify your email and then create a Steam name (your gamer tag) and set a password.**

    Remember to write the password down somewhere safe!

After creating your account, you return to the Steam login page, where you can sign into your new account.

The Steam app has an easy-to-understand layout. You click Store at the top of the page to shop for games (some of which are free, some of which cost money). After you purchase a game, it appears when you click Library at the top. Figure 9-2 shows the screen you see if you download *Dota 2* and then select *Dota 2* in your library. This particular install needs to be updated by clicking the Update button, but when the update is finished, that button switches to Play, which you click to launch your games.

Steam also offers a Friends system and the ability to chat with friends. You access this chat by clicking Friends and Chat at the lower right of the screen. You can add friends, and your friends can add you by using your account name. As shown in Figure 9-2, I didn't follow my own suggestion from Chapter 10 and stick with my customary username for this account; here I use alexanp3 as opposed to DrPhill. I have two Steam accounts, one for showing games when I teach and one for when I play. You could do the same, but make sure that you note which email you linked to each account. Otherwise you might do what I did here and log in to the wrong account.

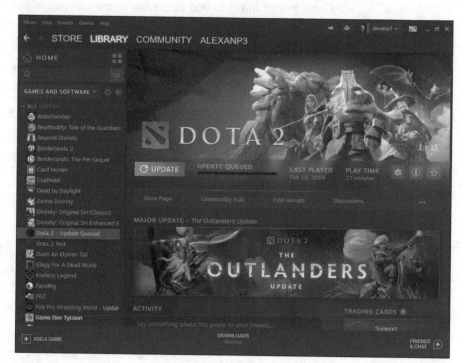

FIGURE 9-2:
The Steam client, open to the *Dota 2* launch screen.

Getting the Epic Games launcher for *Fortnite* and other games

Epic games has its own launcher, which like Steam (described in the previous section), is software that you need to play *Fortnite* or Epic's other popular games, such as *Dauntless*. To obtain the Epic launcher, go to https://www.epicgames.com/fortnite/en-US/download. The download should start automatically, but if it doesn't, click the proper icon for your operating system in the middle of the screen. For most readers, it will be Windows, the first icon. Install and run the Epic launcher.

After the main screen for the launcher loads, follow these steps to create your account:

1. **You can choose to use your login credentials from a number of other places: Facebook, Google, PS Plus, Xbox Live, or Switch Online.**

   Use one of these other sources only if you have played the game on another platform and have progress in the game saved that you want to retain by using one of these login methods.

2. **Click the Sign Up button near the bottom of the screen.**

3. **On the screen that appears, select your date of birth from the drop-down menus and then click Continue.**

4. **On the next window that appears, do the following:**

   a. *Choose your country from the drop-down list.*

   b. *Enter your First and Last name.*

   c. *Choose your display name — that is, your gamer tag.*

   d. *Enter your gaming email address.*

   e. *Create a password. Write it down somewhere safe!*

   f. *Click the link to read the terms of service and then select the box to agree.*

5. **Click Create Account at the bottom of the window.**

   Your account is created and you are taken directly to the Epic launcher.

If you click the Library button on the left of the Epic launcher, you can install *Fortnite* by clicking Get under the word *Fortnite* in the main window, as you can see in Figure 9-3. While the game downloads and installs, you can explore the app. It has a Friends list that lets you add friends based on their display names. It also has a store through which you can buy numerous games. You can change your profile settings by clicking your profile name at the bottom of the left column.

FIGURE 9-3:
The library screen
of the Epic
launcher, ready
to install *Fortnite*.

Connecting your console accounts

Each of the current generation of consoles — PS4, Switch, and Xbox One — has its own online connectivity service. Each service includes some perks, including games that are free periodically, some method of communicating with friends and building friend lists, and other small offerings. The major feature, though, is that these services allow you to play your games online.

Each of these services ties directly to the user account on your console. You can monitor the services online, but the easiest way to set each one up is through the menus on the home screen of your console. On each console, you can select and set up the console's version of the online service through its respective stores, each of which is available through the main screen menus.

PlayStation Plus is Sony's online service for PS4. It is available for $59.99 a year, $24.99 for 3 months, or $9.99 a month. Each month includes free games, cloud space for game saves, and, of course, online play. The PS4 is the favored console of most fighting-game events, so PlayStation Plus is a fighting game must. You can read more about PlayStation Plus online at https://www.playstation.com/en-us/explore/playstation-plus/.

Nintendo Switch online allows for online play on the Switch, a must for fans of *SSBU* or *Tetris 99*. It also allows access to numerous NES and Super Nintendo games, offers cloud space for saved games, and entitles players to discounts on games. Switch Online costs $19.99 for a year, $7.99 for three months, or $3.99 for a month, but also offers a yearly $34.99 family plan that you can spread across eight accounts. You can find more information about Switch Online at https://www.nintendo.com/switch/online-service/.

Fans of *Halo* or the *Gears* series will want to pick up Microsoft's Xbox Live Gold, which offers free games monthly, online gaming, and discounts on various titles. You can purchase Xbox Live Gold for $59.99 for a year, $24.99 for three months, or $9.99 for a month. Microsoft also offers a service called Xbox Game Pass that allows play of more than 100 console games for free each month, and the Xbox Game Pass Ultimate includes Xbox Live Gold. You can read more about Microsoft's offering online at https://www.xbox.com/en-US/live.

Playing all the games

After you have set up your needed accounts and have all your gear in place, you're ready to go. In Chapter 10, I tell you about how to get yourself out on the esports scene through social media, Discord, and related services. I strongly recommend checking out Chapter 10 before you get too deeply involved in competition because it helps you to find opponents and make friends.

REMEMBER

Also, remember that you can play many esports games on your mobile devices. Because of the nature of the platform, mobile games launch within their respective apps, but some of those will tie to your other accounts (for example, you can play *Fortnite* mobile on the same account that you use to play *Fortnite* on a PC). When you download an app to your device, it should guide you through the setup and account creation processes.

TIP

You don't have to set up every single account. If you pick one specific game, you need to set up only the services that relate to that game. All the account information here might seem overwhelming, but generally, registering for accounts is roughly the same in each case. Just make sure to keep track of your user IDs and passwords, and you'll be golden!

Finding Local Competition

Although playing online is great, the energy at live esports events is not to be missed. Depending on the games you play and where you are geographically, you might be able to find numerous local options within driving distance. To find out what is going on in your area, check the following:

>> **Go to your local game stores and ask around.** Game stores often host competitions, but even if they don't, the people who work there are a fantastic resource for finding other gamers and local competitions.

>> **If you have an esports venue, esports café, or other space in your community, check in there often.** Esports cafés and arenas are hubs for competition events.

>> **If your area has a college, see whether it has an esports club or is part of the collegiate esports organization Tespa** (http://tespa.org). Although some events at colleges are likely to be student specific, many may also open to the public, and club members will know where local hot spots are.

>> **Check social media and online spots for your chosen games.** Sites like Smash. gg list tournaments around the country, and you can find *Hearthstone* events through the game's Fireside Gatherings online (https://firesidegatherings. com/en-us/).

>> **Look for local Facebook groups.** Thousands of these groups exist.

>> **If you have a local arcade, hang out there and talk to the locals.** Many retro arcades and fun centers host events regularly.

The real secret to finding local events is getting involved with the local community. After one of the possibilities in the preceding list pans out for you and you locate other local players, following up with them on social media should get you integrated into the scene. If you're in a big city, this integration happens fast. If you're in a smaller community, you might have to drive a bit to find competition, but gamers are everywhere. When you find your local scene, you'll be amazed by how much competition is out there!

IN THIS CHAPTER

» **Creating a gamer tag**

» **Making friends on Twitter**

» **Sharing pictures and video on Instagram**

» **Engaging in discussions on Reddit**

» **Chatting on Discord and watching streamers on Twitch**

» **Checking out archived video on YouTube**

Chapter **10**

Getting Your Name in the Game

This chapter shows you where and how to start establishing yourself in the esports world. Use it as a guide to begin launching yourself into the wild world of esports, staking your claim to your life as an esports superstar in the making.

Each of the websites, services, and tools in this chapter are free and require no specific commitment of time or energy, but you will see as you read that what your teachers told you is true: You get back as much as you put in to something. Esports superstars like Faker or Ninja, who have follower bases in the millions, maintain content as a full-time job, working eight hours a day on gaming, streaming, and posting. That doesn't mean you need to devote that much time to esports yourself, but the more you put in, the more you'll get back out.

Choosing a Gamer Tag That Lets You Be You

When you were born, your parents named you. Love it or hate it, you carry that name around with you, and your friends and family know you by that name. Your name means something. In the esports world, most people don't go by their actual names, although some do. I go by "DrPhill," for example, and one of my varsity *Overwatch* players uses his first name, Sean, as his gamer tag. But the vast majority of esports players are known by names like HungryBox, SonicFox, Faker, LethuL, Scarlett, or something similar. Players also insert numbers in place of letters, hacker style (like Fatal1ty), and use capital letters in nonstandard places, like MinD_ContRoL.

TIP

Give yourself some time to think about your gamer tag. Although you can potentially change it later, any changes can result in lost followers and loss of notoriety. Here are three key things to keep in mind as you develop your gamer tag:

>> **It should reflect you and your personality.** Choosing a gamer tag is all about you, so choose a name you're comfortable with being called.

>> **It should be unique.** You might be tempted to choose a name like MarioLover or RaidenMain, but you will see multiple people online with those sorts of gamer tags. They are too common to stand out.

>> **Don't pick a name already attached to known characters.** Similar to the point above, if your gamer tag depends on the name of an existing character, people will think of that character first and not of you. That's not what you want your gamer tag to accomplish. This is about building an identity for *you*.

When you become heavily involved in gameplay and the various social channels around gaming, you will meet people who will know you as your gamer tag or a shortened version. Before my tag was DrPhill, I went by Ravenos, and even now, tens of years later, there are people who call me "Rav," even when we are talking about things that have nothing to do with games.

REMEMBER

After you've selected your gamer tag, quickly work your way through the list of websites and services in this chapter and claim your name on each.

TIP

Start the whole process of signing up on these sites by first going to gmail.com and creating yourself a new Google Mail address with your gamer tag. Doing so gives you a central mailbox to receive your messages and keeps you from getting all your esports mail mixed into your primary email. It can also serve as your login to YouTube.

Here's a checklist of the sites you sign up for in this chapter:

>> Twitter

>> Instagram

>> Reddit

>> Discord

>> Twitch

>> YouTube

Twitter: Making Friends in 280 Characters

My guess is that you have likely heard of Twitter. After all, Twitter has more than 300 million active users and a global audience. It also seems to have the rapt attention of the media. Twitter limits users to short messages, called tweets, of 280 characters per post. That amount of content sounds like more than it actually is. If this paragraph were a tweet, I would have run out of characters right after the first word of this sentence.

TECHNICAL STUFF

If you want to learn more about the technical aspects of Twitter, I highly recommend *Twitter For Dummies*, 3rd Edition, by Laura Fitton (Wiley). You can learn about what's happening with algorithms and code behind the Twitter machine, for example. But you certainly don't need to understand the inner workings of Twitter to use it masterfully as an esports player.

Both esports players and businesses make heavy use of Twitter to engage with their audiences. The value of Twitter is its high level of interconnectivity. Because the esports community uses Twitter as a primary point of contact, almost all the major figures from game companies to star esports players have a profile. In many cases, you can use one user to find others as well. Many of these users post multiple times a day, offering everything from tournament dates and links to videos to musings about television or day-to-day happenings. The focus of most esports Twitter accounts is to build community and connect to that community. The result is a pleasant mix of informative posts and entertaining stories. And memes. There will be memes.

GETTING THE HANG OF SOCIAL MEDIA LINGO

Throughout this chapter while dealing with social media accounts, you're going to likely encounter some new words and phrases. Here's a quick guide:

- **algorithm:** The underlying sorting rules that determine what content is delivered to a user.

- **hashtag:** A short word or phrase indicated by a # that allows users to label messages so that readers can sort by the hashtag to find posts about that topic.

- **influencer:** A social media content creator with a large number of followers and hence influence.

- **karma:** Another word for likes.

- **like:** A positive vote given to a post, the total of which is generally an indicator of popularity and influence (more likes = more popular).

- **meme:** A humorous post, usually a photo, that is spread quickly via social media. Many memes are quick edits of other existing memes.

- **moderator:** A person or, rarely, an artificial intelligence bot that polices the posts and content on a site.

- **post:** A single piece of content on social media. Can also be used as a verb; the act of creating a post is posting.

- **profile:** The page, or portion of a page, where other users can see the personal information you've created for a site.

- **Reddit:** A service, but also the name of the actual forums the service creates (for example: Reddit is a Reddit).

- **subreddit:** The name of an individual discussion forum on Reddit, indicated in conversation with an r/ before the name (for example, r/esportsfordummies).

- **timeline** (or feed): Your main landing page on Twitter or Instagram, where you see the posted content from the people you have followed as well as responses to your posts.

- **tweet:** A post on Twitter. Can also be a verb (for example, "I'm going to tweet that!").

- **VoIP:** Voice Over Internet Protocol, a technology that allows you to voice chat with people over the Internet.

Creating a Twitter account

If you don't already have a Twitter account, follow these steps to create one:

1. **Click the blue button Sign Up button at the lower right.**

   A screen appears that asks for your name, phone number, and date of birth.

2. **Enter your information and then click Next in the upper-right corner of the window.**

3. **On the screen that appears, choose whether to let Twitter collect data on you and then click Next in the upper-right corner.**

   I recommend deselecting the box that asks about collecting your data.

4. **On the next screen that appears, confirm the name, address, and birthday you entered, read the terms of service and privacy policy (each is a link that opens in a new window when clicked), and when finished, click Sign Up at the bottom of the screen.**

   A new screen appears, asking for a verification code.

5. **Check your email to get the code Twitter sent to you, enter it in the box, and click Next in the upper-right corner.**

   A new screen appears, asking you to create a password.

6. **Enter your chosen password and click Next in the upper-right corner.**

   Make sure to save your password somewhere safe.

Posting a profile picture and editing your bio

Your first step in launching a strong gamer profile on Twitter or converting your current Twitter profile to better fit your esports ambitions is to post a strong profile picture and bio. (You find out how in the upcoming steps.) Including your profile picture and bio is important because in the fast-paced world of Twitter, the new people you meet will build their first impression of you in less than a second. That's quick, right? So you want to present a picture that expresses who you are. The banner space on your main Twitter page, which is the large image at the top, is almost as important as your profile picture. You want your profile picture and banner to fit the image you want to project.

Your profile picture and banner for your account can follow many directions. I've found that gamers who do one of the following tend to draw the most positive attention:

» **Use a clear, striking photo of yourself for your profile picture and some sort of action shot for your banner.**

» **Use a well-designed logo for your profile picture and a larger version of it as your banner.** If you're an artist, make this yourself. If not, I recommend using the website Fiverr.com (www.fiverr.com), where you find a number of freelance creators willing to generate content for you at a decent price. I'm not affiliated with Fiverr, but I have used the service a couple of times and am extremely pleased with the logo I had made for under $50. It's currently the banner on my Twitter page (twitter.com/phillalexander).

» **Use contrasting, vibrant colors that reflect something about you.** A good rule of thumb is to think about your color choices the same way a sports team would. Use no more than three colors (plus black and white). Make sure that two of the colors are close to a direct contrast on the color wheel. (For more details about color, see Chapter 14.) Unless you have a great reason to use them, avoid oranges and browns because they are classically the least popular colors. (Sorry, Cleveland Browns fans.)

» **Complete your bio.** Don't leave your biographical section blank. Remember that if people come to your Twitter page, they look at this information to form their opinion of you. You need only a sentence or two here, but say something that really showcases you. Never overshare by offering sensitive information like your phone number or home address, and if there are things you don't want the world knowing about (remember, this is the Internet), keep those secret.

» **Take the time to edit everything.** You can add website links. Use that function to connect to some of the sites where you have a social media presence. Also, you can edit the colors of the text and links to match your banner. Little things like that go a long way to "branding" yourself.

Follow these steps on the web to upload a profile picture, banner, or both for the top of your personal page and to edit the biographical information on your Twitter account. Please note that the steps for adding these elements in any of the many Twitter apps will be slightly different depending on the software being used.

1. **Go to Twitter.com and log in.**

   Refer to "Creating a Twitter account," earlier in this chapter, if you need to create an account.

2. **Click the Profile button on the left side of the screen.**

3. **Click the Edit Profile button in the middle column of the page, just below the empty banner (which appears as a gray box).**

4. **On the Edit Profile page that appears (see Figure 10-1), scroll down and click each box to fill in your name, bio, and other information.**

Simply adding a picture and a sentence or two about yourself, making sure to mention the games you play and any websites you want your visitors to visit, shows that you're engaged and ready to be a part of the community.

5. **To upload a new profile picture, click the small camera logo inside the circle right above your name.**

A dialog box opens that allows you to select a photo to upload from your computer.

6. **Find your photo and click Open.**

The photo you chose displays as your profile picture.

7. **Click the camera icon in the banner space to upload an image there.**

The banner area is an odd shape, so I recommend using photo editing software to set the size of your chosen photo to be 1,500 pixels x 500 pixels, though you can also upload a larger photo and drag the viewable potion of it to fit what you'd like to display. Make sure that your photo isn't too small! If your photo has to upscale, it will be blurry.

8. **When you finish all those edits, click the Save button at the top.**

Clicking Save commits your changes and returns you to the main Profile page.

9. **(Optional) Click Settings at the lower left of the screen to change the colors and font size on your page and make other little tweaks.**

10. **Click Save when you're done.**

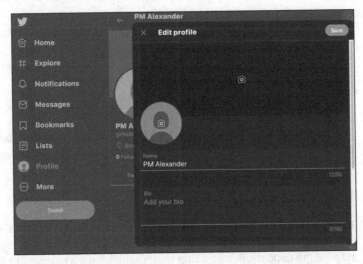

FIGURE 10-1:
The Profile Edit screen on Twitter.

It's time for a quest! Finding people

One of the key features of Twitter is the timeline. This is the page you see when you log in to the site. On this page, Twitter aggregates the posts from all the people that you follow. As a new user, of course, you won't see much content at first. But finding people to follow is as easy as searching for the games, teams, and organizations that you're interested in. For example, in the Search Twitter search box in the upper-right corner, enter **@LeagueofLegends**, the official Twitter account of the game *League of Legends* (or @lolesports for their esports specific account), and press Enter. On the page that appears, click the Follow button next to the *League of Legends* account. You see numerous *League of Legends* players responding to the official League tweets, and by selecting players to follow, you can build an impressive list.

My advice is to locate — through searching Twitter or checking official websites for links — the following types of Twitter accounts:

>> The company that makes the games you play.

>> Any official account for the game itself.

>> The accounts of the professional players and streamers you like. If you're new to a game, determining who is or isn't a professional might be tough, but you can get a good sense of that from the content a person posts. You can also specifically go to pro team pages (like cloud9.gg) and look at player bios to find their Twitter IDs.

>> The accounts of leagues or organizations that offer competition in your chosen games.

>> The accounts of service providers you might use, like Blizzard's Battle.net, which offer you updates on service.

>> The accounts of companies that sell keyboards, mice, headsets, or any other related merchandise you might be interested in.

>> People you play with.

>> People you meet at events.

After working your way through this list, you will have a well-populated timeline and be ready to start thinking seriously about interacting with people.

Getting ready to tweet

When you see the flood of information and wall of memes that will result from following a number of people, you may be tempted to jump right in and start responding to posts. Before doing that, though, take a moment to think about how you want to be received. Although you can delete a tweet, if someone has quoted you and interacted with you, your tweets are essentially out there forever. So give yourself time to get used to how people interact for a few important reasons:

>> Some people interact frequently with people who post in response to them, or tweet at them.

>> Some people post their own content and rarely, if ever, respond to any of the comments.

>> Some follower bases, particularly larger ones such as the followers of a major game or a huge professional star, have their own social rules.

>> Some follower bases welcome questions.

>> Some follower bases might be likely to flame, or attack, a new poster.

TIP

It is smart to post at least a few tweets of your own before responding to someone. When you respond to someone, whether they like or dislike what you have to say, they are highly likely to click your name and look at your profile. If you have only that single response post, the reader will know you only from what you said in that post, leading some people to dismiss you as someone who is brand new. Having some content that establishes who you are helps build your identity and gives the people you interact with something to help visualize the person they are interacting with.

Creating and sending a tweet

Tweeting is easy. That's one of the reasons Twitter is so popular. To post a tweet:

1. Go to Twitter.com or open your Twitter app and log in.

At the top of your screen, you should see your profile picture in a circle next to a text box that says "What's happening?"

2. Click the box and type your message.

A small circle logo in the lower-right corner charts your number of characters and warns you if you go over. (See Figure 10-2.)

3. (Optional) Add media by using the logos that appear below the text box:

- **To add a photo:** Click the icon of the mountains and select the file from your computer.

- **To use a pre-loaded animated GIF:** Click the GIF icon.

- **To add a poll to your post:** Click the bar chart icon and fill in the questions on the pop-up.

- **To add an emoji:** Click the smiley face.

- **To include a hyperlink:** Enter the URL. Twitter converts it to a link automatically.

4. **End your post with any hashtags you want.**

   A hashtag is a label placed on a tweet, following from the # symbol. You can search Twitter for posts with specific hashtags. A popular tag is #tbt (for throwback Tuesday), which people use when uploading old photos.

5. **To tweet to someone, or to mention someone to whom you want the tweet linked, type** @*username* **(the @ sign immediately followed by the person's username).**

   The @username text turns into a link to the person's profile.

FIGURE 10-2:
A Twitter post
interface.

As mentioned in the "Getting ready to tweet" section, earlier in this chapter, you want to post a few tweets before you respond to others' tweets so that people can check out who you are when you start talking to them.

For your very first tweets, you need to put on your thinking cap. How do you want to be known by others? Are you the funny person who posts memes and witty one-liners? Are you the up-to-date active gamer who reads all the blogs and posts links to what you think is the most important news of the day? Are you the strategy nerd who posts theorycrafting (doing theoretical study and then sharing or teaching a game's strategy) about new game developments or changes to the meta? Are you the gamer who posts about nongame-related stuff on Twitter because you're interested in sharing your life or your hobbies?

That question has no right or wrong answer, but you should know the answer before you post some content. Then have at it!

Tweets have to be short. Although you can use 280 characters these days, the service allowed only 140 characters for years, and few people to this day exceed 140 on most posts. Content on Twitter is about being quick, funny, informative, and easy to read and reply to in short order. Although you want to make sure you have a strategy, you shouldn't spend too long thinking about any one tweet. Post! Have fun! Engage!

After you've posted a few of your own tweets, you can start responding to the items that show up on your timeline and customizing your experience. You might find, for example, that some of the choices you made had amazing results and you love the conversations you found, whereas others were a little off the mark. That's fine. No insult is involved in unfollowing a profile. Over time, you'll be able to customize your timeline to serve as a space in which you interact with friends, get quick news at a glance, and keep up with competitions going on both down the street and around the world.

Diving into Instagram: A Picture Says 2,200 Characters

You've heard it a thousand times or more: A picture says a thousand words. In the esports space in particular, the visual nature of Instagram gives your followers a sense of who you are and how you play. Being able to show yourself with other gamers, at esports events, and enjoying gaming is a quick, easy, powerful way to connect. Paired with Twitter, Instagram can give you a solid social network and put you at front-row center in the esports world.

You're most likely familiar with Instagram, but if not, the best way to think of it is that Instagram is Twitter for pictures but also allows for video and for text up to 2,200 characters. Compared to Twitter's 280 characters, that's long! Instagram gives you more than a written page of text for a post. The key difference between the two, though, is that Instagram focuses on the pictures, with the text serving as what Instagram calls a caption, though 2,200 characters can be rather long for what would traditionally be considered a photo caption.

The methods for using Instagram for esports are generally the same as those for Twitter (see the section "Twitter: Making Friends in 280 Characters," earlier in this chapter). You create an account with your gamer tag, post a profile picture before doing any posting, and follow the same sorts of people and companies as you do on Twitter.

Try to stay as consistent across your social accounts as you possibly can. As I explain in the "Choosing a Gamer Tag That Lets You Be You" section, earlier in this chapter, you should select a unique gamer tag that is available on all social sites. Be sure to use your unique gamer tag on Twitter, Instagram, or any of the other platforms I cover in this chapter. Don't make your future fans and followers guess who or where you are on social sites by using different names in different places.

After you register your account on Instagram, you should change your profile picture and bio similarly to how you did for Twitter if you followed the previous section of this chapter. To start, click the icon that looks like a person in the upper right of the Instagram main page. From there, click Edit Profile and you're off to the races.

To create your Instagram account, follow these steps:

1. **Go to Instagram.com.**

   You see a registration screen, shown in Figure 10-3. The easiest option if you have a Facebook account is to use your Facebook credentials (the first button), but I recommend entering all the data instead.

   After you have created an account, Instagram recommends some accounts to follow.

2. **Select Follow next to any that interest you.**

3. **In the upper-right corner, click the icon that looks like a stick figure showing head and shoulders.**

   A new screen appears.

4. **Click Edit Profile next to your username and, on the screen that appears, change your profile picture, bio, and other features.**

5. **When you're done, click Submit at the bottom.**

As you start to create content for Instagram, remember that pictures or video are the key element for this service. The visual element is what people see first when looking at your posts. You can choose from among a few different posting styles to connect with others, such as by posting:

>> Photos from your day-to-day life. Many people build their Instagram presence by taking photos of the places where they travel, the events they attend, and even the food they eat.

>> Clips of your gameplay or compelling screenshots.

>> Memes or other humorous images related to your chosen game or games.

>> Theorycrafting or meta discussions along with helpful photos.

FIGURE 10-3:
The Instagram
Registration
screen.

The fun part of Instagram is that all these methods are effective. There's no one correct way. The best choice is to think about how you can be most visually striking.

TIP

There are many ways to utilize Instagram to connect with audiences for fun, business, or learning. If you're interested in learning more about Instagram, check out *Instagram For Business For Dummies,* by Jennifer Herman, Eric Butow, and Corey Walker (Wiley) and build your brand like a pro.

Using Group Discussions: You Haven't Reddit All Yet

Twitter and Instagram are two ways for you to share information about yourself and follow others, but sometimes you also need a public group discussion. The Internet has always offered the functionality of discussion groups, from Usenet to message boards. These days, the place to be for discussions is Reddit.com.

Reddit is a set of key posts from a whole collection of discussion forums that get aggregated on a front page. That front page is the one you see when you first log in to Reddit, and the content on it changes as you subscribe to individualized forums called subreddits. Although there isn't literally a subreddit for everything,

Reddit is filled with content, particularly for esports and gaming. Each subreddit is designated with an r/ before the name. To offer an example of just how diverse the esports options are, a subreddit exists called r/blazbluetagbattle, which is a community devoted to the lesser-known fighting game *BlazBlue: Cross Tag Battle*. The sub has 12,000 subscribers.

TIP

To get started with Reddit, you register with a username. You should use your gamer tag here, too. Follow these steps to sign on to Reddit:

1. **Go to Reddit.com.**

2. **In the upper right of the screen, click the blue Sign Up button.**

    A sign-up screen appears, as shown in Figure 10-4.

3. **In the text box with the word *Email*, enter your email address and then click Next.**

    Another screen appears.

4. **Choose your username and set a password.**

    Remember to use your gamer tag!

5. **Prove to the captcha that you aren't a robot.**

    The next screen appears, showing some suggested subreddits.

6. **Subscribe to a few of the suggested subreddits or use the search bar at the top to start searching for others.**

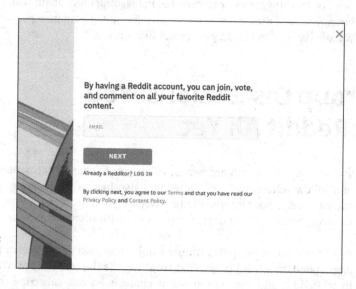

By having a Reddit account, you can join, vote, and comment on all your favorite Reddit content.

EMAIL

NEXT

Already a Redditor? LOG IN

By clicking next, you agree to our Terms and that you have read our Privacy Policy and Content Policy.

FIGURE 10-4: The registration page of Reddit.

After registering with Reddit, you can begin searching for communities that relate to the games you play, the organizations and teams you like, and the events that interest you. Every subreddit has a sidebar on the right side that contains a Subscribe button. Subscribing to a subreddit adds it to a drop-down list on the main Reddit page so that you can easily return to it. When you subscribe, posts from that subreddit get added to your main page. Subscribing also allows you to post to that subreddit. Whenever you'd like to post, just click where it says Create Post at the top of any Reddit page. Doing so opens the post interface page, where you can use the top box to pull down and select a subreddit. In the blank box with Title just below that pull-down menu, you type the title of your Reddit post. In the box just below that, you can add text to your post (but you don't have to; you can post just a title).

Getting your Reddit posts to show up

Some Reddit features take a bit of getting used to before you really get the lay of the land. Almost every subreddit has a moderator or a team of moderators. Depending on the rules of the specific subreddit, a moderator reviews your posts and might remove them if you failed to follow instructions. In rare cases, moderators might review your posts before allowing them to be published for public view, but that practice is uncommon.

Reddit also has a system called karma. People can vote posts up or down, and as you gain positive votes for posting, you gain karma. Your karma score appears as a number next to your name on the main page when you log in to Reddit. As your karma score builds, you also start to build a reputation.

ALWAYS REMEMBER: THIS IS THE INTERNET

Most experiences on Reddit are positive, but you need to remember that Reddit is an Internet forum in which people who seek to remain anonymous can remain anonymous. While engaging with the esports community, you want people to know who you are, but not everyone you interact with on Reddit might have the same goals. You will on occasion encounter trolls or posters who create content only to insult or annoy others. A good rule of thumb is to avoid troll posters and report them to moderators. It's a good idea to *lurk*, or read posts without creating your own, in each of the subreddits you join to get a sense of the personalities of the frequent posters before you engage. And remember, you're here to have fun and enjoy your hobbies. Don't let a rude person ruin the fun!

In addition to building karma, the number of positive votes that your posts receive determines where they are ranked on the subreddit's page. Gather a bunch of positive votes and you'll have the hottest post at the top of the page. If you get too many negative posts, though, your posts disappear for any user not actively seeking you out. Knowing what might result in a down vote can be difficult sometimes, but you should generally avoid arguing with other posters, duplicating existing content, or posting too many messages in a short period. Those are offenses that tend to upset most subreddit communities, and because the communities self-police, sometimes odd things result in down votes.

Running like a kid in a candy store

Reddit has three amazing things going for it. The first, as mentioned previously, is the large volume of active subreddits with a mix of experts, fans, and casual visitors. You can find discussions about just about anything related to esports. The second awesome aspect of Reddit is that you can go to a subreddit and read until your heart is content without having to create a post of your own. And third, Reddit is designed for a low-bandwidth impact, which means that it doesn't take up much space or memory, so the archives are deep and easy to search and access. Reddit started in 2005, and most of those early posts are still there to be read.

TIP

All that open space can be a little intimidating. Here are some suggestions for your initial Reddit use as you develop a sense of how it all works:

>> Subscribe to subreddits for your favorite games and read up on strategies.

>> Subscribe to subreddits for professional teams you're interested in.

>> Subscribe to subreddits that cover esports venues or competitions in your area, like a local arcade or tournament organizer.

>> Find other esports players and personalities you admire, look at their profiles, and see where they post.

>> Consider subscribing to a high-traffic subreddit like r/showerthoughts just to get a look at how people use the platform.

Take advantage of the fact that Reddit is designed to be a discussion forum and doesn't have the same personal focus as Twitter and Instagram. Move at your own speed and have fun reading!

Joining the Horde on Discord

Esports gamers have used numerous Voice Over Internet Protocol (VoIP) services over the years, from Ventrilo to TeamSpeak. A VoIP is a service that allows numerous people to speak via vocal chat over the Internet. The most pervasive, and most functional, VoIP option mixes voice communication with a clean chat interface.

Discord is a VoIP chat service that enables you to chat with other gamers quickly and easily, at the press of a button. People usually use it while wearing a cool gamer headset, though Discord also works with smartphones, and some people set up actual, free-standing microphones to use it.

Signing up on Discord

Discord (www.discordapp.com) is quickly becoming a favorite of all gamers, so you're going to want to join it. It's a free download for your computer or for your phone, and you can register an account by following these steps:

1. **On the main page, click Login in the upper right of the screen.**

2. **On the page that appears, click Register under the Login button.**

   The Registration page, shown in Figure 10-5, appears.

3. **Enter your email, a username, and a password.**

4. **Click the Submit button.**

   Discord walks you through the rest of setup via a series of questions.

Understanding how Discord works

Instead of working as one gigantic system, Discord has servers. A *server* is the basic name for a Discord community and includes a series of text and voice chat "channels" with topics set by the server's administrator(s). Each server is owned by a person or an organization, though the term *owned* can be misleading in that the servers and the service are free. People or organizations with their own Discord server can set the different channels and discussion topics for the server, as well as create a series of user roles or labels that define what a user can do. They can, for example, allow someone to read only and not comment or serve as a moderator with full control. Server owners can also color-code the users, which is particularly useful in helping players of a specific game find other players on a server. For example, all the *Overwatch* players might have a yellow user role label. Because Discord servers are free, anyone can easily start a community. Because of Discord's high usage among gamers, Discord servers are a great way to gain access to the community.

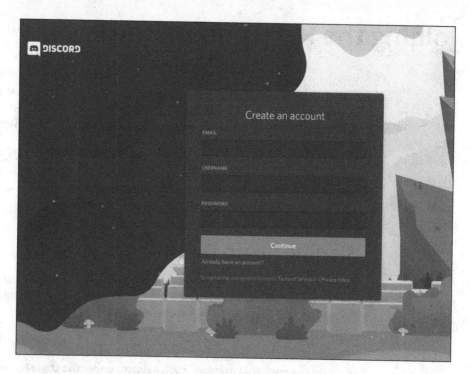

FIGURE 10-5:
The Discord
Registration page.

You're not advised to start by creating your own Discord server, though you certainly could.

Discord is particularly useful for an esports player because of all the communities you can find and join. You can mine your local scene as well as national and world competitions to locate all sorts of clubs and leagues on Discord servers. If you go to a competition, Discord will almost certainly be the VoIP of choice.

Discord gives you a real-time space to look for opponents, friends to team up with, events, and so on. Users who can see you on a public server or who have you on their friends list can see what game you are playing listed under your name and vice versa, which means that you can literally look for people playing the same game you're playing — while you're playing!

REMEMBER

Most Discord servers operate by invitation only. This doesn't mean that they are particularly exclusive, though. Finding communities to join isn't hard at all. However, you aren't likely to find Discord servers within Discord itself. If you look on the other social media platforms discussed in this chapter, you're sure to find people offering links to their Discord servers. Also, if you know someone who has a server or is on a server, don't be afraid to ask to join! Discord communities are welcoming and love getting new members.

TIP

Unlike the other services discussed in this chapter, Discord allows you to change your display username for each server that you join. This feature makes it less important for you to use your gamer tag as your primary account name; also, it gives you the freedom to be known by different names in different places. Remember, though, that if you're building a reputation as a player, you want everyone to know who you are, so I recommend that you still use your gamer tag in some way in your Discord names on each server. For example, on a few servers I belong to whose admins request your full name as part of your tag, my gamer tag appears in the middle of my name, as in Phill "DrPhill" Alexander, whereas on one server that has shorter nicknames, I'm just DrP.

Streaming Games on Twitch (the New TV)

Twitch is the name most often mentioned in esports spaces, surpassing even Twitter. Co-founded in 2006 by Justin Kan and his partners Emmett Shear, Michael Seibel, and Kyle Vogt as Justin.tv — which livestreamed Justin's life 24/7 — and relaunched as Twitch in 2011, Twitch.tv was born from the idea of streaming media live. The site has become quite popular. Twitch has 15 million active users every single day!

Twitch is an amazing resource for esports players because you can find people playing all the most popular games on it 24 hours a day, seven days a week. Professionals stream. Casual players stream. Tournaments and leagues stream. If you want to watch esports, Twitch is the place to be.

Signing up on Twitch

As with all the services described in this chapter, you should use your gamer tag as your name when you register at Twitch.tv. As a viewer, you will be identified in chat and when you interact by this tag, but more important, if you choose to stream yourself, the address of your stream will be twitch.tv/*your username*. You want your gamer tag to show up in your stream address.

To register to start using Twitch:

1. **Go to Twitch.tv (www.twitch.tv).**

2. **In the top right, click the Sign Up button.**

3. **On the screen that pops up (see Figure 10-6), enter your username (gamer tag), a password, your date of birth, and your email address; then click the Sign Up button at the bottom of the screen.**

   Twitch sends you a verification code.

4. Check your email and enter the code into the boxes.

5. Click Submit to complete your registration.

When you're logged in to Twitch, you can click the icon in the upper-right corner and scroll down to Settings to customize your profile. On this screen, you can change your profile picture or banner image by clicking the Update button next to each photo. You can also enter your bio into the bio text box below the images. After making changes, click the Save Changes button at the bottom of the screen to commit your changes.

FIGURE 10-6:
The Twitch
registration page.

Twitching from channel to channel

Twitch functions like a mix of a television network and a social media platform. As a user, you have a channel, and if you are streaming, it appears on your channel. Think of a channel as being like a profile page; it's a landing place for people to see your content. The channel page also has space for text content, a header, and other customization. Each channel also has its own chat room. One of the key aspects of the Twitch community is that a streamer reads and responds to the chat while streaming, creating real-time communication between the viewers and the caster.

When you find a channel that you like, you can mark it as a favorite by clicking the heart icon just above the video feed. Marking a favorite adds you to the notification system for that channel. It also adds that channel to your Favorites menu. The channels you have followed appear in the left sidebar of the main Twitch page when you log in.

TIP

If you love a channel and want to reward the content creator, you can show your love through money. Many channels owned by Twitch affiliates and partners allow you to subscribe using money. In those cases, you also gain special benefits that vary from channel to channel, such as custom emoticons or access to special in-game items or giveaways.

Streaming Games on YouTube

Since it started in 2005, YouTube has been ever present as one of the most popular sites on the Internet, usually second only to Google in network traffic. You no doubt know what YouTube is, and the role of YouTube in esports is exactly what you probably think it is: Gamers upload videos (and sometimes livestream).

To join YouTube, you need a Google account. Earlier in the chapter, in "Choosing a Gamer Tag That Lets You Be You," I recommend that you create a gamer tag Gmail address, and this is a great chance to use it. If you didn't create one, you'll want to do that before joining YouTube. Your Google account is your YouTube account.

Comparing YouTube with Twitch

Many esports content creators prefer YouTube to Twitch. (I cover Twitch in the preceding section of this chapter.) The reasons for this preference center on a few key points:

>> YouTube videos are not usually live, though YouTube does allow for streaming. Still, the focus isn't on live content.

>> Most YouTube videos are edited and then uploaded to be accessed on demand, according to user choice. This approach allows people to edit and craft the specific video they want to put into the world without being listened to live.

>> YouTube's ways of monetizing are different, and YouTube gives more rewards for likes and subscribers than Twitch does. I give more details on monetizing in Chapter 14.

>> YouTube has existed longer than Twitch, so some users have a huge base already installed there.

YouTube is set up with channels, too, which are listed under the content creator's name. (Figure 10-7 shows a YouTube channel page.) You can subscribe to your favorites in the same way you would subscribe to a channel on Twitch. Videos are also accompanied by Like and Dislike buttons. Liking the content you enjoy helps the creator of that content.

For the esports fan and player, YouTube offers a massive library of material. From legendary moments like the Wombo Combo to the finals of almost every major tournament ever, YouTube holds a staggering amount of esports content. And that content increases so quickly that you could never watch all of it. You would never have enough time!

According to a 2017 Think With Google research study (found at https://www.thinkwithgoogle.com/data/youtube-gamers-behavior-statistics/), gamers love YouTube for the following four main reasons:

>> 48 percent of YouTube gamers watch more games than they play.

>> 56 percent of YouTube gamers use YouTube to connect to their community.

>> 74 percent of YouTube gamers watch to get better at games.

>> 66 percent of female YouTube gamers watch so that they can hear someone they can relate to.

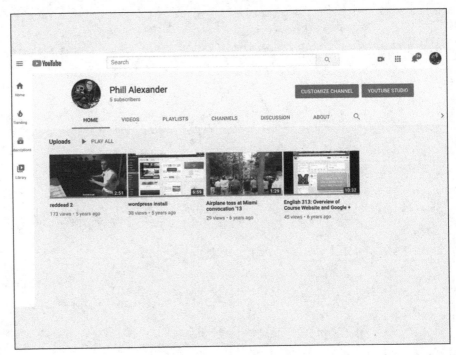

FIGURE 10-7:
A YouTube
channel page.

As you can tell from the preceding list, YouTube serves as a training site, a source of entertainment, and a place to network. YouTube wasn't designed with a gamer focus in mind, but that doesn't prevent it from having a wealth of esports content.

Video is the heart and soul of YouTube, but the comment sections below videos can be as active as any other discussion forum, and reputations can be made, friendships built, and strategy shared in those chat spaces. As with the other sites described in this chapter, you want to use a name on YouTube that's similar to your gamer tag. You use that name when you post to comment sections, and when the time comes for you to upload your own content, that will also be the name of your channel. You need to build a bit of content and gather some followers before you can edit your name on YouTube, though, so early on, your channel ID will be a string of numbers. Don't worry. Everyone starts like that.

WARNING

Remember, again, that you are on the Internet. YouTube comment sections can be filled with trolling, so don't take what someone says too seriously, and if you see a set of comments going bad, remove yourself from the discussion. You're here to have fun! Don't let anyone ruin that for you.

Chapter **11**

Exploring Collegiate Esports

I teach in the games program at Miami University in Oxford, Ohio. I am the codirector of varsity esports there, I am the advisor for three esports related clubs on campus, and I had a key hand in developing the esports coursework that Miami offers. So, of course, if you asked me what was the best college for esports, you wouldn't be surprised if I said Miami. Other sources agree with that assessment, although any of a number of four or five schools could also appear at the top of that list, depending on the source and the criteria being judged.

My experience at Miami is that I've been a large part of the development of collegiate esports and can tell you all about available programs and where collegiate esports is headed in the coming years. But remember, as you read, that even as I try to be objective, I am likely to lean on my own institution. I like the program I've helped build.

I have an obvious bias, and I won't pretend that I don't. I also, however, work with a number of students every year looking for various different esports experiences. I would never say my program isn't amazing, but I would be a bad educator and advisor if I claimed that Miami was the best for everything.

With that said, this chapter gives you the lay of the land for collegiate esports in 2020. Keep in mind that as fast as esports in general are growing, collegiate esports competition is growing *even faster*. The National Association of Collegiate Esports (NACE) notes that it currently has 170 member schools as of February 2020, a massive increase from the 7 (yes, 7) varsity esports colleges in February 2016 (https://nacesports.org/about/). New competitions emerge so quickly that a list of the newest leagues made this week would be out of date within a month. In the last three years, college programs have grown at such an astonishing rate that the growth rate can't be sustained simply because the country will run out of colleges to host them within the next couple of years. Soon, practically every college will have some manner of esports competition.

Taking Stock of Your Options for College Esports

You might be able to find three types of esports competition at a college:

» **Club esports:** Student clubs exist on many campuses and are almost always open to any student. Clubs often have competitive teams that participate in external tournaments, but clubs also sponsor campus-wide events and are a great place to meet and play with other players. Club teams are sometimes casual and sometimes extremely organized and competitive. Some of the teams that compete at the highest levels in national competitions are club teams.

» **Intramural esports:** These esports teams are similar to those of student clubs but are connected to intramural sports. Many campuses offer competitions between teams from their campus, often organized into seasons. These teams are typically casual, but some players take them quite seriously.

» **Varsity esports:** Operating at the most elite level of collegiate competition, varsity teams have competitive tryouts, rigorous practice and competition schedules, and coaches. They also often have their own specific "arena" space on campus where they play. Although varsity collegiate esports doesn't represent a true path to pro, varsity programs are where that level of competition belongs.

If you're considering a college for esports, you should make sure that the campus offers the level or levels of competition you want and expect. A campus with a varsity program will almost certainly have a club program as well because the two often operate in tandem, with the club supporting varsity events and hosting players who don't earn roster spots in varsity on club–level competitive teams. Intramural programs don't have the same connection to varsity programs in most cases because they tend to focus on internal competition with teams from the same school and not with outward–facing competition, so more investigation might be needed if you absolutely want to be at a college with intramural opportunities.

THE BIRTH OF ESPORTS

Esports was born on a college campus. The 1972 *Spacewar!* competition at Stanford University is still recognized as the first gathering of gamers to compete. Fast forwarding to 2009, the Collegiate Starleague began organizing tournaments of *StarCraft*, and campuses began to form esports clubs.

In 2014, Robert Morris University in Illinois was the first college to start a varsity esports program within its athletics department. In early 2016, Miami University and the University of California, Irvine became the sixth and seventh colleges, respectively, to have varsity esports programs, with Miami being the first school with NCAA division I athletics to field varsity esports teams.

In the years since, the varsity esports and club esports programs have exploded. According to the most recent statistics, the United States now has 125 varsity programs (see https://www.espn.com/esports/story/_/id/21152905/college-esports-list-varsity-esports-programs-north-america). Although official documentation doesn't exist at this time, the number of esports clubs in North America, according to Twitch.tv discussions at the 2018 TwitchCon, is 1,600.

You're also choosing a college to get an education, so you want to look at academic programs, location, and other key elements that matter about going to college. A fantastic esports club community can be an amazing draw, but if the college doesn't offer the major you want, that esports scene can do only so much for you.

Knowing the Competitive Opportunities in the Collegiate Realm

As collegiate esports grows, new opportunities to compete are being created and promoted almost every month. Keeping track of all the regional and smaller competitions can be difficult. The HUE Invitational at Harrisburg University is a 64-school invitational that had its second annual competition in the fall of 2019. There are regional events like the varsity- and club-friendly National Collegiate Esports Ohio Region LAN or the Akron Zips Esports Invitational, both of which happened in 2019 in Akron, OH. Being at a college with an active esports scene helps people keep track of events because the players in those clubs are in the social media loop for newer events.

Here are five collegiate leagues to be aware of as you look at schools. You will want to know whether they participate in the following:

>> *League of Legends* **College Championship:** Known as CLoL and now part of the Riot Scholastic Association of America, or RSAA, this tournament is Riot Games' publisher-owned and operated collegiate *LoL* competition. It is, without question, the biggest collegiate *LoL* event of the year, and the top teams are always visible for the annual event, with that visibility starting in January each year and ending as the school year ends. In 2019, Maryville University won the CLoL championship. CLoL welcomes varsity and club-level teams but allows only one team from each university.

>> **Tespa Compete:** Tespa (which started as the Texas Esports Association but now is known just by its acronym) offers competition in all of Blizzard's games. Annually, Tespa has two semesters of competition in *Hearthstone, Overwatch,* and less-hyped titles like *World of Warcraft Epic Dungeon* runs, *Heroes of the Storm,* and *StarCraft II.* Tespa hosts both varsity and club-level teams and boasts more than 200 registrations for its most popular events.

>> **Collegiate Starleague (CSL):** CSL was the first major collegiate esports organization, and in 2019 it offered competition in a wide variety of games, including *CS:GO, LoL, Dota 2, Fortnite, Street Fighter V,* and more. CSL invites all varsity and club teams to compete.

>> **American Video Game League (AVGL):** AVGL offers numerous tournaments in games like *Fortnite, Clash Royale, CS:GO, SMITE, Rocket League,* and more. AVGL welcomes club and varsity teams.

>> **National Association of Collegiate Esports (NACE):** NACE was the first organization to be varsity only, though it has since opened its tournaments to clubs as well as the organization has grown. It offers annual championships in *CS:GO, Fortnite, Paladins, SMITE,* and *Rocket League.* In its first year, NACE competed in *LoL* and *Overwatch,* but in the last two years, those games have not been represented at NACE.

AVGL and CSL are great organizations, and you should look for schools that utilize those two tournaments to build their team tactics and experience for the larger events. If you are serious about esports, however, you want to go to a program whose teams have a history of doing well in CLoL and Tespa. If you play a game for which NACE offers competition, you'll want to find a NACE member school as well.

As you consider potential schools, make sure to also keep an eye on how the esports space is evolving. Although no esports conferences currently take place for esports the way they do for athletics, I've heard many rumblings about such organizations being formed in the coming years. The NCAA is also exploring expanding into esports, though for the short-term future the NCAA appears to plan to stay on the sidelines to see how varsity esports evolves (https://esportsobserver.com/ncaa-nogo-collegiate-esports/).

Scouting a Potential College for Esports

As you consider colleges for esports, think about the college as well as the esports program. You are choosing where to spend four years of your life and where to learn the skills you will take into the workforce with you. Consider the following questions:

>> **Are you looking for a highly competitive program or for a program with lots of opportunities (or both)?** If you're looking to play a specific game at a high level, make sure that the school has a history in that game.

>> **What do you want to do after college?** Majors offered and the quality of the academic programs in specific areas should be as important to your decision as the esports program.

>> **Do you want or need a scholarship to play esports?** Some colleges offer some money, and a few colleges offer quite a bit of money. Is that your deciding factor? According the last numbers from NACE, the average esports scholarship is $5,500 a year (https://nacesports.org/?s=scholarships).

>> **Where do you want to be geographically?** Some of the best esports schools are right where you expect them to be (Southern California) and others are in places you might not expect (such Boise, ID, and Harrisburg, PA).

Numerous colleges are great choices for esports. If you're interested in creating games, both University of Utah and Miami University are good options because the two are ranked tenth and eleventh, respectively, by *the Princeton Review* for game design, and second and third, respectively, among public universities. If you want to look at a career in esports, Boise State has a fantastic esports broadcast program, and Miami and Ohio State are both developing esports management programs. If you want to be attend a college with amazing NCAA Division 1 sports presences, Ohio State and Utah are good bets. If you're looking for a small school experience, Maryville is a good choice. Or, if you want to live in a big city, Georgia State University is in downtown Atlanta.

The following sections go into more depth about each of these and some other highly rated college and university programs. In these sections, I present both the pros and cons of some of the best programs you can find for esports in the United States. These are presented in alphabetical order with no attempt to rank them against each other.

Boise State University

The Boise State University varsity program (https://www.boisestate.edu/esports/) was established in September 2017 and includes the following varsity games:

» *Hearthstone*

» *Heroes of the Storm*

» *League of Legends*

» *Overwatch*

» *Rocket League*

Boise State made a splash when it joined the ranks of varsity esports. Its 100-seat esports Battleground — an Esports Café, or a large sort of deluxe version of what you might think of as a computer lab with high-end gaming PCs that players can rent hourly to play games — is the largest in the nation. As a Mid-Major athletics university with approximately 25,000 students, BSU is the largest college in the state of Idaho and is an esports powerhouse in the northwest.

The BSU program offers five games, placing it among the largest varsity programs in the country. It also has an eye toward expanding to other games in the not-so-distant future. BSU also boasts one of the most impressive video and streaming production facilities in the nation.

Pros

BSU is the premiere program in its region of the country. If you live in Idaho, BSU is the best option for you by far. The university offers a great number of diverse majors, and it's close enough to the west coast to keep traveling to the games and esports industry there from being incredibly difficult.

BSU also has a tradition of being a trailblazer in terms of athletic competition. Its football team was the first school outside of the Bowl Championship Series to make a bid for a national championship, and the blue Astroturf in its football arena marks the team as a maverick. The university appears to be just as dedicated to esports, which is great for anyone involved with the BSU program.

If you're a student who is interested in esports broadcasting or media production, BSU's equipment and facilities are top notch and enticing. Although BSU's esports teams haven't won a national championship —yet —its *League of Legends* team opened the 2019 season on a massive undefeated streak.

Cons

When choosing a school for esports, location is a major part of the decision-making process. BSU isn't in what anyone would call a bad place for esports, but being relatively close to the west coast isn't the same as being on the west coast. If your goal is to be engrossed in the games or entertainment media, as a college student, you might not want to drive long distances for access to the industry.

The other location-based issue is that BSU is one of the few powerhouse esports programs in its region, but they aren't particularly far from the University of Utah in Salt Lake City. For a student interested in a career in games, the lure of Utah's highly ranked program and the industry connections in SLC would be hard to ignore.

Aside from location, there's a lot to like about BSU. Although it's not a top-tier academic institution, it is a fine college offering more than 170 majors, including the only degree in the country in Raptor Biology. Sadly, that means birds of prey and not synthetic dinosaurs, but it's still an amazing offering!

Georgia State University

Georgia State University established its esports varsity program (https://news.gsu.edu/2018/01/30/georgia-state-names-inaugural-varsity-esports-rosters/) in January 2018 and offers the following varsity games:

>> *Brawlhalla*

>> *League of Legends*

>> *SMITE*

Positioned in downtown Atlanta, Georgia State University is a much larger campus than you might initially think. With more than 40,000 students and 11 schools, GSU is integrated into the fabric of Atlanta. Its main campus is downtown but it also has five perimeter campuses located in the suburbs and surrounding area.

GSU looks, demographically, like Atlanta as well, with a "majority minority" student body that is the most diverse in the state of Georgia and among the most diverse in the nation. GSU is also a major player in the National Association of Collegiate Esports, having hosted its first annual conference.

Pros

The southern part of the United States is one of the slower regions to develop major esports programs. GSU is an active, engaged, and growing esports program on a major metropolitan campus in the center of Atlanta, which is a city on the rise with strong ties to industry.

GSU offers more than 250 majors, so students looking for diverse offerings are likely to find something that fits their career goals. If you're interested in esports and want to be located in the south, GSU is a fantastic option.

The diversity of the student body also cannot be ignored. The makeup of many esports programs trend toward the expected stereotype of being white and male. GSU's campus doesn't fit this trend, nor does GSU's esports program. Diversity abounds.

If you want to play the platform brawler fighting game *Brawlhalla*, GSU offers one of the few varsity-level experiences for that title. GSU also offers varsity-level *SMITE* and has strong ties to the game's developer, Atlanta's Hi-Rez Studios and its spin-off esports production company Skillshot Media.

Cons

The location of GSU might make it a bad fit for esports-minded students. For many careers, Atlanta is a fantastic location for real-world experience and networking, but the games and esports industries aren't particularly strong in the southeast.

Another potential issue is living in Atlanta. Paradoxically, its Atlanta location is one of the greatest strengths of GSU, but it could also serve to be a problem in a couple of ways. The first is that living in a major city is in some ways the opposite of the college experience many desire. The second is that campus housing isn't guaranteed, so students might find themselves needing to secure housing in Atlanta in order to attend GSU.

GSU is not a top-tier university, but it is strong and offers a multitude of degrees. Georgia universities appear to be quickly moving forward with esports programs, however, so students with a particular desire to work in computers and technology as well as play esports and be in the south will want to keep a close eye on Georgia Tech over the coming years.

Harrisburg University

The varsity program at Harrisburg University (https://news.gsu.edu/2018/01/30/georgia-state-names-inaugural-varsity-esports-rosters/) came about in August 2017. Its current varsity games are as follows:

>> *Hearthstone*

>> *League of Legends*

>> *Overwatch*

Harrisburg University of Science and Technology went big when it added an esports program. In addition to elite teams for *LoL* and *Overwatch* (as well as its new *Hearthstone* team), Harrisburg is one of the only teams in the nation to have an actual arena, which was converted from an old theater a couple of blocks from the university, and the school is going on a third year of hosting its highly competitive HUE Esports Invitational in late September.

The campus of just more than 5,500 students consists of a single 16-story building in downtown Harrisburg, the capital of Pennsylvania. The university also added a satellite campus in Philadelphia that focuses on Computer and Information Sciences and Interactive Media. Harrisburg's Storm esports is the only competitive unit from Harrisburg, which has no varsity athletics. Its teams are highly competitive and have built their reputation from an impressive win in *Overwatch* at ESPN's Collegiate Esports Championship is 2019.

Pros

Harrisburg's esports teams are among the most competitive of the teams described in this chapter. If you can make the roster, Harrisburg offers the best potential path to professional at the collegiate level, and the scholarship options will mean that you won't pay much for your degree.

If you're an elite player looking to make a big name on the collegiate scene, Harrisburg is a good place to do that. The school is also extremely active in NACE, and its HUE tournament and involvement in the growing Philly esports scene is a major plus.

Cons

Location is a factor for many of the colleges in this chapter, and it plays a major factor in considering Harrisburg. In particular, Harrisburg University is essentially a single tall building in a city that isn't the most desirable location in terms of amenities and safety. It's close to Philadelphia, but getting there would require a car or riding the bus. Here are some major considerations about Harrisburg:

>> **It appears to offer only ten degree options or majors, all of which are linked to science and technology.** This narrow focus isn't a problem if you want to major in one of those subjects because the college does those quite well. But if you want to switch majors, the options are few.

>> **Competition for a team spot is fierce.** If you don't make it onto one of the team rosters when entering the university, the level of competition is such that making a team after you're there would be incredibly difficult.

>> **Housing options exist through the university, but the school has no dorms.** Having no dorms combined with the fact that almost all classes happen in a single building means that the Harrisburg college experience is different from any of the others in this chapter.

>> **Harrisburg is a private school.** It offers no in-state discount for students, and tuition can be pricey.

Maryville University

The Maryville University varsity program (https://news.gsu.edu/2018/01/30/georgia-state-names-inaugural-varsity-esports-rosters/), established in June 2015, plays these games:

>> *League of Legends*

>> *Overwatch*

Maryville is a small college of slight fewer than 10,000 students located in Chesterfield, MO, just outside St. Louis. It's one of the first schools to offer varsity esports, and Maryville's teams often consist of well-known players who are highly ranked and perform well. For example, the Maryville team won a 2017 Collegiate *League of Legends* title and a second-place finish in the 2019 *League of Legends* International College Cup; it was the only U.S. team in the bracket.

Maryville esports is legit. With its commitment and talent base, Maryville is likely to continue to excel. The university itself, however, lacks the reputation for job placement and variety of major programs that some of the larger colleges in this chapter have, so students looking for diverse opportunities might find it difficult to get the education they're looking for. And although it's mighty, the current Maryville varsity program consists of only *LoL* and *Overwatch*, making it the elite program with the smallest selection of competition titles.

Pros

If you want to be an elite collegiate esports player, you get the opportunity and support at Maryville. Maryville is also generous with its scholarship money and emphasizes player preparation and professionalization. If you want to win and you're good enough to make Maryville's roster, you' be in a position to win early and often. The Maryville squad is feared by other competitors. Many of their players refer to themselves as professional esports players, and in fact many of the members of their two rosters have played at the semi-professional level before attending Maryville.

Maryville is far and away the most established and successful esports program in that part of the country, though the University of Missouri, in Columbia, MO, is in the process of building a varsity team, and Columbia College, also in Columbia, MO, have had significant success in *LoL*.

Cons

Here are a few things to keep in mind when looking at Maryville as a potential college destination:

>> Maryville is small compared to many of the other top-tier esports schools. It offers 90 undergraduate and graduate majors combined, and the student body is lower than 10,000. You might therefore find less opportunity than at other schools, depending on your potential area of study, which is an aspect to take into account.

>> Maryville's teams are highly competitive. If you don't make the team before accepting admittance, you might have an incredibly difficult time getting on a team and finding playing time. Maryville has the talent pool to turn away players in the top 1 percent in their games.

>> The school offers only *Overwatch* and *League of Legends* at this point. That situation can change, but no real indicator suggests that Maryville is looking to grow its game base. If you don't play one of those two games, Maryville might not be a wise choice for you to consider.

Miami University

The varsity program at Miami University (`http://redhawks.gg/`) has been going since March 2016 and offers the following:

>> *CS:GO*

>> *Hearthstone*

>> *League of Legends*

>> *Overwatch*

>> *Rocket League*

For people wondering about the name of the university, Miami was a college (founded in 1809) before Florida was a state (1845). Still, a college named Miami in a city called Oxford can be initially confusing, but Miami University is in southern Ohio.

The Miami experience is similar to getting an Ivy League education but at a public university. The campus looks like a college campus from a movie with its brick buildings and beautiful landscaping. Miami ranks highly in undergraduate teaching and offers more than 180 majors. In spite of its size, with a population of just over 16,000 students, Miami steadily ranks in the top 90 colleges in the United States.

With five varsity esports teams, Miami offers one of the largest varsity esports programs in the country. Its *Overwatch* team won the first NACE National Championship, the first varsity-only esports season and playoffs. The program has a mind toward expansion, with new facilities and teams slated for 2020 and beyond.

Pros

You should consider Miami because you've grown to love me as an author and want to take classes with me. I kid, of course, but I want to again recognize my bias. I helped build the esports program at Miami, so being completely objective is hard.

Miami offers the college town experience because Oxford, OH, is a city of 23,000. Factor out the students and faculty, and few people are living in Oxford who don't have ties to the college.

Miami is one of the schools in this list that offers a highly ranked games program — number 11 in the world and number 3 among public universities — as well as a graduate certificate in esports along with numerous academic offerings to help students find careers in the industry. Through the Armstrong Institute, which houses games, esports, and all Miami's digital media degrees, students are offered the chance to study for a semester in Cincinnati; Los Angeles; London, England; San Francisco; Differdange, Luxembourg; and other major cities.

And I can say with 100 percent certainty that Miami is serious about esports. I know a guy.

Cons

Here are three possible deal breakers for you to keep in mind while looking at Miami:

>> **As with other schools described in this chapter, location is a factor.**
   Miami is in Oxford, OH, which is about 20 miles north of Cincinnati. It's a college town to the bone, which can be a great plus for some but could be a problem for others. You have to drive to get to a Best Buy or a movie theater. Also, southern Ohio doesn't have a thriving games industry — yet. Miami balances that lack by offering semesters in other cities and by being the number one school in the country for study abroad, but that doesn't change

the fact that the college is where it is geographically. It's actually close to a number of places, but it's also nowhere. You need a car to do anything that's not school related other than eating and shopping for groceries.

» **Because Oxford, OH, is such a college town, you need to want to be in a college town for the Miami experience to be right for you.** If you thrive on being in the city, or you want to be able to get away from the feeling of being at school, Miami's a bad choice.

» **If you aren't from Ohio, the out-of-state tuition is on a par with what you would expect from an elite college.** The pricey tuition is worth it for some of the best programs Miami offers. If you want to study business and be part of an esports program, Miami is your best bet. If you want to get a degree in games, it's on a short list with Utah. If you want to take multiple classes focused on esports, Miami's your place. If you want to be a teacher, Miami's education program is fantastic for you. For other majors, make sure to do your research and your homework. You could overpay if you're coming from outside the state.

Ohio State University

Ohio State University, located in Columbus, OH, is the newest esports program (https://esports.osu.edu/) described in this chapter, having been created in September 2019. At the time of this writing, OSU's varsity teams hadn't built rosters or held tryouts, decided on games to be played, and or made final decisions on scholarship options.

With an undergraduate student population of 60,000-plus, OSU is the largest campus to offer varsity esports. OSU's esports program, announced in 2018, claims to offer a comprehensive mix of course work, including an esports degree, research involving OSU's medical center, a massive esports club, and a varsity esports program. The university opened a campus esports arena in September 2019.

Pros

If you want to attend a huge school with all the diversity and opportunities that go with a Big Ten campus in the Midwest, OSU is a perfect choice. If you want to be on a campus where traditional sports are an institution, no other school with a competitive varsity esports team can come close to the tradition and success of OSU football. OSU offers a massive number of majors as well, meaning that if you're undecided, or if you are interested in a degree that might not be available on a smaller campus, you'll find what you need.

OSU offers more than 160 majors, and the university is ranked just outside the top 50 in the nation in most ranking lists. Because of its size, the university also manages to offer the college-town experience while being part of a large midwestern city and state capital. OSU is like its own college town sitting on top of the Columbus metropolitan area.

Cons

Here are three items to keep in mind when considering OSU:

>> **At the time of this writing, almost all of OSU's program is hypothetical.** Although the plans are impressive, and no one can question the quality and reputation of the university, the esports program has no track record yet.

>> **A large school has benefits but also drawbacks.** As mentioned at a few points in the book, you have to consider various numbers when determining how many players reach the highest competitive level in a game, OSU has a huge student body, so it likely has more talented players than a smaller campus has. You might therefore have less opportunity because the teams are unlikely to be larger. Also, some people just don't like huge colleges, and OSU is massive.

>> **As of this writing, no one knows what games OSU will offer.** OSU has big plans, but until it fields teams, it could be risky for people who aren't playing *LoL* to commit to OSU. You need to ask questions about how esports plans are shaping up before you commit to this school.

Robert Morris University

Robert Morris University has had a varsity program (https://www.rmueagles.com/sport/0/147) since June 2014 and offers the following games:

>> *CS:GO*

>> *League of Legends*

>> *Overwatch*

>> *Rocket League*

>> *Super Smash Bros. Ultimate*

This university offered the first varsity esports program in the world. That historical status, and the influence that comes with it, is a driving force behind the university's program. RMU is a small campus of slightly fewer than 2,000 students and is located in Chicago, IL. Its athletic teams are part of the National Association of Intercollegiate Athletics (NAIA).

Pros

Having created the first varsity esports program will always make RMU special. Its success is hard to argue with, too; its *League of Legends* team regularly ranks as a favorite in every competition it enters. If you like the idea of attending a small campus and living in the Windy City, RMU is a great option.

Cons

Small schools can offer advantages, but very small schools can also offer limited options. If you're interested in RMU, make sure that it offers the major you're looking for. If you're looking to pursue a career in esports, RMU doesn't provide any academic program that is particularly focused on moving its students into games or entertainment professions.

University of Akron

The University of Akron established its varsity program (https://www.uakron.edu/esports/) in December 2017 and plays the following:

» *CS:GO*

» *Hearthstone*

» *League of Legends*

» *Overwatch*

» *Rocket League*

Akron went big into the esports scene, devoting $750,000 to its facilities and teams. Thanks to that investment and the commitment of its staff, students, and players, Akron has state-of-the-art facilities and put together highly competitive teams quickly. In 2019, the teams won the Collegiate *Rocket League* National Championship. They repeated in 2020.

Pros

It's hard to argue with Akron's beautiful facilities, scholarship options, and that amazing *Rocket League* team. If you're a top *Rocket League* player and you want to make your mark on the collegiate scene, Akron is the place to go. Its young, smart, and energetic esports staff is committed to making collegiate esports better, and the opportunity to do big things is a part of the Akron esports experience.

Cons

Akron, like a few of the other schools in this chapter, suffers from being in a location that isn't ideal for esports because of a lack of major games or esports industry in its general area. The real issue to keep in mind when considering Akron, though, is that the university has cut several academic programs in the last several years — losing more than a fifth of its offered majors — and is predicted to run at a significant deficit over the next several years, which could lead to more cuts. This situation is, sadly, not uncommon for universities in the current economy, but you should look carefully at the relative health of the major you're considering when looking at Akron.

University of California, Irvine

In September 2016, the University of California, Irvine, created its esports varsity program (https://esports.uci.edu/) with these games:

>> *League of Legends*

>> *Overwatch*

I rarely express jealousy, but I have colleagues and friends at UC Irvine of whom I am legitimately jealous. Located in beautiful southern California, just outside of Los Angeles, UC Irvine, or UCI, is within walking distance of both Blizzard and Riot, two of the most important publishers in esports. For all intents and purposes, American esports as an ecosystem is rooted in Los Angeles. Just about everything you could be looking for geographically is there. You're even within 100 miles of top-notch skiing, even while you're on the beach.

UCI's program is also top-notch, with competitive teams, a beautiful public arena space, highly competitive teams that include the 2018 Collegiate *League of Legends* national champions, and connections to an academic program that does great esports research. Up to this point, UCI also hosts the only academic conference in esports, the UCI Esports Conference (UCIESC), which will offer its third meeting in 2020. Classes at UCI are frequently visited by and even taught by industry professionals.

UCI has a diverse campus, with half of its a student body consisting of first-generation students, meaning that their parents didn't attend college. It is regularly ranked as a top-50 university. UCI offers 89 majors and is part of the University of California system.

Pros

Location has to be number one here. Its program is fantastic, and it's located in the epicenter of American esports. If you want the chance to interact with professional teams and visit major gaming companies, UCI is the choice to make.

Also worth noting is that of all the schools in this chapter, UCI has the best weather and is most likely the prettiest location, depending on your preference. It's a jog, but you can walk or ride a bike to the beach. You can also easily take a bus there. Rainy days are rare and the temperature seems to be perpetually 70 degrees.

Cons

I know that the previous section might look like a no-brainer, slam-dunk sales job on UCI, but here are a few things to keep in mind:

>> **UCI offers only 89 majors.** Compared to the other large schools described in this chapter, that number is low. It might not be an issue at all if they offer the major that you want, but if you're undecided about your major, make sure to consider what options might be off the table at UCI that you could find table at another college.

>> **UCI isn't as diverse as some other California schools.** Although it is unquestionably the UC system school for esports, UCI is not as academically diverse or as highly respected as fellow University of California system schools UCLA and Cal Berkeley. If your decision relates mainly to esports, this lack of diversity may not be a major factor for you. But if you're faced with out-of-state tuition, UCI doesn't look better than UCLA, Cal Berkeley, or the private school University of Southern California. USC is particularly important to consider if you're interested in a career in games, as USC's games program is elite.

>> **Living in Irvine is expensive.** Campus housing helps to defray the cost of housing, but regular purchases like food, beverages, and toiletries will cost you significantly more than they would in a place like Idaho or Ohio. Living off-campus might be impossible to afford as a student. If money isn't an issue for you, this aspect isn't a big deal, but if you're a potential student who will need to budget carefully, it's worth researching what a grocery trip might cost you.

University of Utah

The University of Utah's varsity program (https://games.utah.edu/eae-esports/) was established in October 2017 and plays the following:

>> *Hearthstone*

>> *League of Legends*

>> *Overwatch*

>> *Rocket League*

The University of Utah was the first Power Five — meaning large, elite-level athletics program — college to enter varsity esports. Utah has also branded itself Gamer U, and its games program ranks in the top ten in the world.

Utah treats its esports program like its athletics program, building rivalries with other top-tier programs. As is true of only a few other entries on this list, Utah has a full complement of varsity athletics teams, including a football team that consistently ranks in the top 25.

Utah's campus hosts more than 32,000 students and offers 113 majors. The campus is located in Salt Lake City, the capital of Utah. Although the weather gets quite chilly for a large portion of the academic year, Utah is also a literal winter wonderland for those who enjoy winter sports like skiing.

Pros

If you're looking for a school with both a great academic degree program in games and an excellent esports program, Utah is on that very short list of wise choices alongside Miami University. (Keep an eye on the growth of esports at Michigan State University and Rochester Institute of Technology as well in the coming years.) Utah has earned its Gamer U moniker, and you can get a top-shelf education at this school.

If you're looking for a school that is serious about sports and esports, Utah joins that short list with Ohio State University as one of the two schools that is positioned to regularly excel in both categories. Likewise, the sports culture at Utah is strong, so if you want to be able to go to major home football and basketball games, you can do so here.

Utah is also, along with Boise State, one of the few schools in the Northwest with a proven record of esports excellence, and Salt Lake City offers all the benefits of a major metropolitan area, including the presence of a large EA headquarters. Being at the University of Utah might not give you the college town feeling because of the nature of Salt Lake City, but it's also one of the few esports colleges that is within walking distance of top-quality skiing.

Utah is one of those places that doesn't have a number of negatives. It's well ranked as a college in publications like the *Princeton Review*, it offers amazing programs that are attractive to esports players, and its teams are competitive and have maintained a high level of competition since their days as a set of club teams in the early 2010s. Utah's program is likely to expand regularly because its administration is strongly committed to it.

Cons

The negatives are similar to numerous others described in this chapter: location. Being in Utah is great if you don't mind the cold but can be isolating for someone who isn't used to that climate. Also, because the campus is situated in a major metropolitan area, this university might not provide that classic college experience. Beyond those detractors, the University of Utah offers much to like.

Deciding Where to Go: Scholarships and Other Considerations

One of the most frequent questions about collegiate esports is that of scholarships. Each college described previously in this chapter offers scholarships.

Be careful about making scholarship money the primary factor for you when looking at colleges, though. It's easy to be swayed by the offer of partial or full tuition to play esports, but remember that collegiate esports is not a traditional path to playing professionally. You probably shouldn't select your college based just on whether you get to play and get a certain amount of scholarship money to do so. Instead, make a choice based on the information listed here and what you might research on your own about colleges. Yes, scholarship money matters, but you also need to visit the school and consider the following:

>> **Does the college have a quality program in what you want to major in?** This factor should always be your first consideration. It won't matter how happy you are playing esports if you cannot get a degree.

>> **Are you happy with the location?** This issue can be more important than you think. How close will you be to home? Do you like the weather? Do you want to be in the city or in a quieter place?

>> **What are your housing options?** Make sure to check on this. You need to know that you can live comfortably.

>> **Will you be able to study abroad?** This issue comes up more often than I expect when I talk to students. Some colleges have very high numbers of students who study out of the country. Others have fewer programs. If the opportunity to study abroad matters to you, find out before you commit to a school. Also find out how your coaches might feel about your being overseas during a season.

>> **Does the campus offer the college experiences you want?** Activities and organizations like good sports teams, fraternities or sororities, clubs, and other extracurriculars can make all the difference to the quality of your college experience if they are important to you.

>> **Do you like the people there?** Take some time to meet with other players, coaches, and instructors, and spend some time walking around and experiencing the vibe of the campus. If you don't like the people or the feel of the place, you'll never get the experience you want.

Don't let any one factor overwhelm you when making a decision. Collegiate esports is growing quickly. You will have always have viable options to play and compete. You get to be picky. Pick carefully.

4

Making a Life and a Living in Esports

IN THIS PART . . .

Learn about the path to pro in professional esports.

Explore the jobs involved in the ever-growing esports ecosystem.

Craft an identity for yourself as a live streamer.

Chapter **12**

The Path to Pro in Esports

With the massive growth in esports over the last five years, many players dream of becoming professionals. One look at someone like Ninja, Faker, or Sinatraa, and players can't help but want to compete on that same level. To be the best at a game means turning your play into work, though, which in turn means having to consider a number of factors.

Despite the multiple games played and the different criteria for each game, the ever-evolving landscape, and the differing styles of competition, all esports share some common characteristics.

In this chapter, you look at the odds of making it to most elite level of esports and learn about the organization of professional esports. You also get a feel for what life is like for professional players. Some might find that life quite daunting, but this chapter helps you figure out whether playing professionally is for you. Professional esports isn't easy, but it's a tough job that many love.

Calculating the Odds of a Professional Career in Esports

Before you consider the path to becoming a professional, you have to figure out what being a professional means to you. The people mentioned in the opening paragraph of this chapter, for example, earn their money doing different things. Ninja, the *Fortnite* prodigy, makes most of his money from streaming and is only loosely connected to the professional competitive scene. Sinatraa, on the other hand, is a member of the San Francisco Shock and won the *Overwatch* League 2019 MVP award. This chapter talks about the latter option, becoming a high-level professional player. For more information on building your profile as a streamer, check out Chapter 14, which covers building a brand and starting to stream.

A reality of esports is that a marked difference exists between being a great player and being able to play at the professional level. In Table 12-1, you can see the number of players participating in games and how many players are in the top 1 percent, based on best estimates of monthly active users.

TABLE 12-1   **The Number of Players at the Highest Level in Top Esports**

Game	Player Base	Number of Players in the Top 1 Percent
League of Legends	80 million (per https://www.unrankedsmurfs.com/blog/players-2017)	800,000
CS:GO	17.22 million (per https://www.statista.com/statistics/808922/csgo-users-number/)	172,200
Overwatch	40 million (per https://www.statista.com/statistics/618035/number-gamers-overwatch-worldwide/)	400,000
Fortnite	78 million (per https://twinfinite.net/gallery/most-played-games-ranked-monthly-players/)	780,000
Rocket League	50 million (per https://videogamesstats.com/rocket-league-statistics-facts/)	500,000

The table lists only five major titles, and the math is skewed, of course, in that every single player isn't trying to play on the highest competitive level, but look, for example, at *Fortnite*. To win the *Fortnite* World Cup, a player has to be better than 78 million other players and the number of those players who are in the top 1 percent, at the highest level of competition. To get an invite to the *Fortnite* World

Cup, a player must be one of the top 100 in the competition. That comes down to less than half of 1 percent of the 1 percent of the top 1 percent of players. It's tough.

To compare this situation to another professional sport, a prospective NBA basketball player must play at least one year in college. The NCAA has 18,816 basketball players (according to http://www.ncaa.org/about/resources/research/mens-basketball-probability-competing-beyond-high-school) at any given time. Of those players, 175 (plus 58 from international colleges, according to the NBA (https://pr.nba.com/early-entry-candidates-2019-draft/) enter the NBA draft. Of the 233 in the pool, 60 are drafted. Sixty out of 18,816 is just over 0.03 percent of college players who become professional. Bear in mind that all this math deals in averages but is based on the NBA's statistics.

These numbers might seem sort of mind-boggling, but the general point I want to make is that to achieve the highest level of players is incredibly difficult. Here's another example: The *Overwatch* League has 199 players. Four hundred thousand players are at the highest rank, Grandmaster. So only 0.05 percent of Grandmaster *Overwatch* players make it to the league.

So, becoming an elite level pro esports player is a long shot. I don't mean to discourage you or to end your dream. People obviously make it, and you can't tell how good you might be until you put in the effort. Which may leave you asking, "What is the effort?" Read on to find out.

Having What It Takes to Be a Professional

Here are five keys to becoming a professional esports player that apply regardless of the specific game you're considering:

>> **Devote as much time as possible to practicing.** Some pros play 8–12 hours per day.

>> **Know the meta of your chosen game.** You need to know the meta and all current strategies so well that you can watch someone playing a role that you don't play and anticipate their moves and choices because you know the strategy so well.

>> **Avoid other, similar games.** This might seem like a weird concept if you haven't played competitively before, but muscle memory is a huge part of being an elite level player. If you are trying to play *Overwatch* competitively, you cannot play another FPS; your aiming abilities and reaction time will decrease

because of your need to react to multiple games. You want to be able to aim without needing to stop and think about aiming, like a basketball player who dribbles or a cyclist who pedals a bike without thinking about the motion.

>> **Watch all the professional matches in your game that you can.** Many talented esports players in America stay up late so that they can watch the best players in Korea play each day, and pros who aren't in a tournament never miss a chance to watch that tournament.

UNDERSTANDING VIDEO GAME ADDICTION

In recent times, numerous media outlets have reported on the World Health Organization's inclusion of "Internet game disorder" in its most recent International Statistical Classification of Diseases. Although calling this problem a disorder prompted much discussion and concern, it is important to note that the American Psychological Association (APA), which publishes the *Diagnostic and Statistical Manual of Mental Disorders (DSM)*, has yet to consider the available evidence and decide whether such a thing as "game addiction" exists.

The reality is that a person with addictive behavior can become compulsive about games in the same way a person might become addicted to scratch-off lottery tickets or betting on horse races. That condition differs from "addiction" in the sense of the *DSM*, which defines addiction as a neurobiological dependence on a substance (such as drugs or alcohol). The APA has made moves to define behavioral addictions, but the nature of a behavioral addiction (with gambling being the one that the APA focuses on) is quite different from that of substance addictions.

A person can, in fact, play games too often. In rare cases, people have died from playing games and not sleeping or eating (https://venturebeat.com/2015/03/05/man-dies-after-19-hour-world-of-warcraft-session/). A person who tends to succumb to behavioral addictions or compulsions could easily exhibit that behavior toward a video game. Likewise, people who play games so much that they ignore their job and friends, don't sleep, and don't eat are in the danger zone. The picture of a person who plays games for a living can look similar to the one I've just painted because gaming *is* that person's job. Some people work 8–12 hours a day, and pro gamers must do the same.

No evidence exists, however, that playing video games for prolonged periods will somehow *cause* addiction or addictive behavior. Be sure to take breaks as you play for the sake of your body, your eyes, and your mind, but don't live in fear. You have no reason to believe that esports will cause you to become addicted. If you know that you have a predisposition to become "addicted" to other behaviors, though, make sure to have a friend or loved one check in on you as you start playing.

>> **Balance your life and stay healthy.** Playing a game for multiple hours every day can take a toll on your life, body, and relationships with family and friends. It can burn you out. You have to strive to retain a balance while figuring out how to do the other things needed to be a professional. If you play *LoL* for 12 hours every day but you're always exhausted and have stiff muscles from being hunched over your keyboard, you'll never perform at a peak level. Balance in all things should be your goal.

Playing Solo Games versus Team Games

In the professional esports world, the biggest differences are between playing a game in which you compete solo, such as a fighting game, or compete on a team, as in *League of Legends* or *Overwatch*. Teams require organizations, coaches, analysts, and the infrastructure to handle the upkeep of team resources, schedules, and so on. Teams have a great many moving parts.

If you play a game in which you compete solo, all your upkeep and practice scheduling, event planning, and other details of play fall to you unless you're part of a pro team that supports solo games, too (for example, you could be a *Super Smash Bros. Ultimate* player for Team Liquid). As a soloist, you might hire a coach, or someone to help you book events, or just a general assistant, but many solo players run everything on their own. Living the solo life presents a stark difference from the team dynamic.

If you're a solo *Fortnite* player, you play almost any fighting game, or you play a game like *StarCraft II* or *Hearthstone*, the prospects of a life as a pro player depend entirely on your game skills and your ability to navigate the competitive space. To start your career, you're likely to handle everything you do by yourself. From social media and streaming to finding events and qualifying, you deal with everything on your own.

Not every person who competes as a solo player wants to take on the esports world alone. Many esports organizations, such as Team Liquid and Cloud9, have fighting-game competitors on their rosters. Some players, such as *SSB* professional HungryBox, usually compete one-on-one in tournaments, but they reap the benefits of being part of a larger organization, serving as sort of a member of a "team" in the most general sense.

The key to building a solo esports career is finding a way to get sponsorship or to generate revenue by streaming. Prize pools for most single-player games — with *Fortnite* being the current exception — aren't high enough that a person covering all his or her own expenses can go pro without making it to the highest levels. This is true even for top-tier players like SonicFox, who was part of the now disbanded Echo Fox organization.

Joining an Esports Team or Organization

At various times in this book, I refer to esports teams and esports organizations. Although these are not the same thing, they are similar. The difference is in scope and size. In esports, a team is the actual competitive unit, including any substitute players, the analysts, and the coaches. For example, a *League of Legends* team might consist of as few as eight people: five players, a substitute player, an analyst, and a coach. Many teams are larger, but a team includes only the people who are part of an actual competitive unit in a single game.

In contrast, an esports organization is a collection of teams and the staff that supports those teams. For example, Cloud9 is an esports organization. Cloud9 has teams that play *Overwatch* (including the London Spitfire of the *Overwatch* League, which they co-own), *Fortnite, Hearthstone, League of Legends, PlayerUnknown's Battlegrounds Mobile, Rainbow Six Siege, Rocket League, SSB Melee, Teamfight Tactics,* and *WoW,* and solo players in *Dota 2, Call of Duty,* and *Apex Legends.* Obviously, the organization has a massive roster (the Cloud9 stream team on Twitch has 73 team members, and some players choose not to stream) and Cloud9 has a large team of employees to support all that esports activity.

New players don't just walk in and join these organizations. To learn how to get noticed and make your way onto one of these teams, take a look at "Charting the Path to Pro in Your Game of Choice," later in this chapter.

Understanding the structure of an esports organization

The chain of command in esports organizations always starts at the top with the owner or owners. Many esports organization owners are also owners of other professional sports teams or large corporations, and their direct involvement in the organization depends on their expertise and desire to be front and center. Some owners operate in a hands-off manner, whereas others do work similar to that of a general manager in a sports organization: recruit and sign players; talk to tournament organizers; and manage personnel issues such as coaching disputes, salary issues, and so on.

Here are some key professional sports owners who are part of the professional esports world:

» Former NBA Player Rick Fox was co-owner of Team Echo Fox (Echo Fox disbanded in 2019).

» Jeff Wilpon, COO of the New York Mets (a team his father owns), is the owner of *Overwatch* League's New York Excelsior.

- Robert Kraft, owner of the New England Patriots, owns the *Overwatch* League's Boston Uprising.

- Mark and Zygi Wilf, owners of the Minnesota Vikings, owns the *Call of Duty League*'s Minnesota RØKKR.

- Mark Cuban, owner of the Dallas Mavericks, owns Mavs Gaming and its *NBA 2K* League team.

- Dan Gilbert, owner of the Cleveland Cavaliers, owns a part of 100 Thieves' *League of Legends* team as well as the Cavs Legion in the *NBA 2K* League.

- Wesley Edens, co-owner of the Milwaukee Bucks, owns FlyQuest, a *League of Legends* Championship Series team.

Working under the owner of an organization includes the following roles, which are duties that solo players need to handle on their own. These are also potential jobs for those interested in the industry:

- **Marketing manager and team:** The primary job of the marketing manager is to build and maintain the organization's brand and to search for sponsorships. Finding money is a big part of making an esports organization work, so the marketing team is critical to success.

- **Social media manager and team:** Although some teams include these roles in marketing, most organizations have a separate set of employees who are responsible for social media. Social media presence is critically important for esports, and given the number of fans who desire content, no organization can create too much.

- **A game manager for each game played:** This role is the one that most closely resembles that of the general manager of a professional sports team. A game manager is not a coach but rather hires coaches, helps to find players, keeps on top of how teams playing the game are operating, and looks for ways to improve the team's competitive edge. The esports organization Cloud9 probably has ten game managers as well as someone who does the game manager's job for the solo players (likely an eleventh employee).

- **Coaches:** Each team has a coach, and high-profile teams and teams who play games with more complex strategies (like *Dota 2*) often have assistant coaches as well. The coach manages the team's practices, helps to build strategy, and manages on-site or in-game responsibilities, or both. Whereas in physical sports, the coach is pacing on the sidelines, in esports, the coach is walking behind the row of computers or is on the headset talking to the team.

- **Analysts:** Sometimes considered assistant coaches, these are the game experts who watch the team play, review team videos, and scout opponents. Game knowledge is concentrated in analysts, and although being a good analyst and being a good player aren't always the same thing, analysts possess the skill set to break down gameplay and point out everything from major mistakes to slight instances of suboptimal performance.

>> **Team captains:** The captain is a player (or players — but usually just one) who is the team's leader and often also the in-game shot caller, or the person who is responsible for making sure everyone is focused on the correct target or goal.

>> **Players:** These are the members of each team or the solo players. They literally play the games.

Depending on the size of an organization, many also have streaming teams, a web design and development team, a legal team, an accountant, and a human resources team. These roles are also often outsourced, depending on the size of the organization. It might not make sense, for example, for an organization with 30 total employees to have a full-time HR person or legal team when it could simply contract that work as needed.

All the people within the organization have a singular goal: to have their players competing at the highest level. Depending on the size of an organization, some of the teams might only rarely communicate with each other or, on the other hand, all the teams might be closely knit. Regardless of that dynamic, winning is the way to get noticed, get sponsors, and earn money. The more money an organization has, the more it can expand to include more games and teams.

Making the time to play

As mentioned previously, many players practice for multiple hours a day. Issues can arise from that much practice. The first issue is burnout. Some people can, by nature, devote themselves to playing for hours upon hours at a competitive level, just as athletes can. As one of a legion of former high school athletes, I can tell you that I had to draw the line at three hours of high-level practice a day. As a gamer in my late 20s (already beyond the "prime" age of an esports professional), I couldn't hack more than seven hours of highly competitive gaming per day, three times a week. Even short of what it takes to be a pro, that amount of high-level gaming is grueling. Of course, at that time I was also teaching and taking classes, and I was writing a book (for which the gaming was research).

To be the best you can be, and to perform on the level of most professionals, you will likely need to practice at least eight hours a day, five or six days a week. Many pros exceed that, playing so often that they just don't have time for much else. These are players who aren't in school and don't work any other job. Remember, though, that playing games *is* their job. They have to treat it as a vocation.

Contrasting the rigorous schedule kept by professionals to collegiate esports, the varsity teams in the Miami University program practice in three-hour blocks four nights a week, one of which consists entirely of video review of practice and matches. Most of the members of that team are at Grandmaster level, but up to this point, no member of that team has even attempted to go professional. Their college studies would get in the way of practice time and vice versa.

Major aspects to consider in terms of going pro are your current age, your responsibilities, and your natural level of skill. It can be a hard argument to make to a parent that you want to devote your life to playing a game full time, but if you can point to the career that will result, many families will be supportive.

Knowing your game

You need to know as much as you possibly can about the game you want to play. This means that you'll be doing research, watching professional players, asking questions about strategy and the reactions of other players as you play your own matches, reviewing the meta of the game, and exploring what tweaks you can make to your own gameplay to be more effective. The ever-changing meta — or best practices — in games is an aspect of esports that is different from other sports. For example, during a collegiate Tespa *Hearthstone* tournament that spanned a semester in 2018, Blizzard released a new expansion. Players had a week before the first round of the playoffs (from a Tuesday to a Saturday) to learn the effects and values of all the new cards, build new decks, and learn enough of the meta to be ready to compete. Imagine if mid-season in the NFL, the shape of the field and number of yards needed for a first down changed, or the physics of the football were altered. Knowing all the aspects of a game requires constant effort.

Having to quickly master updates to games is, of course, one of the things about esports that is often what draws a player in. Games are about strategy, and if you tend to be good at and enjoy games, you should have no trouble watching matches and learning all the strategy involved.

REMEMBER

Unlike professional sports, the path to pro in esports, at least as of now, does not go through college. Collegiate competition is strong, as you can read about in Chapter 11, but most professional players go pro first and then return to college after they've finished their professional careers. Although research is under way to try to help people play further into their lives, currently the impact of age on reaction time is such that professional esports careers typically end in the mid- to late 20s. This situation, of course, leaves time for college and a successful second career, but to attend college during the path to pro could remove four valuable years from your competitive career.

Being Seen at the Biggest Esports Events

As mentioned elsewhere in the book, specific games have key events, and almost every part of the country has local and regional events. At the pinnacle of the esports world, though, certain major events serve as the most elite and important events on the annual esports calendar. Table 12-2 lists a few of those events.

TABLE 12-2   **Some Top-Tier Professional Esports Events**

Event	Month	Games
The International	August	*Dota 2*
League of Legends Worlds	November	*League of Legends*
Overwatch League Grand Finals	September	*Overwatch*
Evolution Championship Series (EVO) (usually in Las Vegas, NV)	July/August	In 2019: *Street Fighter V: Arcade Edition, Tekken 7, Dragon Ball FighterZ, BlazBlue: Cross Tag Battle, Soulcalibur VI, Under Night In-Birth Exe:Late[st], Samurai Shodown, Mortal Kombat 11,* and *Super Smash Bros. Ultimate*
Fortnite World Cup	July	*Fortnite*
Intel Extreme Masters (IEM)	February	*Counter-Strike: Global Offensive*
Call of Duty League	September	*CoD*
PUBG Global Championship	November	*PlayerUnknown's Battlegrounds*
Rocket League Championship Series World Championship	Varies	*Rocket League*

Almost every esports title has its respective major championship. Even *Clash Royale* and *Arena of Valor* had world championships in 2019.

Charting the Path to Pro in Your Game of Choice

The information to this point in the chapter will help you regardless of your game of choice. After you choose a game, however, the issues become more complicated. Each game has a different path to pro. This book doesn't have the space to cover every single game, but in this section, you take a look at what it means to go pro in the most high-profile games in the current esports environment.

For whatever game you choose, here are a few actions to consider taking that aren't essential but will help along the way:

>> **After you pick a game, consider finding a coach.** You can find coaches offering their services in various online spaces, such as on Reddit, within Discord communities, or through services like Gamersensei.com. If you're starting a game that has existed for several years, a coach can be particularly helpful in getting you up to speed.

>> **Look over Chapter 14 and start creating your brand.** Streaming yourself as a brand will help you to be seen, and being seen is a key part of getting onto a team.

>> **Find other talented players to practice with.** If you can find locals to meet face to face, that's all the better for talking through strategy in the same room.

Going pro in *CS:GO*

The *CS:GO* ecosystem is more complicated than some other games in that it provides multiple ladders and competitive systems to play in. The best place to start is in matchmaking mode within *CS:GO*. You want to rank yourself up in this mode until you reach Global Elite (the top level you can reach). At Global Elite, people view you as a worthy competitor, and you can move into the Esports Entertainment Association League (ESEA), which adds anti-cheat measures and gives you access to higher-level competitors. As you play in ESEA, you should focus on increasing your round win share (RWS) points. RWS is a point system that indicates how much of a round victory was attributable to your actions. Earning a high RWS in ESEA is the quickest way to get on the radar of professional teams. Use this process to get onto a semi-pro team and then continue to impress until you finally get your shot at a spot on a professional roster.

Going pro in *Fortnite*

Going pro in *Fortnite* is, at least structurally, easier than in a game like *CS:GO*. If you play *Fortnite* in Arena mode, you earn "hype" points. You then use your hype to qualify for tournaments. You can also find periodic open events in which to compete to qualify for the *Fortnite* Champion Series (https://www.epicgames.com/fortnite/competitive/en-US/events/). The *Fortnite* World Cup offers multiple weeks of online qualification through which a player can earn the right to be one of the 100 players invited to the final match. If you want to go pro in *Fortnite*, you need to play well and make sure not to miss your opportunities to earn your spot in the tournament. You don't have to earn a spot on a team or to enter any outside tournaments.

Going pro in *League of Legends*

To become a professional *League of Legends* player, you need to be picked up by an LCS team. Getting picked often comes from performing well in the Challenger Series. The Challenger Series is the feeder league for the *League of Legends* Championship Series (LCS), which culminates in League Worlds. Now that teams are franchised, a great deal of the flexibility that once existed is gone. Players cannot form teams and try to make it to the LCS. Players now must impress the existing LCS teams to get recruited.

Going pro in *Overwatch*

The *Overwatch* League system establishes a clear path to pro, and it is similar in many ways to the path for *LoL* players. To get started, you need to find or form a team and enter the *Overwatch* Open Division (`https://playoverwatch.com/en-us/esports/open-division`). Success in the Open Division's six-week season earns your team a chance in the Contenders Trials. The Contenders League is the level below the official *Overwatch* League. Players on Contenders teams are scouted by the League teams and stand a chance of being recruited to the highest level.

The difficult part of this process can be finding a team to enter the Open Division. This is where utilizing social media as discussed in Chapters 10 and 14 will serve you well. Get to know people, practice with people in quick play, and take advantage of the relationships you build to find the best possible teammates.

Going pro in (almost) any fighting game and *Hearthstone*

Because fighting games are one-versus-one matches and so many tournaments occur, no clear path exists for paving your way into the professional scene. Most major tournaments are open compete, which means that you can show up, pay your registration fee, and be seeded into the tournament.

Of course, this lack of a clear path doesn't mean that you want to declare yourself a *Mortal Kombat 11* pro, head to EVO, and throw down your money to enter the field. You need to play in local events and regional events to hone your skills first. No one wants to be the arrogant person who signs up for a tournament and gets seeded against SonicFox, gets beaten in two straight short matches, and has to slink off into the corner to hide. Build your skills first and *then* go big.

The advantage to the more unstructured process of going pro in fighting games is that you can be a relative unknown and score big in a fighting-game tournament if you have the skills. Because you don't need to run through a series of steps and make it onto teams, you retain an element of surprise. You also still have your self-reliance on your side — as opposed to reliance on the other players on a team — in these games.

Becoming a pro by playing *Hearthstone* works in much the same way as with fighting games, though you can also participate in Blizzard-based qualifiers, for which you receive regular notifications in-game.

Contending with Other Day-to-Day Realities as an Esports Professional

For most esports professionals, days are filled with playing games. On the surface, that might sound like a dream come true, but an interesting thing happens when gaming becomes your job. It's still fun because it's gaming, but when your performance matters to your ability to keep your job, and you put in long hours every day in team competition, gaming can turn into work. At one point in my life, I considered playing *World of Warcraft* to be the most fun and relaxing thing I could do. A year into playing competitively at a high level, the idea of running new content that I hadn't seen before was stress inducing. Competitive gaming is a real balancing act.

In the following sections, you learn about a typical workday in the life of a professional player. I also touch on issues involving the inclusion of women in esports, and how the need to acquire and retain sponsorships figures in to a player's career.

Living a day in the life of an esports professional

Many gamers on professional teams live in what is called a gamer house, a multibedroom home with a huge main floor where the players practice. A day in the life at a gamer house looks something like this:

>> **9–10 a.m.:** Wake up. Most gamers are up late practicing with talent from around the world, and early mornings have never been a gamer thing. Most take time to shower and eat breakfast, which is usually prepared for them.

>> **10 or 11 a.m.:** Begin a cycle of scrimmaging or practicing and then talking about performance after a match. A typical team can play two scrimmages with two debrief strategy sessions before lunch.

- >> **2 p.m.:** Lunch time. Lunch is often provided in-house, but many gamers like to leave to get lunch and stretch their legs.

- >> **3 p.m.:** Resume scrimmages and strategy sessions between matches. This cycle continues until 7 or 8 p.m. when the practicing day has ended. During a highly active time of the season, a pro team can scrimmage five or six matches in a single day.

- >> **8 p.m.:** Free time starts. In many gamer houses, players solo queue — play online practice games with random teams — and practice, though it's not a requirement for many teams.

- >> **1–2 a.m.:** Curfew. Most teams have a lights-out time. Presumably, the players sleep from 2 a.m. to 9 a.m. That's seven hours, which isn't quite the eight that is recommended, but it's close. A player can always go to sleep before curfew.

What might be difficult to grasp at first is that in this situation, the players are paid employees. So if your gameplay starts at 10 a.m. every day and ends at 8 p.m., that's what you do as a professional player. You don't have days off, and if you're playing poorly or feeling under the weather, the rest of your team suffers as a result.

This set of circumstances leads to a great deal of potential stress. Players who underperform are likely to be cut. Likewise, players who can't get along with teammates are likely to be removed from the team. And if a player is cut from a high-level team, finding a new team is often difficult. Being cut can mean the end of a career. Players can also lose their spot on a team if the game changes and the player cannot develop new skills quickly enough.

Competition days can be even more stressful, with an intense schedule like the following, which was the day-of-competition schedule for teams at PiViP 2019 in Cincinnati:

- >> **9–10 a.m.:** Wake up, away from home, and find breakfast, shower, and gather gear to head to the venue.

- >> **11 a.m.:** Travel to the venue and move gear into the player area.

- >> **12-1 p.m.:** Tour the venue, look at the competition computers, and ask any questions of venue managers.

- >> **1-2 p.m.:** Meet with the team and discuss strategy.

- >> **2–3:30 p.m.:** Set up on stage and play warm-up matches.

- >> **3:30 p.m.:** Eat a light lunch.

» **4–7 p.m.:** Play best-of-three match on stage with no more than a ten-minute break between matches.

» **7–8 p.m.:** Talk to media and fans. Post to social media.

» **9–10 p.m.:** Team dinner.

» **10:30 p.m.–1 a.m.:** Free time.

» **1 a.m.:** Curfew.

The days in professional esports are long. Here are the critical considerations when thinking about a career in professional esports:

» **Can you handle playing at a high level, under competitive stress, for eight hours a day?** For most people, engaging highly competitive gaming for eight hours a day has never been a reality before attempting to be an esports professional. It's rigorous.

» **Are you good enough to maintain elite-level gameplay on a grueling schedule?** The traits of being good enough and able to play for long hours aren't sufficient. A pro esports player must be able to balance energy and avoid fatigue. A pro has to be as good at hour eight as he or she is at hour one.

» **Does your life allow for you to put this much energy into gaming?** People regularly ask me whether I want to go back to playing *WoW*. My answer is always that I don't have the time because I now run an esports program, teach, and write books like the one you're holding. And I'm not going to sacrifice time with my wife, family, and friends to play. I'm also probably too old to have the reaction time I had back then. No longer participating as a game player doesn't mean that I cannot have an esports career, however.

Confronting gender imbalance in esports

The general trend in esports is that participation by female players increases markedly each four years in direct correlation to classes of students moving through high school. In numerous interviews, female players have indicated to me that their ability to get involved in gaming in high school, and then in college, had a profound impact on their competitive gameplay.

Although the collegiate esports organization Tespa doesn't publicize the numbers, internally it has indicated to chapters that membership in their college-level clubs is nearly 60 percent male and 40 percent female, and the organization has seen a dramatic upward trend in female leadership. This same trend holds when looking at collegiate esports clubs. For the past eight years, the clubs at Miami, where

I advise, and at surrounding schools like the University of Cincinnati and The Ohio State University, have seen significant gains in female officers within clubs.

This trend has yet to impact professional esports, however, or even the highest level of collegiate competition. Based on my current research, the reasons for the lower participation of women include:

>> Not feeling welcome in competitive gaming situations (because of sexist and lewd comments from male players)

>> Not wanting to play in situations in which other gamers are overly aggressive

>> Not having the same requisite experience as some other gamers because of their lack of involvement in esports in high school and younger

>> Not feeling represented because of the lack of female game characters

Slowly, these conditions are changing, and over the last several years, the collegiate level has seen a rise in female competitors. It remains to be seen how quickly change will occur at the professional level. The rise of new stars like Chiquita Evans in the *NBA 2K* League will no doubt help women to feel more welcome in the esports world. You can read more about Evans in Chapter 6.

Change can't come fast enough, though. As you enter the esports space, here are things to consider and behaviors you can adopt to create a more inclusive space:

>> Any time you hear or see someone behaving in a sexist, racist, homophobic, or otherwise rude way, call it out. When one person is cruel in a group of ten, but no one asks that cruel person to stop, it can feel to the person being targeted as though everyone else agrees with the aggressor. Intervening by telling offenders to stop makes a big difference.

>> If you're a male player, be encouraging to the female players you meet, your female relatives, your female teammates, and female players you see at events. Although male players commonly trash talk, remember that your trash talk feels much different when you're directing it at someone who feels like an outsider.

>> When you see a female player (or any player who is being excluded, for that matter) at a tournament or event, introduce yourself and make it clear that you're interested. Sometimes all it takes is a smiling face to ease concerns.

>> Always take time to point out that your gaming events and gaming areas are safe spaces. Even if you're just inviting people to a small LAN, make it clear that everyone is welcome.

>> Make sure that your organization — regardless of size — reaches out to female players. Always remember that growing up female around gamers can lead to a preconception of not being welcome. Outreach means everything.

>> If you can volunteer, work with junior high and high school girls who are interested in esports (or even be the one to introduce them to esports). The greatest impetus for change in the esports landscape comes from high school clubs and players moving into the professional and collegiate spaces.

>> At the more extreme end, be ready to boycott events, teams, and games that behave badly. Esports is a business, and in business, money talks.

Understanding the importance of sponsors

One of the major elements of being a professional player is having sponsors. Sponsors, which are usually major companies who produce products, have expectations for the people they sponsor. In gaming, this can sometimes mean a culture clash because gamers don't always exhibit the best behavior. Bear in mind that pro players who are sponsored by a companies like Red Bull, Geico, Coke, Alienware, and similar companies have to behave in ways that those brands find becoming. A large part of being a pro esports player is learning to avoid toxic online behavior and producing engaging, appropriate social media and stream content.

With the rise of professional streamers, more people are finding sponsors on their own. For the typical pro player, however, sponsorship comes through the team, a league, or a tournament. It is critical that players understand the expectations of their sponsors, because sponsorship is where 40 percent of esports revenue comes from (according to Newzoo (`https://newzoo.com/insights/trend-reports/newzoo-global-esports-market-report-2019`).

One of the major time commitments that pro players have to make involves attending to sponsors through posting to social media, going to events, and mentioning sponsors on streams and similar events. Keeping a good relationship with a sponsor is a key part of the professional esports lifestyle, and it can sometimes mean that a player can wear only certain clothes, use certain equipment, or be seen on camera drinking certain beverages. In almost all cases, sponsors expect players not to use extensive profanity while streaming and to avoid controversial content that might alienate viewers.

Living Your Life after Professional Esports

As mentioned earlier in this chapter, the average age for professional esports careers to end is somewhere between 25 and 30, depending on the game and what experts you ask. I've met players as young as 23 who were already considering their next career move. Esports, even more than professional sports, ends for a player long before a typical career would end.

The options for a career after esports are many. You can read more about some of those potential careers in Chapter 13. The single biggest piece of advice I can offer you, though, is that if you make it as a professional player, use that skill set to get yourself into a good college at the end of your playing career, and then play as a college student so that your college is free and you can train for the career of your choice. Because of the inverted structure of playing as a pro and then going to college, no rules are in place like those of the NCAA for professional athletes. You can play as a pro for a decade and then play four years of collegiate esports while on scholarship. Pro players should take advantage of that situation. You can end your pro career at 26, get a four-year college degree, and move into your second career at 30 with all your esports earnings and little, if any, student debt. It's a great move!

Chapter **13**

Getting Involved (or Finding a Career) in Esports

When considering the esports ecosystem, particularly at the professional level, the reality is that the players represent only a small portion of the people who make competitive events come together. From volunteers to fully employed professionals, a massive network of people with varied skill sets get involved to make sure that an event like EVO, The International, or BlizzCon goes off without a hitch.

This chapter tells you about the various jobs — both volunteer and paid — that exist around esports, making the system go. Although salaries vary greatly, if you have a desire to work in the esports realm, work is available.

Getting Involved as a Volunteer

If your goal is to get a foot in the door of the esports world, or if you're not necessarily looking for a career path but want to help make esports happen, a good move is to look at volunteer options. Although esports is an ever-growing industry, the real spending on events and staff happens mostly at the international, or at least national, level. A relatively small amount of money is currently being spent on local events, such as on high school and collegiate esports.

What that means for someone trying to get a start in esports (you, for example) is that plenty of opportunities exist to start getting work experience as long as you're not trying to make a living wage doing it.

On the local level, you should be able to easily find experience offering the following services to small local/regional events, to high schools, or even to your local college. (Though most colleges start by looking to their students, having nonstudents volunteer is not uncommon.) Here are some services you can offer:

>> **Help to organize local events.** Although the actual organizers of local events are often paid, and you shouldn't volunteer yourself to run an event, sometimes everyone but the main Tournament Organizer (TO) are volunteers or interns.

>> **Work as street team members for a team, a game, a club, or an organization.** One of the biggest areas of need for smaller-scale events is publicity. Although some people are always "in the know" for local and small regional events, many events wouldn't draw attendance without the help of people spreading posters, posting to social media, and facilitating word-of-mouth publicity. The idea behind "If you build it, they will come" works only if they know you built it.

TIP

If you're interested in streaming a channel of your own eventually, smaller events can provide you with a gold mine's worth of experience. I could tell you all about this, but instead, here's what one of my students, who is now the streaming coordinator for our varsity team, told me: "When I wanted to get started streaming, I just popped onto different Discord servers and looked for whoever was handling streaming or PR and asked whether they needed help. It took only a couple of messages to find a gig, and once I had clips to show people, I could get gigs easily."

>> **Help with the nuts and bolts at esports events.** Someone has to set up the machines. Someone has to register people and check them in at the door. Someone has to make sure that all the machines work, answer questions from players, help with catering, and so on. Willing hands are rarely turned away from an event.

Going local to help with esports events

Regardless of the size of the event — whether it's a four-team tournament or a huge, multi-day festival involving 100 teams — a small army of volunteers and interns is almost always helping to make sure the event happens. In esports right now, few organizations have large staffs. A group like AllMid, for example, which operates tournaments in the Ohio River Valley, has a decent-sized group of experts on its team, but to run an event, AllMid needs help. I use one of its events as an example here to show how people contributed their time and skills.

In May 2019, AllMid worked in conjunction with a group called PiviP to put on a one-day esports event at a Cincinnati, OH, amusement park called King's Island. AllMid had almost its entire staff of 15 on the ground at King's Island as well as 30 volunteers. Those volunteers were members of one of the Miami University's esports classes on hand to help with the event in the following ways:

>> Handling talent relations and making sure that people like celebrity guest Markiplier had everything he and his team needed to stream his live podcast

>> Working with King's Island's catering to make sure that the competitors and guests had access to food, water, and quiet areas to practice

>> Managing the competition stage and making sure that the computers were ready as teams rotated in and out to complete

>> Managing audio and video hardware and production

>> Taking tickets and staffing the information desk

>> Handling tech support throughout the day

>> Handling duties like on-stage introductions and stream management

>> Assisting with setting up and tearing down stages, casting rigs, and seating

REMEMBER

As a volunteer, you can contribute without having any existing event-management or technical skills. Volunteering is a great way to start learning about what's involved in handling esports events. After you establish a specific set of skills, you become even more valuable as a volunteer and can become a key part of your local scene, which could, in turn, lead to paid work. It could also just make you someone whom everyone in your esports community knows, which is also pretty cool, plus it can help you to find opportunities to enjoy the esports world!

Interning to develop a deeper skill set

As a new industry, esports needs more people power than it currently has. If you're interested in working for a prolonged period with an organization or team, you may be able to find a position as an intern, and internships almost always lead to job opportunities at the end of the stint if you do well.

Internships can exist at every level of an organization, and the duties an intern might be responsible for are similar to the list offered in the previous section for volunteers. The difference between an intern and a volunteer is that an intern wouldn't work for only a one-off event. Interns stay with the organization for a certain period of time that the parties agree to before the internship starts.

An intern is like an apprentice. In esports, the point of an intern is to learn and develop skills over the course of numerous events. For example, the varsity team I direct has a team of interns that we hire at the start of each school year for a nine-month period (from the start of school until the end of that school year). During that period, most interns go from being new to their duties to being ready to move to another organization and handle whatever they worked on for our team. For example, one of our former student analysts, Haitham Algbory, spent two years as a student analyst and assistant coach for our *League of Legends* team. He now works as the assistant coach for Team SoloMid's (TSM) League Championship Series (LCS) team. He credits his experience with us with getting him the job, but in truth, he's an amazing talent who just needed a chance to show what he could do. That's how internships work. They offer you a way in and a means to show what you can do.

In addition to the items mentioned in the previous section, interns often handle the following duties for teams and organizations under the supervision of a mentor:

>> **Social media presence:** Almost every team and esports organization needs more social media content. In most cases, younger people who are new to the scene are much better with social media than some of us (like me). Social media internships offer a great way for a young person to break into the esports world.

>> **Analytics:** Most teams have coaches, and coaches have assistants whom most people refer to as "analysts." An analyst's job is to watch the team play, scout upcoming opponents, and help with video review, among other tasks. Interning as an analyst is a great opportunity for someone who knows a game really, really well. It could also open the door to a potential career in coaching.

>> **Media production:** Organizations usually don't have photographers and videographers at events, and even when they do, players rarely have time to go through their streams and pick all the best clips. Having an intern who possesses camera and editing skills take the time to create photos and videos is important to publicity, and smaller teams (particularly high schools and colleges) rarely have a full-time employee to handle those duties.

>> **Webmasters and content creators:** Large teams have a number of people on staff to handle webmaster duties and content creation, but smaller teams often look to interns to handle these tasks. College teams, in particular, often need to find someone willing to do this work as an intern to avoid having their team page added into a university page and lost stylistically in the university's default template.

Paying the Bills: Jobs in Esports

Although the realm of esports abounds with volunteer and internship possibilities, those opportunities won't help you pay the bills. Fortunately, an ecosystem as large as esports provides plenty of paying jobs for people with the right skills. Some of those jobs might even surprise you.

At BlizzCon 2018, thanks to a friend in the industry, I was given a full tour behind the scenes and had the chance to check out the production team for the event. The *Overwatch* World Cup was happening at that BlizzCon, and the production team for that event was operating outside the arena in two trucks as big as the trucks needed for a major football broadcast.

Another team of four or five people ran the video feed to the big screens inside the arena. A team of five or six ran the broadcasting desk, and tens if not hundreds of employees were spread out around the arena. BlizzCon 2019 employed 33 in-game observers, 26 editors, and 48 camera people who were involved in getting the video feed to the broadcasters (per `https://www.sportsvideo.org/2019/11/01/blizzcon-2019-as-esports-presence-grows-so-too-does-size-of-blizzard-entertainments-production/`). In other words, many, many people work in paying jobs at these large events.

More interesting still is the skill gap that currently exists. There are directors who understand how to handle broadcast sports, and there are players or former players with expert level understanding of esports games, but few people possess knowledge of both areas. Those who have the broadcast training and are well-schooled in the games are highly desirable and receive multiple job offers at any given time.

Table 13-1 presents a list of potential jobs in esports along with the skills needed to do the job. Although some of these jobs require a college degree (see Chapter 11 to find out how esports can help you go to college), some of them are based on skills that you can build without needing to go to college.

TABLE 13-1   **Major Esports Jobs**

Job	Skills Needed	Requires College?
Analyst	Mastery of game meta, good communication skills, high level of organization (for data)	No degree needed
Coach (team)	Game experience and good understanding of the meta (can lean on analysts as needed), good leadership skills, discipline, some experience managing people	No degree needed
Coach (individual)	Should have analyst-level game skills and good communication skills; must be a self-starter (coaching people one-on-one requires the ability to multitask and to schedule)	No degree needed
Team Manager	Administrative skills (for handling money, scheduling, booking travel, making sure supplies are on hand, and other tasks)	No degree needed
Social Media Manager	Expert skills with all social media platforms; writing and verbal communication skills; good understanding of the game(s) your organization plays	No specific degree needed, but marketing majors and English majors excel at this position
Public Relations Director	An understanding of branding, communication, and external relations	Degrees in PR, marketing, management, or communication fit the required skill set best
Tournament Organizer	Event planning, understanding of game metas, understanding of tournament formats (brackets, platforms like Challonge.com, and so on), mastery of competition rules	No degree required, but many TOs have trained in Sports Management
Broadcast Director	Understanding of broadcasting and media content creation	No degree required, but a degree in broadcasting, mass communication, or communication arts is highly beneficial (or experience working in television)
Videographer	Filming and capturing media	No degree required, but a degree in broadcasting or film is useful
Video Editor	Similar skills to videographer and broadcast director, but with a focus on manipulating the video after capture	No degree required, but a degree in broadcasting or film is helpful, and game knowledge is extremely helpful at this level as well
Caster (a broadcaster or "shoutcaster")	Elite level of understanding of game meta and mechanics; has done vocal training or has a good voice; the ability to think quickly and react	No degree required, but communications and English majors do well in these positions, as do former professional players and people with experience in front of a camera or on the radio (or podcasting)
Streamer	The same skills as a caster plus the ability to play a game or games well; also requires having a personal brand	No degree required, but experience with media design or broadcast is helpful

In addition to the jobs described in Table 13-1, a large network of people is involved in selling and supporting hardware and software as well as providing peripherals. In the past few years as well, a number of jobs have started to materialize in advertising through esports in what are called non-endemic brands, or brands that aren't related to esports, like McDonald's or Geico, who often need consultants and sometimes even new staff members to help their companies strategize how to enter the esports space.

Plotting the Path to an Esports Job

If you'd like to work in esports as something other than a professional player, the path in is to figure out what you think you might want to do and then:

>> **Look for local places to volunteer.** Try whatever you want to do without investing much in it before you move forward.

>> **If you liked volunteering, look for an internship.** An internship gives you a way to get more experience and start getting to know people in the field. The best way to find internships is to monitor the social media of teams and organizations that you know need the skill you want to provide. Also, as bold as this might seem, don't be afraid to ask whether an organization needs someone. Most esports organizations don't have an intern manager, for example, so they might not realize that they need an intern until you express interest in being one.

>> **If you will need a degree for the job, look at colleges.** Chapter 11 of this book tells you about collegiate esports programs. If you know that you want to have a career in esports, make sure that you go to a college with a program and, before you accept an offer for admission, ask whether you can work with the team.

>> **Get yourself out there.** Look at Chapter 10 for information about how to establish yourself on social media and in game spaces, and take advantage of social media to show off your developing skills. Be creative, but be persistent and vocal, too. Show people what you can do. Assemble highlight reels or examples of your work.

>> **Make connections and keep active in the esports world.** Go to events. Volunteer when you can. Interacting with people and making your presence known is a key part of esports longevity.

>> **Look for job openings.** If you see that an organization is hiring, apply. After you've gained experience from following the preceding recommendations, you'll be a quality candidate.

>> **Work your personal network.** Let people know that you're looking for work. Don't be obnoxious about it, but make sure that the people you meet along the way know.

REMEMBER

With the massive growth in esports, this is a rare time in history for you to safely assume that if you have dedication and flexibility, you are likely to find a job in the industry if you want. The real trick is to determine what you're best at and how to transform that into a career!

Chapter **14**

Creating a Brand for Streaming

Short of becoming a high-profile professional player, the most surefire way to get involved in esports quickly, and to find places to make money for your efforts is through streaming and creating video content. If you purchase or build an esports gaming PC similar to the ones discussed in Chapter 2 of this book, you need to make only a few additions to be up and actively streaming in no time.

This chapter tells you about the key streaming services, how to set up your own hardware and software for streaming, and some of the basics for branding and creating an identity for yourself as a streamer. Remember as you read that the idea of streaming is to share yourself and your enjoyment of gaming, so don't think that you need to do everything listed here right away (or ever).

Understanding Your Equipment Needs

When it comes to streaming, the most important element to your overall presentation is the quality of your source material. Playing well and being charismatic are important, to be sure, but how entertaining or engaging your stream is won't matter if your video quality is bad, your sound is muddy, and you are uploading at a speed that causes your stream to hiccup and time out. This section sets you on the path to getting all the right equipment for streaming success. That starts with a camera.

Finding the right camera

Casual streamers often run streams with a built-in camera from a laptop or with a relatively cheap webcam. If you're just looking to dabble and test your feet in streaming, you can get by with any webcam that captures video. If you're serious about streaming, however, you don't want to stick with a cheap camera for too long because the quality of the input will turn off viewers.

The best bet for someone starting out streaming is to find a camera that will capture in 1080p, which is at the high end of standard high-definition video. Depending on your upload speed, you might end up broadcasting at a lower resolution, but having the ability to downscale — to move from 1080p to a lower resolution — will result in more crisp video than if you capture at a lower level. You never want to resize smaller video to larger when creating your video output because doing so degrades your image quality.

You can purchase quality webcams that capture at 1080p for $50–$100. The most popular current model is the Logitech C920 Pro HD, which has a suggested retail price of $99 but often runs cheaper. Prices fluctuate, but at any given time, a Google search should yield a vendor selling this model at around $60.

If you're looking for the highest-quality video input, or if you just happen to have a high-quality still camera that you use for other purposes, you can attach any DSLR or mirrorless still camera to your computer via a capture device like the Elgato Cam Link (https://www.elgato.com/en/gaming/cam-link-4k). You can buy the Elgato for around $100. Unless you are looking to produce higher-quality videos in addition to your streaming, however, going over 1080p is essentially overkill. You won't need any higher resolution for streaming or for video sites like YouTube until network speeds significantly increase.

Knowing your bandwidth needs

In the previous section, I suggest using a webcam or camera that allows streaming in 1080p. Be aware, however, that streaming like this requires significant upload bandwidth, and if you don't have sufficient bandwidth, you will have to lower your graphical resolution (making your video more blurry) and won't be able to broadcast as many frames per second, thereby making your video animation look "choppy." The biggest difference in the quality of your video playback comes from maintaining 60 frames per second (fps). The difference between 60 fps and 30 fps is such that no rating is given for 1080p at 30 fps because it would require the same bandwidth as streaming 60 fps at 720p would take. The loss of those frames would make the 1080p at 30 fps so much less desirable in spite of the extra resolution that no one would choose 1080p at 30 fps over 720p at 60 fps. In short, the number of frames is more important than overall resolution because the frames result in smoother animation.

Table 14-1 gives you a sense of the upload bandwidth you need for various streaming video resolutions.

TABLE 14-1   **Upload Speeds Needed for Streaming***

Resolution	Frames per Second	Upload Speed Needed
320 x 240 pixels (low quality)	30	200 kbps
740 x 480 (480p-standard TV resolution)	30	350 kbps
720p (1280 x720)	30	3000 kbps
720p (1280 x 720)	60	4500 kbps
1080p (1920 x 1080)	60	6000 kbps

*https://stream.twitch.tv/encoding/ and https://support.streamspot.com/hc/en-us/articles/215567677-How-fast-does-my-Internet-need-to-be-to-stream-

TECHNICAL STUFF

For broadband Internet (cable, DSL, or fiber), the Federal Communications Commission dictates that your upload speed must be at least 3,000 kbps. That should mean that streaming at 720p, 30 fps is possible. In most cases, you will have significantly higher upload speeds with commercial broadband. You cannot simply trust the numbers listed on your Internet plan, however, because those aren't always accurate. You can determine your home Internet speed by going to www.speedtest.net and running a test. (Just click the Go button in the middle of the screen.) Running on a basic Xfinity cable package, in the middle of a Saturday afternoon, my home office upload speed is 18,000 kbps, which far exceeds the required bandwidth for 1080p at 60 fps.

Listening for the right microphone

Microphones for streaming depend largely on the desires of the streamer. If you picked up a high-quality headset like those discussed in the peripherals section of Chapter 2, and you aren't opposed to appearing on-stream with a headset on your head, a good headset will suffice. I teach online classes using the SteelSeries Arctis headset that I also use while gaming, and the sound quality is comparable to when I use an external microphone.

You might not always want to have your headset on while streaming. Perhaps you need to move in ways that cause your headset microphone to bump against objects or slide out of position. Or you might find the attached microphone to be a problem in some way. Fortunately, you have multiple options for external microphones that can give you great sound without breaking the bank.

One of the most popular microphones among streamers, and among podcasters, is the Blue Yeti (`https://www.bluedesigns.com/products/yeti/`). Available for around $100, the Yeti is a quality microphone that runs directly through a USB port. This feature is important because most condenser microphones (which get superior sound reproduction) require some sort of pre-amplifier or other external power. The Yeti takes care of these issues through the USB port, which makes the device plug-and-play.

You can obviously look into more expensive microphones to get even better sound quality, but unless you are planning to include musical performance (vocal or instrumental) as a part of your stream, you are unlikely to need anything more powerful than the Yeti for streaming purposes.

Setting Up to Stream

To be an active streamer, you need to know and work with three sites: Twitch, YouTube Gaming, and the newest streaming site, Microsoft's Mixer. Chapter 10 provides directions for setting up accounts with Twitch and YouTube. In this section, you see how to set up an account at Mixer and how to gather the information you need from Twitch and YouTube so that you can get started streaming to your audience.

Obtaining a Mixer account

Chapter 10 tells you how to set up accounts at Twitch and YouTube. Added to the mix now is Microsoft's streaming site, Mixer. (See what I did there? Mix — Mixer. com?) The setup process at Mixer is similar to Twitch, but Mixer also sets you up to stream as you create your account. Here are the steps to sign up to use Mixer:

1. **Go to** `www.mixer.com` **and click Sign In at the top right.**

2. **On the screen that appears, select to sign in with your Microsoft account if you have one.**

   If you don't have a Microsoft account, click Create One.

3. **If you have a Microsoft account (perhaps through an Xbox or from playing a Microsoft game online), skip to Step 4.**

   If you don't have a Microsoft account, go back to Chapter 9 for information about getting directions in the section about connecting your console accounts. The same Microsoft account that you use for Xbox Live will control your Mixer account.

4. **On the main Mixer.com page, click the icon inside a circle in the upper right.**

   A new screen opens.

5. **Scroll down to the Broadcast Dashboard entry on the menu and click it.**

6. **On the next screen, read the paragraph above the Get Started button that's midway down the left column; then click Get Started.**

   A new screen opens and begins a series of videos that orient you to how Mixer works and what the rules are.

7. **(Mandatory) Watch each video and click the Next Step button at the bottom when a video completes.**

8. **On the next screen, click the blue Request Your Stream Key button to request your stream key.**

   I explain stream keys in the following section of this chapter, "Gathering your stream keys."

   Clicking this button triggers a review process, and Mixer takes about a day to send your key to you. At this point, you need to stop and wait for your stream key. I recommend leaving that browser window open so that you can go back later, or if you want to power down your computer, bookmark the site in your browser.

   When your account is ready, you can copy your stream key from the page located at Broadcast on the menu at the top right of the Mixer screen that you used to get started in the list above. If you just completed the preceding steps, you might currently have a timer onscreen telling you how long it will be until your key is available. Go back when that timer reads 00. Copy that code. As I say elsewhere, I recommend creating a file with all your stream keys for easy access.

9. **After copying your stream key (you'll need it later), click the Next button.**

10. **Read the Streamer's Pledge and click the Accept button at the bottom of the screen if you agree.**

11. **Click the Finish button.**

    Clicking this button returns you to your Mixer dashboard.

Gathering your stream keys

After you have your accounts set up at each site, you need to collect a set of codes called *stream keys*. Think of your stream key as a pregenerated password that indicates where your account is and gives external software (like OBS, which you can read about shortly) permission to access your page on the streaming service. The stream key is what enables you to broadcast live content.

If you opened a Mixer account, as described in the "Obtaining a Mixer account," earlier in this chapter, you either have that stream key or are awaiting it. Now you need to get your keys from the other major streaming sites, Twitch.tv and YouTube.

REMEMBER

All three of these major streaming sites frequently update their user interfaces, so this book's instructions for obtaining their stream keys might not lead you directly to what you need by the time you're reading this. In such a case, you can find the new location of your stream key by typing **stream key** into the help system on any of these three sites.

Getting your Twitch.tv stream key

If you have a Twitch.tv account set up, you're ready to get your stream key for that site. If you don't yet have an account, you can find out how to set one up in Chapter 10.

To obtain your Twitch stream key, follow these steps:

1. **Go to twitch.tv and click Login or your profile picture in the upper-right corner to log in.**

   A pop-up window appears in which you can enter your username and password. If you're already logged in, a menu appears below the profile picture.

2. **Navigate the menu below your profile picture, scroll down to Creator Dashboard, and click Creator Dashboard.**

   On the screen that appears, you see the Dashboard menu on the right.

3. **Click Channel under Settings near the bottom of the menu.**

   On the screen that opens, you see the heading Stream Key and Preferences. The first entry is your stream key for Twitch. Copy it and save it to your file of stream keys. Make sure that you're specifying which keys are for which sites on your list! You can now close the window.

Getting your YouTube stream key

If you have a YouTube account set up, you're ready to get your stream key for that site. If you don't yet have an account, you can find out how to set one up in Chapter 10.

To get your YouTube stream key, follow these steps:

1. **Go to YouTube.com and click the Login button in the upper right of the screen.**

If you're already logged in, your profile picture appears there instead.

2. **On the screen that opens, click your profile picture in the top-right of the screen and then, in the menu that appears, select YouTube Studio (see Figure 14-1).**

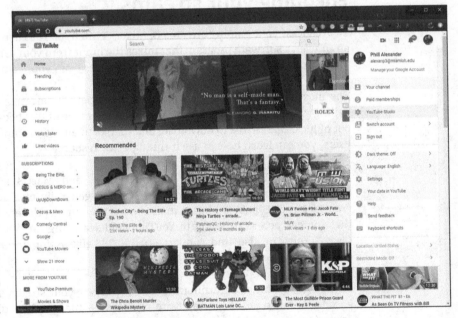

FIGURE 14-1:
Locating the
YouTube Studio
page from the
User menu.

3. **Click the image of a red circle with black arcs radiating from it (a broadcast symbol) that appears just below your profile picture.**

If this is your first time looking at live streaming on YouTube, you will have a 24-hour wait, similar to the one on Mixer.

4. **When your account is ready, click the broadcast symbol just under your profile picture to launch the livestream dashboard.**

5. **Near the top of the screen, you see three options: Webcam, Stream, and Manage. Click Stream.**

6. **Give your stream a name in the blank at the top of the next screen. Also select the radio box next to Yes, It's Made for Kids or No, It's Not Made for Kids based on whether your content is kid friendly. When finished, click the Create Stream button at the bottom.**

    A pop-up window appears. Next to the number 2 on that list is your stream key. Copy it. You can now close this window.

With your stream keys in hand, you're ready to set up an encoder on your machine where you can mix the input from your camera and your games along with any other graphics or audio you might wish to offer.

Encoding your streams

To broadcast your gaming streams to Mixer, Twitch, or YouTube, you need to use an *encoder*, a software program that mixes the input from your camera and microphone as well as your games, sound, and pictures from your computer itself.

The most common choice for an encoder is Open Broadcaster Software (OBS). Telling you how to use an encoder is beyond the scope of this book, but you're not out of luck. OBS is free to download, and thanks to an active community of expert users, you can learn how to use it through free resources.

You can download OBS for Windows, Linux, and MacOS at https://www.obsproject.com. In addition, master user and generally nice guy Adam Taylor (YouTube user EsposVox) has compiled a lengthy, in-depth set of video tutorials that you can access by going to YouTube and searching for "OBS Studio Master Class." You can also find support on the OBS discussion forums at https://obsproject.com/forum/.

There will be a bit of a learning curve as you create your stream setup within the encoder because you need to create overlays — the graphics that are situated around your gameplay window, your camera window, and any other information or imagery you choose to use. The number of graphics you want or need depends on the game you choose to stream, but if you want to be taken seriously as a streamer, you need to do more than just stream your face on camera or yourself playing a game. I give you some ideas about what to include in your stream in the following "Mastering your layout" section.

Mastering your layout

The *layout* is the arrangement of items being displayed onscreen, and esports streamers have basic layout standards that they attempt to maintain. To see an example of a layout, take a look at Figure 14-2, which shows a stream of the Miami University varsity esports team playing *League of Legends.* As you can see, the majority of the screen is devoted to the game itself. Insets show the team names next to each score, and statistical blocks help the viewer follow the action, but the overlay additions are minimal. *LoL* streamers tend to keep their additional graphics small and few so that the viewer can see the game being played. Most solo streamers also include a webcam in one of the four corners of the screen so that the viewer can see the player. In a five-versus-five match, having ten of those windows would greatly detract from the ability to follow the action.

FIGURE 14-2: Streaming a *League of Legends* game with five players on each team.

Figure 14-3 shows a clip from a streamed Tespa *Hearthstone* match. A casual first look might leave you with the impression that this stream is highly similar to the *LoL* stream shown in Figure 14-2, but they differ in several key ways. First, the left third of the screen is devoted to nongame match graphics. You can see the logo of the tournament organizers in the center, and to the top and bottom are video feeds of the teams playing. The team images display the number of victories (currently zero for each) and the class of their *Hearthstone* decks. (You can read all about classes in *Hearthstone* in Chapter 8.) The rest of the screen shows the entire game board, but because this feed comes from the tournament organizer, the display includes an inset at the top showing the opponent's cards so that the audience can follow along. Because *Hearthstone* happens in such a small space compared to a game like *LoL*, in which players could be anywhere on a huge map, the smaller play space works here, and the ability to see the competitors adds to the viewers' enjoyment.

FIGURE 14-3:
Streaming a team
Hearthstone
game.

For your streaming display to look professional, you need to include the following elements. You can hire someone to create these elements through the website Fiverr (`www.fiverr.com`) or Upwork (`www.upwork.com`) by searching for **Streaming Overlays** or **Streaming Kits**.

>> **Background:** You need a background or set of background images to use as a base when you use multiple windows so that you don't leave blank space. The background is also useful for intervals between action, such as for a "Stream Starting Soon" screen. I recommend that you use a high-resolution still image that doesn't have any intricate details that could clash with the elements you place over it. You could even use a solid color or gradient.

>> **Theme:** Choose a theme for how you will handle framing or decorating the various elements. For example, you want something to surround your video camera image so that it isn't just a rectangle sitting on top of whatever else is onscreen. See Figure 14-4 for an example of a frame around a camera window.

>> **Color scheme:** Choose a color scheme and font (or fonts — but never use more than two different fonts — okay, maybe a third one as well, if used sparingly) for creating any onscreen text you want or need. This will include buttons that you might place on your Mixer, Twitch, or YouTube account pages. I go into more detail about colors in fonts in the section "Working with colors and fonts," later in this chapter.

>> **Logo:** Choose a key graphic to use as a logo, a thumbnail, or both. (See Chapter 10 for a discussion about crafting or purchasing a logo or getting a professional headshot taken.)

>> **Game logos:** You need clean images of the logos for any games you plan to play or organizations you plan to stream through. You should look for high-resolution PNG files of these logos with no backgrounds so that you can place them anywhere you might need them.

Your initial stream "scenes," or the collections of images and video inputs that you assemble like those shown previously in Figures 14-2 and 14-3, will likely be minimal. That's okay; it's a learning process. You want to keep four ideas about your stream in mind, though:

>> **Keep it simple.** More often than not, the biggest problem that new streamers have is trying to put too much information on the screen at one time. Think about how the viewers see the screen. Ask a few friends if your layout looks too busy when you first start streaming. Always lean toward having less on the screen at any given time.

>> **Keep the image and sound quality high.** Make sure that you're using high-resolution images and video input, and light yourself well while using your video camera. Likewise, don't use music that makes hearing your voice too difficult, and set the audio levels on your games high enough for people to hear the game while also being able to hear and understand you.

>> **Be consistent with your "brand."** Viewers will think of your stream the same way they might a television program. As you move from game to game or from topic to topic, give your layouts and screens the same basic style and colors. Viewers should never feel like they have changed channels.

>> **Make your design match your tone.** The style of your design work should be consistent with the tone of your streaming and should match the style to your chosen game. If you're trying to be funny and entertain with humor, your graphics, colors, and fonts should reflect that, though I recommend never, ever using Comic Sans. You can choose among numerous playful fonts with soft edges that will serve you well if you're going for a humorous look, like the font Slugfest (`https://www.1001fonts.com/fun-fonts.html`). If you're trying to be ultra-competitive and serious, you should likewise have serious graphics and fonts. The standby font Helvetica is a great choice because of its clean lines and neutral styling. Figure 14-5 shows an example of a stream logo using three different fonts to give a humorous feel, a serious feel, or a game-centric feel for a stream. The serious font is Arial; the fun font is called CC Jim Lee and is free for use from DaFont (`www.dafont.com`); and the game-styled font that mimics Pac-Man is called Crack Man and is free for use from Fontsc (`https://www.fontsc.com/font/crackman`).

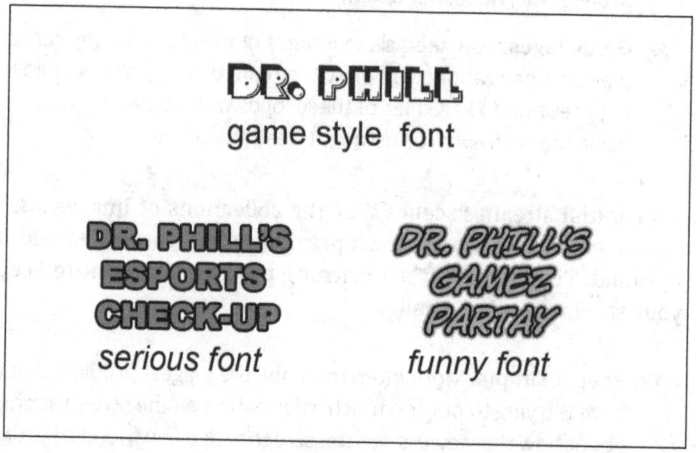

DR. PHILL
game style font

DR. PHILL'S
ESPORTS
CHECK-UP
serious font

DR. PHILL'S
GAMEZ
PARTAY
funny font

FIGURE 14-5:
Fun text,
game-styled text,
and serious text
examples.

The ultimate goal of your streaming is to produce the sort of quality content that results in a healthy and growing viewer base. The path to quality content is paved with careful consideration given to yourself and your audience.

Establishing a Theme for Your Stream

After you've assembled your various accounts, set up an encoder, and thought about how you want to present your content, the next step is to make decisions about your "brand" — that is, specifically what you plan to produce and what your streams and social media profiles will look like. To figure out the best way to present yourself, you want to think carefully about the audience you want to attract.

TIP

Don't make the mistake of thinking, "My stream is for everyone!" Although you might create a stream that could appeal to a wide audience, part of the process of focusing your branding and overall streaming plan involves picking a specific audience to serve as your primary user. For example, *Hearthstone* streamer Firebat narrows his audience to *Hearthstone* fans and players, which he further narrows by talking about competitive decks that are standard for competition, offering the sort of detail that someone trying to learn to construct and play those decks would need. Although his stream might still be appealing to someone who isn't a competitive *Hearthstone* player, Firebat creates content with that competitive player fan base in mind.

Sorting through potential stream themes

You can choose among a number of tried-and-true themes adopted by other streamers to use as a basis for your own streaming endeavors. You might even combine a couple of themes, or use them as models to brainstorm your own original contribution. Table 14-2 presents the style or theme of some of the most frequently viewed streams.

FREQUENCY VERSUS QUALITY

How quickly you build an audience and develop your skills will depend partly on how often you stream, but the most important factor by far in building a reputation in the community is the quality of what you stream. Presenting two or three excellent hours a week will take you much further than 20 hours of haphazard and low-quality streaming. Scale your streaming activity to your available time and desired commitment. Exhausting or overloading yourself won't benefit you. You need to find your own balance and stick with what works for you. Remember: There's no one right answer to how much to stream!

TABLE 14-2   Themes for Streaming

Focus	Activities	Example
Competitive play of a single game title	Sharing expertise; documenting as you climb the ranking ladder; documenting a team's matches	*League of Legends* pro Faker `https://www.twitch.tv/faker)`
Play a single game without being particularly competitive	Taking on random opponents; telling stories as you play; talking about the game (lore, current news, the professional scene) as you play	Ninja (`http://mixer.com/ninja`)
Be a "variety streamer" who plays multiple games	Offering game opinions and reviews; building your persona and then applying it across different game titles (in other words, selling "you"); moving from a set game that you play most days to having a day or two a week when you play something brand new to show a different side of your gaming personality	SodaPoppin' (`https://www.twitch.tv/sodapoppin/`)
Play a character while streaming	Often comical; can be based on game lore; sometimes is based on subverting the game (for example, playing *Grand Theft Auto* but doing only the taxi, firetruck, or police car side missions while role-playing as if that were your job)	Dr. Disrespect (`https://www.twitch.tv/drdisrespect`)
Create a "show"	Report news or interview other players (not focused on gameplay)	The Game Grumps (`https://www.twitch.tv/gamegrumps`)

If you choose to follow one of the themes described in this section, you should set a schedule for your sessions, which will clarify what you should do with each streaming session based on your goals.

Working with colors and fonts

In Chapter 10, I recommend that you choose a gaming name to use consistently in all your gaming and streaming spaces (including social media). Likewise, I recommend that you adopt a logo or have a professional headshot photo taken to use in all your online spaces. Having a logo or professional photo is an important aspect of establishing your brand as a streamer and esports professional.

Another aspect of making all your online spaces and stream elements look professional and draw an audience is to choose a color palette and a set of fonts to use across all your public sites (from Twitter to Twitch).

Figuring out your fonts

Sometimes people aren't as careful with fonts as they should be, but choosing your fonts well will help you stand out from the pack. You can find a wealth of information about fonts, including articles like this one on web fonts from Dummies.com (`https://www.dummies.com/web-design-development/site-development/how-to-choose-fonts-for-your-website/`).

Choose fonts that suit the personality and theme of your stream. To keep your display from being distracting and looking amateurish, limit yourself to two different fonts, or three at the absolute maximum. You want to have the following kinds of fonts (see Figure 14-6 for examples):

» **Styled for large items:** Use a styled font for big text items (like buttons), headings on larger blocks of text, and anything that is highly decorative. A good choice would be a font with unique-looking letters or that matches well with the game you've chosen to play. A good example of a styled font is The Wild Breath of Zelda (`https://www.dafont.com/the-wild-breath-of-zelda.font`), which is font styled after *The Legend of Zelda: Breath of the Wild's* logo.

» **Standard for main text:** Use a standard, sans serif font for all the main text in your display. San serif means that it has no decorative feet or edges, such as Arial or Helvetica. A san serif font is more readable than a serif font, especially online.

» **Decorative (optional, and to be used sparingly):** If you want to add additional flair, you might use a decorative font for keywords or specific items such as captions. A good example of making a font decorative is to switch your standard font to bold and italic so that the text stands out. You can also select a similar but slightly different font to do this same sort of work. The key is to not use decoration in standard text too often because you want the decorative element to draw attention to key ideas.

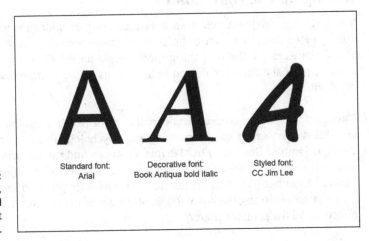

Standard font:
Arial

Decorative font:
Book Antiqua bold italic

Styled font:
CC Jim Lee

FIGURE 14-6:
A standard, decorative, and styled font choice.

Your primary styled font — that is, the one you choose for large items — needs to convey something specific about your stream and about you. For example, if you want to stream *Overwatch*, your style font should probably be something that looks high tech and angular, like the free font Hyper Helix (found at `https://www.dafont.com/hyper-helix.font`).

Another option for your primary stylish font is to tie it directly to your gamer tag. If your tag was, for example, MilkMan, you might want to go with a font like Chocolate Drink (`https://www.dafont.com/chocolate-drink.font`).

Note that some of the fonts you find online will not be free. There is some gray area concerning whether a small-scale stream is considered commercial, but if you choose to use a font that is not free for commercial use, it's a good idea to pay the money to get a license. Plenty of fonts are actually free, too. You just have to read carefully to make sure you understand how and where you can use a font.

REMEMBER

Readability matters! Although some fonts may look awesome, you don't want something so stylized that reading the text is difficult.

Likewise, your standard font should be crisp and clean. Almost anything from the Google Fonts Sans Serif collection (`https://fonts.google.com/?category=Sans+Serif`) will work well. Try to select one that matches well with your styled font.

Your computer likely has numerous fonts preinstalled, but you can find free fonts online at a number of sites, including free-for-use Google Fonts (`https://fonts.google.com/`) and DaFont.com, which includes both free and purchasable fonts.

Mixing up the right colors

The last major element you need before creating graphics for your stream is a color palette. Color can make or break your stream because the color aspects of the visual elements are the first thing most people notice. Choosing colors is also a highly personal element of design because your colors communicate what you're all about.

This section takes an ever-so-basic look at color psychology. Table 14-3 offers a simplified overview of sports-related color psychology from an article published through Samford University in Alabama. (You can find the full article at `https://www.samford.edu/sports-analytics/fans/2017/Wear-Red-and-Youll-Win-Gold`.) Although the article relates to uniforms for physical sports and focuses on research regarding the color red, it offers some insight into the psychological effects of all the primary colors.

TABLE 14-3

Meanings of Primary Colors in Sports

Color	Means	Could Also Mean
Green	Balance, support	Nature
Red	Stamina, vitality	Fire
Blue	Stability, calmness	Water/ice
Yellow	Fun	Light (sun, lightning)
Orange	Productivity	Caution
Violet	Imagination, art	Royalty

You may notice that black, white, and gray are not included here. Logos often include black and white because they work as neutral colors, and the same is true of most visual online layouts. Each of those shades has a meaning, but unless you make one of them your dominant color, their meanings as accents don't overpower the other colors you choose.

Another important aspect of color in design is that opposites on the color wheel create the most obvious and pleasing contrast. So, for example, you often see blue paired with orange, green with red, and yellow with violet.

People make entire careers of developing color palettes and creating effective designs, but you don't have to have years of experience to create an effective design for your stream. The following tips can help combine color choices that will work well for your needs.

>> **Pick a primary color based on your streaming identity.** Look at Table 14-3 and the above to give you a general sense of what might be your best "main" color and consider the following:

- **Colors that make sense with your gamer tag.** If your tag is GreenRanger, for example, you might want green.

- **Colors that make sense for the game you play.** *Overwatch*, for example, is associated with orange and black, so maybe you want to go with the bright orange that is on so much *Overwatch* material.

- **Your favorite color.** I use blue in my branding. I've always used blue, all the way back to my time in high school. I picked it back then because it was my favorite color.

>> **After you choose a primary color, play with shades of it.** I mentioned that I use blue. There are hundreds of shades of blue whose differences range subtle to major. The Carolina blue used by the *Carolina Panthers* NFL franchise, for example, is wildly different from standard navy blue. Find the perfect shade for what you want to portray about yourself and your stream.

>> **Look at logos that use that color.** Color theory can be difficult, but you can find numerous examples of major sports teams and corporations that have done this work already. If you go to Google Images (https://images. google.com/) and type **green logo**, you see thousands of examples of logos with a variety of shades of green. Companies like John Deere, Land Rover, and Starbucks have spent big money figuring out how to pair the green in their logos with other colors and shades. Scroll through the many examples for inspiration.

>> **Look to nature.** This suggestion might seem a little strange as a design inspiration, but nothing is better at putting colors together in ways that the human eye finds pleasing than nature, and you might find inspiration from the natural world. Look at photos of birds, flowers, fish, insects, foliage, and so on and sample colors from them. If you select colors that appear in nature together, they will almost always appear complementary; the very fact that they appear together in nature makes our minds recognize the relationship.

>> **Use online tools.** After you have nailed down your primary color or colors, use online tools to develop a palette. Here are some available tools:

- colormind.io uses machine learning to match colors. Input your primary color or colors to the site and let it suggest palettes to you.

- canva.com pulls a color palette from a photo (especially useful for when you are sampling colors from nature).

- paletton.com allows you to select one color and then see how it compares to various relationships based on color opposition or harmony (like monochromatic, dichromatic, and the like).

Equipped with your theme, fonts, colors, with your encoder set up and with your stream keys handy, you're ready to start streaming.

REMEMBER

Although the idea is to create a great stream, streaming should be fun! Don't stress out if you feel things don't go perfectly from the start for you, and don't treat it like drudgery. Enjoy what you're doing, and tinker with all the ideas suggested here. Also remember that you can hire people to help with designing graphic assets through sites like fiverr.com and Upwork.com. Have fun putting your content out there!

5 The Part of Tens

Discover ten esports games everyone should know.

Take a look at several esports games you might have missed.

Get to know some key esports influencers.

Chapter **15**

The Ten Games Every Esports Player Should Know

This book means to offer you an overview of the competitive esports land-scape. If you want to get up-to-speed a quickly as possible, though, you can use this chapter to get a quick rundown of the most important esports games. A description of every game here appears in other sections of the book, where you can find additional details on its genre or competitive scene.

Counter Strike: Global Offensive

Released: August 21, 2012

Publisher: Valve Corporation

Platform(s): PC (primary), Mac, Xbox 360, PlayStation 3

Available from: Steam (www.store.steampowered.com) or console online stores

Counter Strike: Global Offensive (CS:GO) is the tactical first-person shooter (FPS) with the longest current life. It has been in regular competition for so long that the generation of consoles it was released for has been replaced, though Valve has to this point not made the game available on the Xbox One or PS4.

In CS:GO, players compete in teams of five, either as terrorists or counter-terrorists. The goal is to defeat the opponent by achieving a goal (typically defending or diffusing a bomb or defending and reclaiming hostages). The combat is meant to be as realistic as possible, and gameplay focuses on team coordination so that advances or defensive stands are made in coordination. A player going "rogue" usually means defeat.

CS:GO gained its greatest exposure through play in ELEAGUE, with regular matches televised on basic cable network TBS in 2018 and 2019. Valve, the game's developer, sponsors two major championships every year, each with a $1 million prize pool. Numerous minor events and other tournaments are hosted by organizers such as ESL and RFRSH Entertainment's BLAST brand.

You can find more information on CS:GO in Chapter 4. CS:GO is now free to play.

Dota 2

Released: July 9, 2013

Publisher: Valve Corporation

Platform(s): PC (primary), Mac

Available from: Steam (www.store.steampowered.com)

The Multiplayer Online Battle Arena (MOBA) genre was born in a *Warcraft III* mod called *Defense of the Ancients (DotA)*. *Dota 2*, Valve's MOBA, was created by a team that included *DotA*'s last online curator, a developer known only as IceFrog. It is believed that IceFrog himself is still the one and only person to handle balancing the heroes and units in *Dota 2*, though to this day he has still not revealed his real name to the community.

In the MOBA world, *Dota 2* is considered the most complex and interesting title. In terms of popularity, *Dota 2* lags well behind Riot's *League of Legends (LoL)* in the United States, but in many regions *Dota 2* is competitive with — and even, in some cases, more popular than — *LoL*. MOBA masters credit the depth of gameplay and the less clearly structured roles for the game's success.

Dota 2's major annual competition is an event known as The International. Presented by Valve with a prize pool that is at least partially crowdfunded by selling in-game cosmetics and other gamer goodies, The International has had the highest prize pool every year since its inception in 2011 (when it was played using a preview version of the game). The 2019 prize pool for The International was more than $34 million, with Valve providing only $1.6 million of that.

You can find more information on *Dota 2* and the origins of the MOBA genre in Chapter 3. *Dota 2* is free to play.

Fortnite

Released: July 25, 2017

Publisher: Epic Games

Platform(s): PC (primary), Mac, Nintendo Switch, PlayStation 4, Xbox One, iOS, Android

Available from: Epic Games (`www.epicgames.com/fortnite`) or console/device online stores

In July 2019, 16-year-old Kyle "Bugha" Giersdorf won $3 million at the *Fortnite* World Cup. That event capped a two-year period during which *Fortnite* — the most popular battle royale game in the world — saw explosive growth. The game's 1-versus-99 quick-paced matches, in which players build structures and hunt for other players in their attempt to be the sole survivor, offers a sometimes problematic but undeniably popular esports experience.

Fortnite is almost as well known for its cosmetics and dances as it is for its gameplay. From the colorful Loot Llama to dances like the floss, *Fortnite* references are numerous in popular culture and all over the various social media sites.

Fortnite also had a direct impact on the career of the most successful esports influencer in the world, Tyler "Ninja" Blevins. Once the most popular streamer on Twitch.tv with more than 13 million followers, Ninja, in August 2019, exclusively switched to Microsoft's streaming service Mixer. Although Ninja's overall viewership has reduced since the move, his presence gave Mixer just over 3 percent of all streaming audiences in September 2019.

Fortnite's major event is the *Fortnite* World Cup, which had a $30 million prize pool, with $3 million awarded to the winner. Given the success of the event, *Fortnite* will likely become even more prominent on the esports scene in coming years. Epic Games pledged $100 million toward *Fortnite* prize pools during its first year-plus of competition, which includes the World Cup.

For more on the battle royale genre and the problems that 100-player events can cause for esports, as well as for more details about *Fortnite*, check out Chapter 7. *Fortnite* is free to play.

Hearthstone

Released: March 11, 2014

Publisher: Blizzard Entertainment

Platform(s): PC, Mac, iOS, Android

Available from: Blizzard's Battle.net (http://playhearthstone.com) or device app store

A video game that simulates a collectible card game has a certain novelty. By mixing the idea of building decks from collecting cards, opening packs to obtain even more cards, and borrowing the stories and characters from its popular game *World of Warcraft*, Blizzard managed to create a card game that has had significant esports legs.

At the heart of it, *Hearthstone* is a simplified version of something like *Magic: The Gathering* or *Yu-Gi-Oh*. Players start with a basic collection of cards and must build a 30-card "deck" to take into gameplay against other players. The gameplay is slow and requires a mind for strategy.

Hearthstone's major events each year are linked to Blizzard's annual convention, BlizzCon. That event, called the *Hearthstone* Global Finals, is the culminating event in a lengthy *Hearthstone* system, found at www.playhearthstone.com.

Hearthstone was in the news in late 2019 because of the six-month ban of a player named Blitzchung for comments he made about Hong Kong at the end of a live event broadcast. You can read more about that incident, and more about *Hearthstone* in general, in Chapter 8.

Hearthstone is free to play, but to have access to all game content, players must purchase "expansions." Players can also purchase card packs to obtain cards quicker than they would by simply opening the packs they earn in-game. For that reason, most people consider playing competitive *Hearthstone* to be an investment.

League of Legends

Released: October 27, 2009

Publisher: Riot Games

Platform(s): PC, Mac

Available from: www.leagueoflegends.com

The MOBA genre was custom-made by esports fans for esports competition, and the current king of the hill is *League of Legends (LoL)*. The third-person isometric MOBA, built by members of the team who created the original *Defense of the Ancients*, is currently the most popular esport based on viewership. The 2019 *League of Legends* World Championship (*LoL* Worlds) garnered more unique viewers than all other esports events and all traditional sports championship events other than the NFL's Super Bowl. *LoL* Worlds had more viewers than the NBA Finals, the World Series, the Bowl Championship Series championship game, or the last Olympics. *LoL* is a big deal.

LoL's success is often credited to Riot's game design philosophy. Instead of attempting to saturate the market with numerous releases, Riot spent a decade focused primarily on *LoL*, resulting in frequent content updates, quality-of-life improvements, and balance patches. Though the game is free to play, Riot's cosmetic add-ons and other purchases — none of which impacts the ability to win at the game — generated revenue of $2.1 billion in 2017 and $1.4 billion in 2018.

Interestingly, in October 2019, Riot announced a host of new titles, most of which are within the *LoL* universe. Included in the company's upcoming offerings are a mobile MOBA called *Wild Rift*, a fighting game, a collectible card game, and a free-roaming dungeon crawler–style game (with the latter three being based on the *LoL* universe). Riot also announced a squad-based FPS that will be an entirely new IP. How these developments will impact *LoL* remains to be seen, but the addition of their auto battler *Teamfight Tactics* has only meant new players and growth of the player base. You can find more information on *LoL* and the origins of the MOBA genre in Chapter 3.

Overwatch

Released: March 11, 2014

Publisher: Blizzard Entertainment

Platform(s): PC, Mac, iOS, Android

Available from: Blizzard's battle.net (http://www.overwatch.com) or device app store

Overwatch is a First-Person Shooter (FPS) with a focus on heroes that possess diverse character traits and abilities. In some ways, the characters are more like those in a MOBA like *LoL* than of an FPS, but one look at the first-person six-versus-six squad-based combat game will cement your view of the game as an FPS.

Overwatch has a rich competitive base, with a strong collegiate presence through Tespa and a clear-cut path to pro and ladder system. (See Chapter 1 for more about the ladder systems in professional esports and Chapter 4 for more on the *OW* ladder.) The most interesting, and so far the most innovative, aspect of *Overwatch* is that Blizzard founded its own official *Overwatch* League for professional competition, complete with geographically located franchises. You can read much more about the *Overwatch* League in Chapter 4 and Chapter 10.

In November 2019, at Blizzard's annual BlizzCon, the company announced *Overwatch 2*, offering a video trailer that included familiar fan-favorite heroes from the first game. *Overwatch 2* has no official release date as of this writing. Until *Overwatch 2* releases, and perhaps even after the release of the sequel, *Overwatch* is sure to remain among the top esports titles on the scene. You can find more information on *Overwatch* in Chapter 4. The game retails from $29.99 to $59.99 with no additional subscription fees.

Rocket League

Released: July 7, 2015

Publisher: Psyonix

Platform(s): PC, Mac, Nintendo Switch, PlayStation 4, Xbox One

Available from: Rocketleague.com, console app store, or retail stores

Rocket League (RL) is a fascinating game. Describing it makes it seem so simple, but seeing it in action shows its complexity. *RL* is soccer, but instead of players, the game involves rocket-powered cars that can drive up walls and soar through the sky. The resulting gameplay is a mix of a racing game, a soccer game, and an advanced trick-based physics engine in the spirit of a game like *Tony Hawk Pro Skater*.

Along with its genre-bending nature — is it a sports game or a car game? — *RL* is also one of the few top-tier esports to come from a relatively small developer, San Diego's Psyonix. The designers often joke that *RL* is living a charmed second life after its brief early release as *Supersonic Acrobatic Rocket-Powered Battle Cars* in 2008 on PlayStation 3.

RL has a particularly competitive collegiate scene, with Psyonix running a successful annual *Rocket League* Collegiate National Championship. You can find more information on *RL* esports at www.rocketleagueesports.com. Also, Chapter 6 provides more details about *RL*. The game retails for $29.99 ($19.99 digital download) with no additional subscription fees.

StarCraft II

Released: July 27, 2010

Publisher: Blizzard Entertainment

Platform(s): PC, Mac

Available from: Blizzard's battle.net (http://starcraft2.com) or device app store

StarCraft II (SCII) is a game that has entered its esports twilight in 2019. In its earliest days, though, SCII was the game that brought competitive esports out of Korea and to the west. At its release in 2010, SCII was an esports powerhouse because of its high skill ceiling and almost perfect balancing. Even with the time required to develop units as part of the Real Time Strategy (RTS) genre, matches were fun for fans to watch and highly competitive for the most talented players.

SCII also separated the truly gifted from the casual players. Although a casual player can play the game at a relatively slow pace, professional *SCII* players commit more than 1,000 actions per minute, which means that in every second, they input and complete 16 separate actions while still concentrating on high-level strategy. If you read that last sentence out loud at normal speaking speed, in the same time that it takes you to learn those statistics, a professional *SCII* player will have taken 112 in-game actions. If you're like me, you will have already lost that match-up.

You can find more information on *StarCraft II* in Chapter 3. The game is now free to play.

Street Fighter V

Released: February 16, 2016

Publisher: Capcom

Platform(s): PC, PlayStation 4, Arcade

Available from: Retail stores, PlayStation online store, streampowered.com

The fighting-game world has essentially three pillars of the competitive genre. There are 2-D fighting games, 3-D fighting games, and platform-style brawlers. In the realm of 2-D fighting games, no company has had the success or built the reputation that Capcom has. The jewel in Capcom's fighting-game crown is the *Street Fighter* series.

Street Fighter V (SF V) is the most recent entry in the series, and since its release in 2016, it has been a major part of the yearly Evolution Championship Series (EVO) tournaments in Las Vegas. Always a favorite for local fighting-game competitions, *SF V* retains many of the long-time favorite combatants like Ryu, M. Bison, Chun Li, and company.

Known for its brutal combos and special moves called V-Triggers, *SF* has been a part of numerous historic esports moments, not the least of which is the famous EVO Moment #37 (https://www.youtube.com/watch?v=klaWV-szmnY), wherein a player named Daigo pulled off a seemingly impossible series of parry attacks that required ultra-precise timing with not even a millisecond of flex room. If you're reading this in a hard copy book and can't click the link in this paragraph, stop reading right now and go to YouTube to search for EVO Moment #37. I'll wait here.

You can find more information on *SF V* in Chapter 5. *SF V* retails $29.99 to $59.99 with no additional subscription fees. You can obtain additional fighters as in-game-purchases.

Super Smash Bros. Ultimate

Released: December 8, 2018

Publisher: Nintendo

Platform(s): Nintendo Switch

Available from: Nintendo Shop (online, accessible from the home screen of the Switch console) or any retail store that sells video games

In the previous section, which is about *Street Fighter V*, I mention the three types of major esports fighting games. *Super Smash Bros. (SSB)* was the game that established one of those three genres, the platform-style brawler. Since its first release on the Nintendo 64 in 1999 to 2018's *Super Smash Bros. Ultimate (SSBU)* for the Nintendo Switch, the series has been catapulted into the spotlight by the talent and devotion of the player base.

SSBU is different from most fighting games in that it also incorporates into the game's combat the reality of a platforming game. The game has numerous spaces where a player can stand in the various levels of *SSBU*, but in almost every case, the player can be knocked from those spots and tumble off the screen to its death. The game doesn't just allow a player to fall, however, because it provides a number of mechanics that allow you to rescue your player from the tumble into the cold unknown at the bottom of the screen.

Another contributor to the success of *SSBU* is that the roster is made up of the cast and characters of numerous Nintendo gaming properties, allowing players to finally find out whether Luigi can best his brother Mario, or how Samus from *Metroid* would fare in combat with Link from the *Legend of Zelda*. The cast includes numerous wacky fan-favorite characters, including the recent addition of Banjo and Kazooie from the cult favorite game *Banjo-Kazooie*. You can find more information on *SSBU* in Chapter 5. *SSBU* retails for $59.99. You can obtain additional fighters as in-game purchases.

Chapter **16**

Ten Esports Games You Might Have Missed

The esports world is full of games. Some are so important that they command attention, like *League of Legends*, *Overwatch*, or *Fortnite*. Others are newer, or are a bit quirky or off the beaten path. In this chapter, you check out a few of the newer or suddenly surging esports games.

Apex Legends

Released: February 4, 2019

Publisher: Electronic Arts

Platforms: PC, PlayStation 4, Xbox One

Available at: `https://www.ea.com/games/apex-legends/play-now-for-free` or via console online stores

At the time of this writing, *Apex Legends* (AL) is the newest entry into the battle royale genre. *AL* also represents Electronic Arts' (EA) first nonsports simulation entry into the competitive esports world. With a first-person viewpoint reminiscent of popular FPS games, *Apex Legends* makes a few changes to the standard battle royale format.

AL matches have 60 players, which are divided into 20 teams of 3. In addition to the standardization of teams of squads, *AL* also has a variety of heroes that each player can select, which allows for each team to have specific roles and for team composition to be a part of character selection.

EA will launch an *Apex Legends* Global Series esports series in 2020, which will include four major events and $3 million in total prizing. *AL* is currently free to play. You can read more about *AL* in Chapter 7.

Arena of Valor

Released: December 19, 2017 (North America)

Publisher: Tencent

Platforms: Android, iOS, Nintendo Switch

Available at: App stores and console online stores

With the announcement of *League of Legends: Wild Rift*, all indications are that the mobile device MOBA *Arena of Valor (AoV)* might have a limited remaining shelf life in North America. What it represents, however, shouldn't be taken for granted. In China, Korea, Thailand, and other countries outside North America where esports are popular, *AoV* has more than 200 million active players. The player base is absolutely massive.

Mobile gaming is red hot, but American players in particular have yet to offer the buy-in for mobile that the PC has. As devices improve in quality and networks advance with the dawn of 5G coming soon, the popularity that mobile esports have seen in the East may well migrate west. The Chinese version of *AoV, Honor of Kings (HoK)*, has a massive player base and professional league, King Pro League, rivaling most PC and console esports titles.

If any mobile game has been designed to pull in traditional esports players, it's *AoV*. The map is identical in structure and in art style to *League of Legends (LoL)*. In fact, Tencent, the maker of *AoV*, also owns Riot Games, the maker of *LoL*. Although the heroes are different from *LoL*, the skill sets are strikingly similar and the play style, likewise, is a bit stripped down but still feels shockingly like *LoL*. *AoV* is free to play. It is also the only traditional MOBA available on any console available in America.

BlazBlue: Cross Tag Battle

Released: June 5, 2018 (NA)

Publisher: Arc System Works

Platforms: Nintendo Switch, PlayStation 4, PC, Arcade

Available at: Steampowered.com or retail stores

The fighting-game genre is filled with interesting variations on traditional styles and tropes for gameplay. The 2-D, side-scrolling, two-versus-two game is certainly nothing new; Capcom has utilized that style in its games since the second generation of *Street Fighter* and the first of the Marvel versus Capcom series titles. But *BlazBlue: Cross Tag Battle* is different in that it pulls fighters from Arc system games and anime, providing a unique cast of characters. The fighters are interesting and, in contrast to Marvel characters, are less familiar to most American gamers.

BB: CTB offers classic, anime-style 2-D art and complex but satisfying combos and mechanics. With a collection of characters including BlazBlue, Under Night, RWBY, Atlus, and Rooster Teeth, the 68-character roster offers at least one character that plays in every classic 2-D fighting game style.

Some uncertainty surrounded how well *BB: CTB* would fare in America, but after inclusion in both the 2018 and 2019 EVO championships, it appears that *BB: CTB* will continue to see regular competition at the highest levels as Arc System Works rolls out an actual arcade cabinet version of the game to accompany the console and PC releases. *BB: CTB* retails for $49.99.

Clash Royale

Released: March 2, 2016

Publisher: Supercell

Platforms: iOS, Android

Available at: App stores

In 2012, the relatively unknown Finnish developer Supercell released the surprise mobile hit *Clash of Clans*. Although *Clash of Clans* appealed to many players, it played more like a Real-Time Strategy (RTS) game than something that was quick and easy to pick up and play. To remedy this drawback, Supercell developed a much faster-paced game based on the same universe: *Clash Royale.*

Clash Royale is the classic easy-to-play, hard-to-master game. Each player has three towers, one with a king and the others with defenders. These towers also represent lanes where units can be placed. The units a player can deploy come from a small deck that each player builds before the match. Placing a unit in any of the three lanes uses mana, which generates over time. Although this formula has complexities that make it a viable esport, after the player puts together a deck, competing is as easy as dragging the card of a unit into a lane and letting go. A new player can be in-action in a matter of minutes. Most matches last less than 5 minutes. *Clash Royale* is an extremely approachable game.

In America, the game has been popular among casual players but hasn't found the strong competitive base that many popular PC titles have. Some regions, however, have had major tournaments with significant prize pools. The *Clash Royale* League World Finals 2019 took place in Los Angeles in December and had a prize pool of just over $1 million. As mobile esports grow, *Clash Royale* is a game to keep an eye on because Supercell understands how to run competitions within the space. *Clash Royale* is free to play.

Gears 5

Released: September 10, 2019

Publisher: Xbox Games Studio

Platforms: Xbox One, PC

Available at: Steampowered.com, Microsoft.com, or retail stores

In the esports world, most shooters are FPS, but one third-person franchise that has always maintained some level of traction is Microsoft's *Gears of War*. Though it has never been a top-tier esports title, the *Gears* series has always seen healthy competition, and the newest entry, *Gears 5*, is sure to do the same.

An often overlooked reason for the game's popularity is that a number of players cannot play FPS. They experience motion sickness from the attempt to simulate the first-person perspective. People who suffer from this condition can, however, play a third-person shooter, which allows players to see their player-character. The strategic difference of being able to see your player-character, which is absent from an FPS, is also a factor in the game's popularity.

Gears 5, which is in an early stage in its life as a major title, has had minimal competition to this point, but based on the structure outlined on the web at http:// gears.gg, Microsoft has big plans for the game, including regional professional leagues and a world championship to come in 2020. *Gears 5* is a title to watch, particularly for console players who enjoy shooters that focus on controller-based play. *Gears 5* retails for $59.99.

Killer Instinct

Released: November 22, 2013

Publisher: Xbox Games Studio

Platforms: PC, Xbox One

Available at: Microsoft.com or Xbox console store

Killer Instinct (KI) lived its first life as an arcade fighting game in the mid-1990s. It was developed by Rare and eventually positioned as a major Nintendo 64 game. As arcade popularity faded and the 64-bit generation of consoles gave way to the PlayStation 2, *KI* disappeared. But as is true of many games, a strong title couldn't continue to gather dust, and in 2013, Xbox Game Studios revived *KI* as an Xbox One exclusive fighting game.

KI is a game of insane combos and input precision, and its popularity among fighting game fans cannot be denied. The relative price of the game has helped it as well; its retail price of $39.99 is often discounted as part of Microsoft's Xbox Live service. As a member of that service, I've managed to get every piece of *KI*, including bonus downloadable fighters, for free. *KI* also bridges a nostalgia gap, bringing back a title that was popular during the height of arcade competitions and placing it once again beside its then-rivals *Mortal Kombat* and *Street Fighter*.

Although *KI* is no longer part of the main slate for games at EVO, and the *KI* World Cup has been discontinued, *KI* remains a popular game for local tournaments and online competition. It would make a suitable starter game for someone looking to break into the fighting game scene but not start with a title for which local competition would include the most elite fighting gamers in the area (as a title like *Mortal Kombat* or *Street Fighter* would). *KI* with a minimal set of characters is free to play on Xbox One. It can be purchased with all available downloadable content for $39.99.

Teamfight Tactics

Released: June 26, 2019

Publisher: Riot Games

Platforms: PC, Mac (with Android and iOS anticipated in 2020)

Available at: Leagueoflegends.com (Teamfight Tactics is part of the *LoL* Launcher)

Throughout this book, I refer to the battle royale as the hottest new esports genre of the last several years, but it's not the newest thing on the scene. That honor goes to a game type called "Auto Chess," or auto battler. Although Auto Chess started as a modded mode for *Dota 2* that was developed by Drodo Studio, the most popular auto battler–style game in the world is currently *Teamfight Tactics (TFT)* from Riot.

An auto battler happens on a map that resembles a chess board built from hexagons in rows. The game involves eight players who play one-versus-one match rounds on separate boards. Each round, both players place their champions in hexagons on the board and anticipate how the champions will interact (in a manner akin to chess pieces). After both players have placed their champions, an automated fight takes place, with the results giving gold and taking health from both players. This process continues until seven players have run out of health and a single winner emerges. A match often takes many rounds to complete. A typical one-versus-one board takes around a minute, and a full match lasts about 35 minutes.

Four months after its release, *TFT* already boasted 33 million active players. The game's popularity is based on its strategy and the fact it doesn't focus on reaction time and speed of input. Riot announced in late October 2019 that a competitive scene for *TFT* would be developed in 2020.

It's too soon to know if the auto battler will be the next game genre to disrupt the esports ecosystem the way the battle royale has, but with 33 million players, *TFT* is absolutely a title to watch. The game is free to play.

Magic: The Gathering Arena

Released: June 26, 2019

Publisher: Wizards of the Coast

Platforms: PC (with Mac anticipated in 2020)

Available at: Magic.wizards.com

The biggest complaint leveled against Blizzard's Collectible Card Game (CCG) *Hearthstone* is that it's too simple compared to real-world CCGs like *Magic: The Gathering (MTG)*. In the summer of 2019, Wizards of the Coast, the makers of *MTG*, decided to find out whether digital was what audiences wanted by launching a digital version of its game, which it called *Magic: The Gathering Arena (MTGA)*.

MTGA is exactly what an *MTG* player would expect. It follows all the rules of the physical game but does so within a digital space. For those not familiar with *MTG*, the game can seem complex from the start, but the steep early learning curve is rewarded after about an hour of tutorial play when the complexity and flexibility of the system become apparent. Unlike *Hearthstone*, which simplifies things like the amount of mana a player has or the conditions needed to activate a card's abilities, *MTGA* requires that players manage resources and plan their turns carefully. The result is a complex but multifaceted card game.

As is true of several of the games in this chapter, *MTGA* has been live to play for only about five months as of the time of this writing. It remains to be seen as to whether the game will rise to the popularity of Blizzard's *Hearthstone* and become part of the top-tier esports scene. Wizards of the Coast has a strong track record with its *MTG* events, however, and its early plans for *MTGA* esports can be found at Magic.gg. *MTGA* is free to play, but as with *Hearthstone*, players can spend money to gain packs and cards faster. Many believe that to be competitive at the highest level requires spending money to earn cards quickly enough.

Mortal Kombat 11

Released: April 23, 2019

Publisher: Warner Bros. Interactive Entertainment for NetherRealm Studios

Platforms: PC, Nintendo Switch, PlayStation 4, Xbox One, and Google Stadia (announced but not released as of this writing)

Available at: Retail stores or console app stores

The original *Mortal Kombat* game, released in 1992, was an arcade stalwart and led to the creation of the Entertainment Software Rating Board (ESRB) for rating games because of what was considered ultra-realistic gore and violence at the time. Now a trademark of the series, *Mortal Kombat 11 (MK 11)* came out of the gates so strong that it was named as a title for EVO 2019 before it was officially released to the public.

Known for punishing kombos (with the trademark *k* replacing the *c*) and now-infamous kombatants like the fire-wielding ninja Scorpion or the ice ninja Sub Zero, *MK 11* is considered one of the top fighting games in the world. Less than a year into its competition cycle, *MK 11* drew in most of the heavy hitters at the 2019 EVO, with The Game Awards Esports Player of the Year SonicFox winning the grand finale.

MK 11 amped up its competitive scene by developing a multi-pathway to its major event Final Kombat 20 with a full, rather complex schedule and standings available at www.mortalkombat.com/esports. In addition to Final Kombat 20, *MK 11* offers an online mode called Kombat League that allows players to climb a competitive ladder to earn rewards and points toward placement in other esports events. *MK 11* retails for $59.99 and includes additional downloadable fighters, including the Terminator and the Joker.

Rainbow Six Siege

Released: December 1, 2015

Publisher: Ubisoft

Platforms: PC, PlayStation 4, Xbox One

Available at: https://www.ubisoft.com/en-us/game/rainbow-six/siege/ or retail stores

It is rare in esports for a title to release, acquire a solid but not outstanding player base, and then to surge years after release. But that's exactly what happened with *Tom Clancy's Rainbow Six Siege (Siege)*. The reason for this surge in popularity was a choice by Ubisoft to release a number of high-quality free updates in an attempt to keep what was a well-received game viable in a crowded marketplace.

Siege is a five-versus-five tactical FPS in which the environment can be destroyed and the characters — called operators — have a variety of unique skills that are customized to specific jobs like setting explosives or operating surveillance. Each map has a mission for each side, similar to *CS:GO* (which you can read more about in Chapter 4). The high level of specialization for each operator adds complexity to the game, and the ability to shoot through and destroy almost anything makes the maps more wide open and difficult to control. The resulting gameplay appeals to those who favor a more active game experience that requires adapting on the fly as opposed to developing a plan to unfurl slowly over the course of a match.

The popularity of *Siege* soared among collegiate players in 2018 and 2019. On the professional scene, *Siege* has blossomed to include an official Pro League, a series of major invitationals, and a tiered system that allows for players from amateur to experienced professional players to compete. You can find out more about *Siege* esports at www.rainbow6.ubisoft.com/siege. *Siege* retails for $20.

Chapter **17**

Ten Esports Influencers to Follow

I n esports, it's often about who you know. Because of how the Internet distributes the scene, allowing people to play from practically anywhere, the major seats of influence aren't particular geographical locations. You find the key influencers — the tastemakers and game meta builders — through social media and streaming. This chapter tells you about ten heavy hitters who deserve your attention as you enter the esports landscape. If you decide to be a player and pick a particular game to focus on, the influencer scene will constrict because you'll want to focus on the best players of that game. To start, though, here are ten people to know.

Chopping It Up with Ninja

Gamer tag: Ninja

Full name: Richard Tyler Blevins

Primary game: *Fortnite*

Where to find online:

Mixer: www.mixer.com/ninja

Twitter: @ninja

Instagram:@ninja

YouTube: https://www.youtube.com/user/NinjasHyper

Ninja is one of the most well-known gamers and esports players in the world. He most recently made esports headlines in August 2019 when he left the world's biggest streaming site, Twitch, to join Microsoft's new streaming platform Mixer. At the time of his departure, Ninja had 14 million Twitch followers, a number that was almost double that of the second most popular streamer (Tfue, who had 7.01 million followers). Within a week of joining Mixer, Ninja had a million followers on the new site. In December 2019, he had 2,600,000 followers on Mixer to go with his 22 million YouTube followers.

The rise of Ninja as an influencer coincided with the rise of *Fortnite* as the biggest game in North America. Ninja's popularity is based on not just his skill but also his personality and the level of interaction he maintains with his fans. He participates in events like Ninja Vegas '18, a tournament in Las Vegas that let anyone who came compete for a chance to play against Ninja and in the process appear on his stream and win money including special bounty prizes for taking out Ninja himself in any match. Participating in such events cements his place as one of the most engaging influencers in esports. He's also an aspirational figure for streamers because he reportedly made $500,000 a month from his gaming activities when he streamed for Twitch (https://www.businessinsider.com/ninja-tyler-blevins-twitch-subscribers-fortnite-drake-youtube-2018-3).

Guarding Lanes with Arteezy

Gamer tag: Arteezy or RTZ

Full name: Artour Babaev

Primary game: *Dota 2*

Where to find online:

Twitch: www.twitch.tv/arteezy

Twitter: @ arteezy

Instagram:@ arteezyarteezy

YouTube: https://www.youtube.com/channel/UCybsCNFXLPUHhpkuPIKWatw

Arteezy is an example of someone who has risen to prominence in the streaming community through the sheer skill of his gameplay. As a *Dota 2* player, Arteezy participates in a game that isn't as popular in the United States as many other titles are, but his level of play mixed with an entertaining gaming persona keep people watching his streams to learn, to enjoy, and to gather material to make memes for various *Dota 2* online forums and Reddit.

Arteezy's Twitch numbers are modest compared to someone like Ninja, but with almost 550,000 followers, the Canadian is the most-watched *Dota 2* player on Twitch. His YouTube channel has far fewer subscribers than his Twitch channel. In fact, his YouTube channel has so few followers that he couldn't get the channel renamed, so you find a long string of characters in his YouTube channel address. If you're a *Dota 2* fan, though, he's the one to watch.

Faking the Funk with Faker

Gamer tag: Faker

Full name: Lee Sang-hyeok

Primary game: *League of Legends*

Where to find online:

Twitch: www.twitch.tv/faker

Twitter: @faker

Instagram:@faker

YouTube: https://www.youtube.com/channel/UCpJw2H9KKqwCCGQKRh1Bf2w

Faker is the mid laner for Korea's SK Telecom T1 team, one of the most dominant teams in *LoL* Worlds competition, having won in 2013, 2015, and 2016. Although no standard way exists for determining "the best" *LoL* player ever, Faker is one of only two players to win three *LoL* Worlds championships, and most members of the community call him the GOAT (greatest of all time).

Watching him stream is a master class in how to mid lane, and fans follow to see what Faker will pull off next. Although no one has officially confirmed this claim, people believe that his most recent contract with T1 was for $2.5 million a year. Faker has professed to play 12 hours a day to keep his skills sharp.

Knocking 'em Down with FalleN

Gamer tag: FalleN

Full name: Gabriel Toledo de Alcântara Sguario

Primary game: *Counter Strike: Global Offensive*

Where to find online:

Twitch: www.twitch.tv/gafallen

Twitter: @fallencs

Instagram:@fallen

YouTube: https://www.youtube.com/falleninsider

FalleN was named the most influential person in Brazillian esports in 2015. A seasoned *CS:GO* pro, FalleN is one of the few professionals ever to be an AWPer (a sniper) as well as a team leader. His streams are a testament to his talent in aiming and carefully reading a combat situation. Most of his streams are in Portuguese, however.

With the popularity of *CS:GO* still on the rise, the number of FalleN's 815,000 Twitch followers may grow. For anyone looking to learn more about AWPing in *CS:GO*, FalleN is the one to see.

Dealing a Hand with Firebat

Gamer tag: Firebat

Full name: James Kostesich

Primary game: *Hearthstone*

Where to find online:

Twitch: www.twitch.tv/firebat

Twitter: @firebat

YouTube: https://firebat.tv

Firebat was the first ever *Hearthstone* World Champion. He is, in fact, one of the few people specifically called out in a *Hearthstone* card's flavor text (the short story or narrative bit included at the bottom of each card); the "Fiery Bat" card reads "he will always be our first." A native of Detroit, Firebat has played the game since just after its release in 2014.

Known for content like his "Deck Doctor" YouTube videos through his team, Omni, Firebat's personality and knowledge of *Hearthstone* makes him a key figure in the *HS* community. He often provides strategy videos and help for other players. When not competing, Firebat is known to take on casting duties for *HS* tournaments.

Fighting Like a Girl with Mystik

Gamer tag: Mystik

Full name: Katherine "Kat" Gunn

Primary game: *Dead or Alive* series

Where to find online:

Twitch: www.twitch.tv/katgunn

Twitter: @MystikGunn

Instagram:@mystikgunn

YouTube: https://www.youtube.com/LadiesofLT3

A former professional *Dead or Alive* player, Mystik is a games content creator, gamer, active streamer, and *cosplayer,* someone who designs costumes and dresses up as a game character. She was listed in the 2016 *Guinness Book of World Records* as the highest-earning female gamer. She currently runs the gaming and cosplaying team Less Than 3 (LT3), through which she generates all manner of gamer content on YouTube.

Mystik is active daily on Twitch as a variety streamer, playing any of a number of games. At 11 p.m. on a random weeknight, I found her streaming a match of *Call of Duty: Modern Warfare.* Her production schedule and the variety of content she creates is a model for anyone who wants to be a major part of the esports scene without trying to be a top-level player.

Hiding in the Shadows with Shroud

Gamer tag: Shroud

Full name: Michael Grzesiek

Primary game: *Counter Strike: Global Offensive*

Where to find online:

Mixer: www.mixer.com/shroud

Twitter: @shroud

Instagram:@shroud

YouTube: https://www.youtube.com/shroud

When Ninja left Twitch, Shroud, a former *CS:GO* pro who is more of a variety FPS streamer now, became one of the top streamers (if not the top) on the site, with 7 million followers. In late October 2019, however, Shroud, like Ninja, left Twitch for Mixer. In the time between his move and the time of this writing, Shroud has collected almost 998,000 followers on Mixer.

Shroud's skill at FPS, particularly with aiming, has led to his ability to pick up and play a number of games at a high level while entertaining people on his stream. Newer releases like *Apex Legends* and *Call of Duty Modern Warfare* come easily to Shroud, as does speaking to his audience while playing. Paired with Ninja, Shroud gives Mixer a solid foundation from which to build its fledgling streaming platform, and anyone who enjoys FPS will find something to like on his streams.

Zerging with Scarlett

Gamer tag: Scarlett

Full name: Sasha Hostyn

Primary game: *StarCraft II*

Where to find online:

Twitch: www.twitch.tv/scarlettM

Twitter: @onfirescarlett

As mentioned in other places in this book, esports still tends to be male dominated at the top levels. Scarlett, however, is a shining example that esports isn't a boys club. This Canadian-born *StarCraft II* pro is the only woman to ever win an international *SCII* tournament, but she excels to the point that she's been referred to as "the queen of *StarCraft*" and "Korean Kryptonite."

Scarlett occupies an interesting position in esports in terms of diversity and inclusion. As a Canadian — or, really, anyone outside of Korea — she is viewed as a "foreign hope," one of the few non-Korean players able to stake a claim to being among the best in the world. She is also trans, something that Scarlett herself rarely brings up but which is important in a gaming environment in which issues of intolerance abounded for years. Scarlett's presence in competition and the chanting crowds who cheer her victories are a welcome sight as esports continues to move toward being more inclusive.

Stringing Together Combos with SonicFox

Gamer tag: SonicFox

Full name: Dominic McLean

Primary game: *Mortal Kombat/Injustice*

Where to find online:

Twitch: www.twitch.tv/zsonicfox

Twitter: @ SonicFox5000

YouTube: https://www.youtube.com/SonicFox5000

When it comes to fighting games, SonicFox is the name to know. Usually found wearing their trademark blue, furry, fox-ear hat, SonicFox (who recently began self-referencing using the plural pronoun as a nonbinary person) is the fighter who is beating everyone at pretty much everything. Ranked as the greatest *Mortal Kombat X* and *Injustice 2* player of all time, SonicFox made esports waves by winning the first ever *Mortal Kombat 11* championship at EVO 2019.

Their many wins have led their fans to refer to SonicFox as the LeBron James of gaming. But another aspect of SonicFox's life and career is equally important. After being named the top esports athlete of 2018 at The Game Awards, SonicFox said, "I'm gay, I'm black, a furry, pretty much everything a Republican hates. And the best esports player of the year, I guess!"

Although none of those aspects of their identity were a secret to their fans or to the games community, their willingness to announce their difference in front of such a large crowd illustrates their desire to increase representation and understanding in games. SonicFox's talent cannot be silenced, and their matches always excite.

Smashing Goals with SquishyMuffinz

Gamer tag: SquishyMuffinz

Full name: Mariano Arruda

Primary game: *Rocket League*

Where to find online:

Twitch: www.twitch.tv/SquishyMuffinz

Twitter: @SquishyMuffinz

Instagram:@squishymuffinzrl

YouTube: https://www.youtube.com/SquishyMuffinz

Many people regard *Rocket League* as the little esport that could, a game run by a smaller studio that emerged from a niche audience to stand on the big stage with games like *LoL*, *Overwatch*, and the like. If *RL* is the little game that could, SquishyMuffinz and his team, the Muffin Men, are the little esports athletes who did.

The Muffin Men, led by SquishyMuffinz, won DreamHack, Atlanta's *RL* tournament, in 2017 and were signed a week later by esports juggernaut Cloud9. Within months they were playing in the *Rocket League* Championship Series World Championship.

Squishy was a professional *RL* player at age 17, and now at 19 is viewed as one of the best in the world because of his amazing mechanical mastery of the game. He regularly pulls off moves in-game that make viewers and seasoned players alike gasp. Aspiring *RL* players will learn much from his streams and YouTube videos.

Index

N

National Association of Collegiate Esports (NACE), 178, 180

National Basketball Association (NBA), 201. *See also NBA 2K* League; *NBA 2K* series

National Collegiate Athletic Association (NCAA), 180–181

National Football League (NFL). *See Madden NFL* series

National Hockey League (NHL), 112–113

nature, colors from, 242

NBA 2K League
 first woman in, 112
 importance of, 111
 joining, 111
 overview, 103–104, 109–110

NBA 2K series
 creating your own player, 108–109
 first woman in *NBA 2K* League, 112
 NBA 2K League, playing in, 109–111
 overview, 108

networking card, computer, 21

nexus, in *LoL*, 58

NHL 20 game, 112–113

NHL Gaming World Championship, 113

Ninja (Tyler Blevins), 122–123, 200, 247, 263–264

Ninja Las Vegas, 123, 264

Nintendo esports offerings, 31. *See also specific games*

Nintendo GameCube console, 31, 32

Nintendo Switch console, 31, 69, 121, 125, 150–151

Nintendo Switch Online, 144, 151

Nintendo Switch Pro Controller, 44

noise, protecting others from, 143

NVIDIA graphics cards, 21, 26

O

Ohio State University (OSU), 181, 189–190

OLED TV (LG), 35

Omen system (HP), 26–27

1 versus 1 Solo Mid mode, *Dota 2*, 67

1-versus-99 format, battle royale games, 118, 123, 125–126

online Cheat Sheet, 3

Open Broadcaster Software (OBS), 232

Open Division, *Overwatch*, 210

operators, *Siege*, 84

Opto-Mechanical switch, Huntsman keyboard, 38

organizations, professional esports, 203, 204–206

overclocked processors, 21

overlays, stream, 232–236

Overwatch Contenders League, 210

Overwatch game
 console versus PC-based play, 29
 criteria for qualifying as esport, 10–11, 12–13, 14–15
 going pro in, 210
 as hero shooter, 75
 number of players at highest level, 200, 201
 versus other FPS events, 81–82
 overview, 77, 80–81, 249–250
 services needed to play, 143

Overwatch League Grand Finals, 208

Overwatch League (OWL), 80–81, 83, 201, 210, 250

Overwatch Open Division, 210

owners, esports organization, 204–205

P

Paladins game, 77, 85

paletton.com, 242

PCs. *See* computers

peripherals
 controllers, 43–45
 headsets, 42–43
 input devices, 39–42
 keyboard, 36–39
 overview, 36
 player preference for, 25

phones, gaming, 70

photos
 sharing on Instagram, 163–165
 Twitter profile, 157–159

physical position, awareness of in FPS games, 75–76

pick phases, of *LoL* competition, 59–60

PiviP, 219

platform brawlers, 88, 89, 92–94

play modes, 58, 66–67, 84, 109

player characters
creating in *NBA 2K* series, 108–109
in *Dota 2*, 65, 66
in *League of Legends*, 58
in MOBA games, 53–54
players. *See also* brand, player; playing esports; professional esports; streaming
in battle royale games, keeping tabs on, 126
criteria for games qualifying as esports, 10–11
versus gamers, 15–17
isolating opposing, in *LoL*, 62
picking and banning, in *LoL*, 59–61
in professional esports organizations, 206
PlayerUnknown (Brendan Greene), 118
PlayerUnknown's Battlegrounds (*PUBG*) game, 118–120, 208
Playground mode, *NBA 2K* series, 109
playing esports. *See also* collegiate esports; esports; professional esports; *specific games and genres*; streaming
accounts, setting up, 143–151
checklist for, 141–143
finding local competition, 152
overview, 141
time dedicated to in pro esports, 206–207
tips for, 151
PlayStation 4 Pro (PS4 Pro) console, Sony, 29–30, 44, 144, 150. *See also specific games*
PlayStation Plus service (Sony), 144, 150
Pokémon Go game, 16–17
polling rate, mouse, 39
posts, social media, 156, 160–163, 164, 167–168
power, levels of PC, 24–27
power converters, 142
practice, importance of, 17, 201, 206–207
prebuilt computers, buying, 23
primary colors, in stream, 241–242
prize money, for most popular esports, 11
pro draft, *LoL*, 58, 60
Pro League, *Quake*, 86
Pro-Am mode, *NBA 2K* series, 109
processors, computer, 20–21, 24, 26
professional competitions. *See specific competitions*; tournaments

professional esports
biggest events in, 208
calculating odds of getting into, 200–201
career options after, 216
charting path to, 208–211
collegiate esports after, 207, 216
day-to-day realities in, 211–215
joining teams or organizations, 204–206
keys to getting into, 201–203
knowing your game, 207
making time to play, 206–207
overview, 1, 199
solo versus team games, 203
professional sports, 111, 201. *See also* sports simulation games
profiles, social media, 156, 157–159, 164, 172
Project A game, 63
Project F game, 63
Project L game, 63
pseudo-3-D FPS games, 74
Psyonix, 115, 250–251. *See also Rocket League* game
PUBG game, 118–120, 208
PUBG Global Championship, 120, 208
PUBG Global Series, 120
public group discussions. *See* Reddit
public relations directors, 222
publicity, volunteering in, 218
publisher support, as esports criteria, 9–10
pushing lanes, in *LoL*, 61

Q

Quake Champions game, 74, 86
Quake Pro League, 86
qualifiers, *NBA 2K* League, 111
quality, of stream, 236, 237
Quinn, Zoe, 16

R

racing games, 114–116
Raiju controller (Razer), 44
Rainbow Six Siege (*Siege*) game, 77, 83–84, 262
Random Draft mode, *Dota 2*, 67

T

T1 team, 265

table, for playing, 142

tactile switches, keyboards, 38

Take-Two Interactive. *See NBA 2K* League; *NBA 2K* series

tanks, 54, 82

taunt dances, *Fortnite*, 122

Taylor, Adam, 232

team captains, 206

team managers, 222

Teamfight Tactics (*TFT*) game, 63, 259–260

teams, professional esports, 203–206. *See also specific games*; *specific teams*

Tekken series, 89, 97–99

televisions (TVs), 32–35

Tencent, 55–56, 63, 68, 256. *See also Arena of Valor* game; Riot Games

Tespa Compete, 180, 213, 233–234

Tetris 99 game, 125

themes, for stream, 234, 237–242

theorycrafting, 162

third-person games, 55, 74, 86, 258–259. *See also* Multiplayer Online Battle Arena games

3-D art, in 2.5-D fighting games, 91

3-D fighting games, 88, 89, 90–92

3-D FPS games, 74

tier lists, *League of Legends*, 60–61

timelines, social media, 156, 160, 163

Titan RTX Ultimate Gaming PC (iBUYPOWER), 27

Toledo de Alcântara Sguario, Gabriel (FalleN), 266

tone, stream, 236

top lane, MOBA games, 53, 54

tournament modes, sports simulation games, 102

tournament organizers, 222

tournaments. *See also specific competitions*; *specific games*

    battle royale games, 126

    collegiate, 179–180

    controllers approved for, 44–45

    fighting games, 100

    local, finding, 152

    professional esports, 202, 208, 212–213

    volunteering at, 218, 219

toxic behavior, 57, 104

tunneling, in *LoL*, 63

turrets, in *LoL*, 58

TVs, 32–35

tweets. *See* Twitter

Twisted Treeline play mode, *LoL*, 58

Twitch.tv

    channels, 172–173

    impact on esports, 173

    Jacksonville Landing shooting, 107

    Ninja on, 122, 264

    overview, 171

    signing up, 171–172

    stream keys, gathering, 230

    streamers and viewers for popular esports, 10

    YouTube streaming versus, 174–175

Twitter

    account creation, 157

    finding people, 160

    getting ready to tweet, 160–161

    overview, 155

    profile picture and bio, editing, 157–159

    tweets, 156, 161–163

2.5-D fighting games, 88, 89, 90–92

2-D fighting games, 88, 89–90

2-D graphics, 74

2K, 103–104. *See also NBA 2K* League; *NBA 2K* series

U

Ubisoft, 83, 262. *See also Rainbow Six Siege* game

Under Night In-Birth Exe: Late[st] game, 89

University of Akron, 191–192

University of California, Irvine (UCI), 179, 192–193

University of Michigan, 100

University of Utah, 181, 193–195

unranked modes, *Dota 2*, 67

updates, of esports games, 9–10

upload bandwidth, for streaming, 226–227

V

Vainglory game, 68

Valve Corporation, 246. *See also specific games*

Vantage controller (Scuf), 44

varsity esports, 178, 179, 207. *See also* collegiate esports; *specific colleges*

About the Author

Phill Alexander is an Assistant Professor of Game Studies and the Co-Director of Varsity Esports at Miami University. A lifelong gamer who has competed with others since the days of *Pong*, Alexander has spent the last 20 years working in education. His first book, *Identity and Collaboration in World of Warcraft*, emerged from years of researching and playing as part of a progression raid group in *WoW*.

With the exponential growth of esports, Alexander has become a frequent consultant and contributor to various conversations, appearing on various local news programs and in publications like *Variety*. After his Game Developer's Conference presentation last year, he checked off one of the items on his bucket list that he never thought he'd hit when he was interviewed for *Rolling Stone* magazine.

When he's not writing about himself in the third person, not teaching class, not coaching or advocating for his esports team, and not sleeping from all that work, Alexander is a huge fan of professional wrestling and attends local shows whenever he can. He can also be found consorting with his wife and his family of dogs: Boo-Boo, Cody, Wagnar, and Wiggles.

Dedication

This book is dedicated to my mother, my wife, and all the members of my RedHawks family. Game on!

Acknowledgments

A book like this one is a labor of love, but it is labor. A number of people helped to get this book into your hands. First and foremost, I want to thank Susan Christophersen, the editor of this book, who had to read over every single page more than once, had to deal with learning gamer lingo on the fly, and had to shepherd me through running a deadline while I was fighting a terrible flu. She's amazing. I also want to thank Andrew Heyward, who had the unenviable job of serving as technical editor on a book for which so many things changed between drafting and reviewing chapters (esports comes at you fast!). I also want to extend my sincere thanks to Steve Hayes and Wiley for having the vision to suggest this title and honoring me with the chance to write it.

Above all, I want to thank my mother, Susan, for making sure that a poor kid had access to video games and computers growing up (and for always knowing I should be writing books) and my wife, Julie, for supporting my gaming adventures.

Publisher's Acknowledgments

Executive Editor: Steve Hayes
Project and Copy Editor: Susan Christophersen
Technical Editor: Andrew Hayward
Proofreader: Debbye Butler

Production Editor: Mohammed Zafar Ali
Cover Image: @RyanKing999/Getty Images

Leverage the power

Dummies is the global leader in the reference category and one of the most trusted and highly regarded brands in the world. No longer just focused on books, customers now have access to the dummies content they need in the format they want. Together we'll craft a solution that engages your customers, stands out from the competition, and helps you meet your goals.

Advertising & Sponsorships

Connect with an engaged audience on a powerful multimedia site, and position your message alongside expert how-to content. Dummies.com is a one-stop shop for free, online information and know-how curated by a team of experts.

- Targeted ads
- Video
- Email Marketing

- Microsites
- Sweepstakes sponsorship

20 **MILLION** PAGE VIEWS **EVERY SINGLE MONTH**

15 MILLION **UNIQUE** VISITORS PER MONTH

43% OF ALL VISITORS ACCESS THE SITE VIA THEIR MOBILE DEVICES

700,000 NEWSLETTER SUBSCRIPTIONS TO THE INBOXES OF

300,000 UNIQUE INDIVIDUALS EVERY WEEK

# of dummies

Custom Publishing

Reach a global audience in any language by creating a solution that will differentiate you from competitors, amplify your message, and encourage customers to make a buying decision.

- Apps
- Books
- eBooks
- Video
- Audio
- Webinars

Brand Licensing & Content

Leverage the strength of the world's most popular reference brand to reach new audiences and channels of distribution.

For more information, visit dummies.com/biz

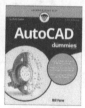